Susmita Mukherjee is an actor. A graduate of the National School of Drama, she has done pioneering work in her 35-year-long career in theatre, films and television. She founded the Natak theatre company in 1988 and her script, *Nati*, has played to full houses at Prithvi Theatre in Mumbai and elsewhere. She has acted in over 100 films. Her most recent, *Sold*, deals with child trafficking. It was directed by Oscar-winning director Jeffery Brown, and released in the US in 2016. Susmita has also written several short stories, and is working on her second novel.

MEE AND JUHIBABY

Susmita Mukherjee

SPEAKING
TIGER

SPEAKING TIGER PUBLISHING PVT. LTD
4381/4, Ansari Road, Daryaganj
New Delhi 110002

First published in India by Speaking Tiger in paperback 2018

ISBN: 978-93-88070-87-4
eISBN: 978-93-88070-88-1

10 9 8 7 6 5 4 3 2 1

Typeset in Garamond Premier Pro by SÜRYA, New Delhi
Printed at Gopsons Papers Ltd

For
Raja, Rudransh, Rudranuj
My microcosm

For
Didi and Bhai,
as self-respecting siblings
we fought,
till we scrambled
up to the light

And
for
Maa

Contents

Prologue

'My mother died yesterday...or was it today?'

When Meehika had first heard these words, back in college almost three and a half decades ago, she had winced. She had just turned sixteen and was startled out of her reverie by the authoritarian voice of Mrs Subramaniam who taught them Modern English Literature.

'What? How retarded is this Camus? Doesn't he remember when his mother died?'

Sudanshree, her best friend for the last seven and a half months, a feisty girl of peasant origin who had studied her way up from the backwaters of a small south Indian village to the prestigious Jesus and Mary college in one of the poshest areas of New Delhi, had whispered back, 'Meehika...stop dreaming! Concentrate on Camus's existentialism!'

'Stop calling me Meehika—haven't I said so before? Call me Mee. I dislike Meehika. Makes me sound like an old maid. Way too many ee...hii...aas...'

The rest was cut off by a sharp look in their direction from Mrs Subramaniam. Their poker faces hid the giggles threatening to burst out.

Now, years later, Meehika watches her mother lying supine on the grimy floor of her rented apartment. Hysterical thoughts rush through her head.

'She doesn't look dead. How is one supposed to look when one is dead? I mean how dead is dead? Newly dead, half-day dead, one-day dead or yesterday-dead like Camus's mother? I can't believe this is happening. Not now, after I finally found what I had been searching for.'

She glances at her mother again and stops short. Her mother is glowing. How is that possible? Can a corpse glow? Could she be alive after all? Had there been a mistake? How utterly strange. Ma was fine this morning... could she not have had the courtesy to give me a warning... some kind of gesture to say 'Beta, I'm off, cheerio!'

A faint smile touches Meehika's face—Ma could be so cute when she wanted.

Meehika's stomach takes the cue from her mind and starts to churn and she finds herself crouched on her knees in front of her mother's body. Her knees crush her belly, uncomfortable and painful. She shifts her weight on her buttocks, cursing herself for not exercising her fifty-year-old body.

'Funny... here I am sitting in front of my mother's dead body and all I can think about is why I don't exercise enough.'

She looks down at her mother again. This time it seems that her mother sighed...ever so softly. Meehika cranes her neck to stare at her. Ma, as she and her brother had been trained to call her, was looking white, so clinically white. A sob rises from within Mee, she thinks, 'How can this be? How can my beautiful Ma be covered in this blanket of white. She *hated* white. No, this just won't do!'

Ma used to say that white depressed her. She was a striking figure, not because she was glamorous or cultured or erudite but by her utter disregard for the rules of colour coordination. She would wear a yellow blouse with a pink saree, under which glared a purple petticoat and accessorize it with a multi-beaded drawstring purse. And she would look stunning!

And the sindoor...Ma loved her sindoor. The blood red powder pinched between her thumb and index finger flew with fierce pride in the air before settling itself in the parting of her jet-black, faintly oily hair. She would declare with passion, 'Our sindoor...Bengali sindoor, is very different from Madrasi sindoor which is maroon. And the bhaiyyani sindoor worn by Hindustani women is a cheap fluorescent colour. Our sindoor is by far the best.'

Meehika would listen wide-eyed, a little thing all of five, as she stood atop a wobbly stool. Ma would tame her hair and pin it into a plastic hairband and then hastily put up her own in a neat knot. Then she would take Afghan Snow from a pink pot and smooth some into both their cheeks and dab it down with a fluffy pink powder puff. Once this daily ritual was done, mother and daughter would wait in the drawing room for Bapi to come home. Bapi—Mee's wonderful, loving, always supportive father. Meehika's thoughts rush to her father...her Bapi...the grave, soft-spoken bhadralok.

'Thank God he exited this earth before his Juhibaby. Thank God he did not have to cope with her yo-yoing, her abrupt and random entries and exits from her dark personal tunnel, woven by the web of her own past. How strange of her to hold the "secret" to her bosom. I mean, it was hardly such a big deal. She could have shared it with me. After all, I am her daughter...I was her daughter... till this morning. Till I left for work, till I said "aashcchi" to her and did not wait for her "aesho". She is my mother damn it...my mother... Juhibaby.'

Meehika's thoughts float chaotically around her. She had so much to do. Once again she stares at her mother. And freezes. Juhibaby seems to be smiling. Ah, she looks so beautiful!

Meehika cannot help feeling a stab of self-hatred. Why had she let herself go? She twists her greying hair and stares at the veins on her hands... an old woman's hands, gnarled and bony. Her eyes pull her towards her mother. She looks so ethereal, glowing like a million suns. Was it because of this great beauty that Juhibaby, her mother, was pulled out of Bengal at the tender age of sixteen, to be married off to a stranger?

'Ma! Come on,' thinks Meehika desperately. 'Can't you get up? Can't I hug your frail old bones, kiss your sightless eyes, one last time?'

1
Juhibaby

Beautiful Juhibaby was the fifth daughter of a jatra singer. She had come in unannounced and unwelcome. Her father had been an accomplished singer, who knew the difference between a 'raga' and a 'tala' but here in rural Bengal, at the turn of the century, who really cared? He was part of a very shabby jatra troupe who eked out a living, giving performances of mythological plays on makeshift platforms to a medley of unenthusiastic villagers who only gathered together to see who could heckle the loudest.

Being compelled by circumstances to sing his refined songs to an undeserving audience had soured and embittered him. His wife, the sexy Ruma, whom he had eloped with at a tender age, had become bellicose and obese after giving birth to four daughters in a row. Much fun was poked at this unfortunate couple who struggled along the periphery of the jatra troupe, lugging along four scrawny, underfed girls.

So, when Juhibaby came along, nobody even reacted—as if she hadn't come. As if she didn't matter! The midwife cut the cords off Ruma's belly as she lay whimpering. She was too tired to even feel pain. At the back of her mind she knew that she had to put on the pot of rice to boil. The eldest girl was close to fourteen, when Juhibaby was born. This one was the prettiest, because the mother had been wooed and fed before her conception. Now, she quickly went about looking after the younger siblings, attending to their needs. Nobody went to school. With parents travelling in a junket for a living, where did they put up their boots long enough in order to go to school? Some days they slept in an open field, other days they would be packed like sardines in the small wagon, as the oxen lugged them along to the next village in time for the performance. But Ruma had a few books in an old trunk and these would be ritually passed around every evening when the children had finished with the chores of cooking, cleaning and winding up for the day.

The responsibility of washing their parents' costumes lay with the second daughter. Every night, she would wake up to the smell of warm, sweat-laden costumes being flung towards her. She would get up and sleepwalk her way to the bucket where she would dutifully wash the clothes and hang them up on the wagon to dry.

The third daughter had the responsibility of looking after the family finances. Though not yet ten, she was the accountant in the family and always saw to it that the tin box which housed their meagre funds never went empty. She never let the box out of her sight and would often choose not to join her siblings in their rural games of 'gaua-goi' or 'dabba-dabba bhio' for fear that her mind may be diverted from the precious box. It was from this box that her father would cajole her to give him an extra anna for his drink. Though she would give in occasionally, the matter would be discussed openly with her mother and other sisters, for they were all deeply connected with each other through the box.

During the annual Durga festival, each sister got one new

cotton saree and blouse. They had never seen footwear in their lives. Nobody seemed to wear it. Only the actor playing king used to tie his legs in a strange kind of contraption, sustained together by frayed golden tassels and leather thongs.

The fourth daughter was six and asthmatic. No one knew when she would give up her struggle. Sometimes the mother secretly prayed that this child of hers should pass on. After a strenuous night of performing to a heckling audience, trying to keep greedy paws away from her luxuriant bottom, it was difficult to even keep her eyes open let alone administer to her sick child. Her husband would be drinking with the troupe members, exchanging abuses. The sounds of raucous laughter and cheap jokes would float into the wagon as Ruma valiantly tried to stay awake and help her little girl to breathe. She was not maudlin, Ruma was a tough bird, a survivor. She was hell-bent on keeping her family going, hoping beyond hope that a son would come along who would then be her ticket to retirement.

She longed to own a small piece of land and grow her own vegetables. They never stayed long enough anywhere to be attached to anything but somewhere in the back of her mind, Ruma dreamt of an emerald green patch of earth.

She was lucky in having a good husband. Though it was a hard life, he was essentially a good man who did not trouble her too much. His wants were few and they managed to eke out a little intimacy now and then in the wagon when they thought that the girls were sleeping. Once when they were locked in each other's arms, Ruma happened to see a pair of wide eyes gazing at her in shock. Without breaking movement, she had turned and covered the eyes and had kept them like that, till she and her husband were done. Afterwards, when she had withdrawn her hand, she had found the eyes closed as if in deep sleep. Nothing was mentioned the next morning.

Thus when Juhibaby came into the world, she was not welcome. She was yet another girl. This time her father shot a baleful look at his wife as if she were to blame for the chromosomes. This time, she too had hung her head in shame as if this transgression was of her making. Thereafter, to show her remorse, she never picked up Juhibaby, except to occasionally put her to her breast. She was virtually raised by the eldest sibling, Chhayamoni, who by now was bursting into puberty and already drawing attention to herself. Every time she carried the little infant with her, she would be stared at. Some even dared to make harmless advances but these were met with downcast eyes and a stoic silence.

The little infant had no name. Being so unwanted and unwelcome, it was left to the eldest sister to call her something. So, somehow, the name Juhibaby fell on her. Juhi was the name of the heroine of the jatra performance. Her actual name was Mrinmoyee but since she was doing the role of the Western-educated city-bred girl Juhi (flower of eternity) everyone called her Juhibaby.

Juhibaby was the star attraction of the troupe. Tall for her age and buxom, she should have been in a better place, but as everyone around her would murmur, 'Karma... karma... nothing but rotten luck! She was born for something else. Why is she here with us menials?' And Juhibaby would revel in their adulation. She had a raucous voice, a big appetite for life, and was a threat to all the women associated with the troupe, including Ruma. But Ruma had a native intelligence and never exposed her vulnerability. Only in the privacy of the wagon would she whisper to her husband and warn him against any attraction to Juhi. Her husband, tired after a sad night of singing for plebians, would nod drunkenly and while half-heartedly attempting to grab her, slip off into peaceful slumber. Ruma would then pick up Juhibaby at the end of her day and put her to her breast.

One day, she looked deep into her daughter's eyes and became alarmed. My God, this is not an infant. She has grown up.

'How old is she now?' she asked her firstborn.

Chhayamoni absently asked, 'Who?'

'Your sister, who else?' said Ruma.

'Oh, you mean Juhibaby?' Chhayamoni casually responded. And that is how the mother learnt that her youngest daughter had been christened 'Juhibaby' by her siblings. For the first time her eyes had moistened on seeing the beautiful chiselled face of her baby. She averted her face quickly but not quickly enough. The eldest one saw her mother's guilt, and rejoiced.

Chhayamoni was growing tired of her life. She wanted to settle down. She wanted a man's touch. Above all, she wanted her mother to love the little one. This youngest one had been like her own child. From the time she was born, it was she who had bathed her and cleaned her bottom and fed her. She was truly her mother. Juhibaby thought so too! When the other siblings called Ruma 'Ma', Juhi would call Chhayamoni 'my Ma' and everyone around would laugh. Even Juhibaby would gurgle, pleased to have been the cause of so much mirth.

And then, one day, without warning, the troupe was asked to disperse. They had to close shop. There was too much competition from the Bioscope, as the cinema was called those days. The manager could not make ends meet. It was a bad time for all. Ruma and her husband were torn in despair. What could they do? They had no other means, assets, abilities. All they could do between the two of them was to sing and dance. But now there were no takers. Besides which they had five other hungry mouths to feed.

With a heavy heart, they parted with their costumes, carefully worn and maintained over all these years. And they put all their personal belongings in two small steel trunks. They did not have much—some clothes, utensils, jars for spices and a few well-preserved books. With these worldly possessions, they stumbled out to the vast unexplored world to eke out a living.

It was surprisingly Juhibaby, the original prima donna of their drama, who landed them their first job. Though not particularly fond of Ruma who she suspected was spreading rumours about her behind her back, Juhibaby was nonetheless sympathetic to Chhayamoni. She had liked the girls' demure behaviour and had openly expressed her pleasure when told that the little sibling in her arms had been christened Juhibaby after her. This had flattered her no end and she was looking for a way to repay the compliment.

So, when she heard that someone in Calcutta was desperately looking for an honest housemaid, Juhibaby wrote the address on a piece of paper and handed it to the father. 'You can tell them that I sent you,' she said somewhat imperiously. Of course, the family of seven had no choice. Numb with shock and terrified by the prospect of imminent starvation, they thanked her profusely and set out to the distant land of Calcutta, the land of opportunities, the land that would calm the leaping frogs in their stomachs.

156, Rashbehari Avenue stood out from amongst the other equally august mansions that dotted the tree-lined avenue. Though suitably subdued from the exterior, the children marvelled at the blue-painted windows, set against lilac walls. Chhayamoni was presented first—beautiful, with a flawless skin and a wonderfully curvaceous body—and the

Mitra family welcomed her warmly. They had no daughter and they had to find help for their paraplegic twin boys who were around the same age as Chhayamoni.

Why they should open their hearts out to a beautiful girl, traumatized by poverty and despair, is another story. But as this particular story goes, Mrs Mitra suffered from 'alasya', a respectable disease prone to attack people of high birth, a malaise involving complete non-action. Mrs Mitra hated to wake up in the mornings, she hated to cook, she even hated to supervise the cooks as they went about their chores—cutting, chopping, grinding. She hated to be woken up at 5 p.m. for evening tea, and 'jolkhabar' replete with piping hot snacks. She hated to go for the 'ga-dhua', the evening ablutions, prior to lighting the lamps at the altar. And most of all, she hated to tend to her paraplegic boys. She loved them in her own way—but with a distanced, detached curiosity, as one would love a diseased pet.

When she was younger, things had been better. Mr Mitra's business as a retail textile merchant had been flourishing and she had an army of servants. But as time went by, Mr Mitra succumbed to the tough labour laws of the times and now they had pretty much nothing left but this mansion at 156, Rashbehari Avenue, to fall back on.

Mrs Mitra hated to have to comb her long tresses, hated to keep hunting for her large, heavy bunch of keys which, when found, were tied to the end of her saree pallu, only to be misplaced yet again. She hated to have to rush to the sound of falling plates and glasses as the twins whooped clumsily around the verandah. Of late, she had even started hating the evenings, when she would sit fanning Mr Mitra after his hard day at the shop, complaining about the neighbours and the twins' erratic behaviour.

No servant was willing to stay beyond a week. She overworked them enormously, not lifting a finger, not even to get a glass of water for herself.

It was therefore a godsend when a poor family of seven descended on their house. Right from the start Mrs Mitra had made things clear. They could use the servants' quarters behind the house, provided they used electricity only at night, while sleeping. She would provide food only for the eldest daughter, Chhayamoni, who was the official servant of the household. The rest of the family had to fend for themselves by looking for jobs outside the mansion. Chhayamoni had to be at the big house by 6 a.m. and could return by midnight. She had an hour off after lunch provided she stayed on in the mansion and kept an eye on the twins. After the deal was struck, Ruma moved in with her relieved family. They had journeyed for miles, part of the way on foot.

When she entered the servants' quarter, Ruma was speechless with joy. For the first time in her life she had a permanent place to call home. The room was quite large and airy and had a small anteroom which the previous servants had used as a kitchenette for there was a broken stove and some utensils lying carelessly around. There was also a toilet attached to the room—a luxury indeed for those used to the open fields and a quick dip in a nearby pond. Quickly, Ruma set about fixing the stove. Being trained all her life to combat adversity, she managed to fix it soon enough by twirling around small pieces of wire that her probing eyes had located under the stairwell. There were enough rations for two days—a kilo of rice, a half bottle of salt and some chickpeas. Ruma yearned for some eggs and clarified butter that would go so well with the boiled rice. But that would have to wait. Today she would manage to feed her family.

And so the Small House and the Big House settled into a peaceful co-existence.

✦

Ruma goes out and finds herself surrounded by a green lawn. It is unkempt, with flowering bushes and tall trees. She knows them—coconut, guava, mango. Tentatively, she plucks a ripe guava and then immediately tenses. Could the Mitras have seen her? Could this small transgression amount to thieving? She quickly covers the guava with her saree and goes back to the Small House.

Chhayamoni wakes up at the crack of dawn. This place smells so different from the fresh air that she has experienced all her life. There she would wake up to the smell of rajnigandha or the warm smell of crackling firewood or the cool breeze of a stream. Here the morning hangs on her like a damp shawl. The skies are overcast and moisture-laden; the trees numbed by the nightly dewdrops stand silent, humble, head bowed. The street is already stirring with activity. She can hear the sound of feet as someone pulls a cycle rickshaw. She had seen one for the first time in Calcutta. In her sojourn with her parents in rural Bengal, she had never seen a human being pull another human being sitting primly in a carriage. She had been at first aghast and then faintly amused, as if it were a joke. But then for the poor, poverty is not that hard-hitting. One grows up with it, is used to it and does not know anything different.

A dog whimpers and a loud sound is heard from the Big House. She looks up anxiously as a light is switched on. The twins are up to something. Quickly she bathes and with wet hair, she steps out of the Small House and tries to find her way into the Big House. As she leaves, Ruma stirs. Their eyes meet for a moment. Neither greets the other, just a look which holds the moment together. Chhayamoni leaves and Ruma turns her back to grab a a few more moments of sleep before she wakes up to the reality of hunting for food for her family.

The house, which had looked friendly in the day, has an eerie appearance at dawn. Chhayamoni quietly tiptoes her way across the lawn and enters from the side door which opens into the stairwell. It is dark and Chhayamoni's heart is beating rapidly. Softly, she inches her way up, her hands groping the banister till she comes to a landing and faces a vast corridor. In her entire life she has never seen such a huge house. The balcony has a scalloped balustrade curving out into a central courtyard. Huge diamond rocks glinting, multi-hued, are suspended from the ceiling. She has never known chandeliers. She tiptoes towards the room to her left which has a slab of light spilling under the door. Her feet glide over marble floors at once cold and impersonal.

Shivering slightly with fear and excitement, Chhayamoni reaches the door. Now she stands confused. What is she expected to do? She looks to her left and right. No one in sight. Suddenly, the air is rent with a bloodcurdling scream which is cut short by a sharp sound of what seems like a slap. Horrified, she is frozen to the spot. Just as quickly two voices in unison start to sing in a high-pitched voice. A few doors away, a female voice calls out sharply. Chhayamoni scurries towards the door.

Mrs Mitra, dishevelled, paan-stained mouth opening into a huge yawn, comes lumbering out, her pallu with the heavy bunch of keys trailing on the floor behind her. As Chhayamoni bends to pick it up and help put it on Mrs Mitra's shoulder, the latter slumps down clumsily on the floor. Chhayamoni is baffled but Mrs Mitra nonchalantly instructs her to finger-comb her long tresses and massage her scalp. Ignoring the twins' eerie morning litany, Mrs Mitra closes her eyes while accepting Chhayamoni's gentle administration on her scalp. That done, the girl is instructed to go to the kitchen where she will meet the head cook, and serve as her assistant.

✦

By the end of the first month, Chhayamoni was bone-tired but had got the hang of her responsibilities. Mrs Mitra, abdicating hers, took to her bed, fanning herself, making paan from her ornate paan box, and giving half-hearted and incoherent instructions to Chhayamoni. With the experience of helping her mother raise four children under harsh circumstances, Chhayamoni found working in the mansion a huge luxury. The only difficult time was when Mrs Mitra closed her door for her afternoon siesta and Chhayamoni had to keep an eye on the twins. The elder twin was more seriously paraplegic than his brother and had to be propped up in a wheelchair. The younger one moved around with a gliding limp. But they were so energetic and active that Chhayamoni had to be on her toes all the time though this was officially her 'rest time', when she could stretch out on a mat in the balcony. Though she couldn't understand their chatter or the meaning of their raucous laughter, she nonetheless found herself laughing with them. Initially, Mrs Mitra would be around while Mr Mitra bathed the twins. But now she had begun to make excuses and discreetly disappear, leaving Chhayamoni with the embarrassing task of handing over items of clothing to the wet and naked twins.

Time passed quickly for the residents of 156, Rashbehari Avenue. Mr Mitra, to his utter astonishment, found that his business had suddenly picked up. Once more he was able to provide more servants to his wife, who by now, lived in a more or less torpid stupor. The entire household was in Chhayamoni's care and Mr Mitra gave her full credit.

'She is our Lakshmi sent by God,' he told his listless wife.

Mrs Mitra agreed by nodding, too tired to do anything more than chew her betel leaves.

'She is the daughter we did not have,' continued Mr Mitra, waxing eloquent.

Suddenly, Mrs Mitra artfully positioned red spittle into the spittle bowl, and slowly turning to her husband, remarked, 'But she can be our daughter-in-law!'

Mr Mitra stared, confused, at his wife. 'You're right, why didn't I think of it earlier?'

To which his wife replied laconically, 'Because we have forgotten that six years ago she came with her family as a servant.'

Mr Mitra recoiled as if the thought itself was unbearable. 'No need to bring that up! She is a good girl and perfect for our little master. Go and talk to her mother.'

Mrs Mitra managed a torpid nod.

Ruma had been carefully cleaning the aubergines that she had harvested that morning from her emerald patch of green when she was hugely astonished to see Mrs Mitra standing at her doorstep. Open-mouthed, Ruma silently prayed that any lapse of duty on Chhayamoni's part was not responsible for this early morning visit.

So imagine her shock when Mrs Mitra, without any preamble, without even sitting down, blurted out, 'I want Chhaya to be my son's bride.'

Ruma turned red, then deathly white. How was she to react? Happiness or despair? Happiness that her daughter was going to be the mistress of this stately mansion, or despair that the bridegroom in question was a paraplegic?

Minutes passed. Both women just stood in front of each other, caught in a time warp. The silence was broken by

Juhibaby, now a cute girl of six years, bursting into the room, singing a film ditty at the top of her voice. Mrs Mitra started faintly and mustered up the energy to ask her, 'Do you want your Didi to marry my son?'

Upon which Juhibaby burst into loud lamentations and ran all the way up to the Big House where on finding Chhayamoni, she clung to her and wept copiously.

It was thus through Juhibaby that Chhayamoni heard about the marriage proposal. She was not perturbed. In fact, she was expecting it sooner or later. She was in any case older than the other marriageable girls of her age who she had grown up with. But she had no choice. She was the chief breadwinner, a mantle forced upon her by circumstance. Her father, growing increasingly despondent over the years, had totally given up singing and would lie on his iron cot for hours, staring at the ceiling. Her mother cleaned floors and washed clothes in two of the mansions down the street. But Ruma was aging rapidly. Giving birth to five children, with little or no care, had taken a toll on her and except for her obsession with her vegetable patch, she too had started to spend her days listlessly.

The second daughter dutifully helped her mother, still following the pattern of washing the household clothes. The third daughter, the bright one, did not bother with the tin box any more. Mr Mitra had got a bank account opened in Chhayamoni's name and hence she was the one who dealt with all financial matters related to her family.

The fourth daughter had had a remarkable turn of fortune. Having discovered a knack for sewing, the girl had made a name for herself in the municipal school in which Mr Mitra had got all the sisters admitted, and, basking in the adulation, asthma had left her forever.

Which brings us to Juhibaby. Knowing only Chhayamoni as her mother, Juhibaby had grown up in the mansion in the shadow of her older sister, 'Mamoni', as she used to lisp adorably. In the early days of moving into the Small House, Juhibaby could not bear to leave her beloved Mamoni, even for an instant. She had been a toddler then and whenever she could escape, she would make her way towards the Big House. Chhayamoni would hear the tinkling sound of her anklets rhythmically making 'chhan chhan' sounds as little Juhibaby came searching for her Mamoni.

Then, Chhayamoni would panic and sneak her little sister away to a remote part of the mansion. She was too new and perpetually in dread of losing her job. Hiding young Juhibaby in the folds of her saree, she would pet her and croon to her, sometimes sneaking out a sweetmeat or a biscuit which she would break up into pieces and feed her with her own hands.

Once, she had managed to save one plump yellow mango for her Juhibaby. Skilfully ripping off the top with her teeth, she was preparing to scoop out the pulp to feed her when she froze. Someone was sniffing her back and before she could react, a neighing sound exploded around her. Shocked, hand squeezing the pulpy mango, she stared at the apparition in front of her. He was of medium height, with a smooth hairless complexion, oval face with a high brow, bright-eyed, but he was standing at a forty-five degree angle and was neighing like a horse gone berserk. And then he moved and the sisters watched in horror as the apparition limped away, gliding across the marble floor at an alarming angle. He stopped and turned and they saw two eyes filled with laughter. He approached them once more, eyed the mango, neighed again and lurched away. Both the girls remained there for a long time, the mango forgotten and reduced to a soggy mess, dripping on the polished floor. That had been Juhibaby's first encounter with Benu, the younger of the paraplegic twins.

Now, as she wrapped herself around her sister, tearfully telling her about the marriage proposal, Chhayamoni gently reminded her of the day when she had first met Benu, and had forgotten to eat the unfortunate mango. Juhibaby consented to laugh and both sisters hugged and rocked each other, one twenty years of age, the other just six.

After that, the two were inseparable. Juhibaby would not leave Chhayamoni. She sensed that things would change. Her biological mother Ruma would not stop blabbering, unable to contain her excitement. 'Now she will be sleeping in the west wing with Benu sahib. Her mother-in-law has already made plans to break down the wall and create a big living and bed unit for them. She does not want the elder son, Bonju sahib, to feel envious. Poor thing, how can he marry, he can't even straighten his legs, poor soul.'

Juhibaby would hear this and sundry other pieces of information that her mother would divulge to all who cared to listen. By now, Ruma had made a lot of friends in the neighbourhood. All the servants would meet at the gate or sit on the verandah outside the Small House and envy Ruma her destiny.

'Imagine, you came here as a servant, and now you will be the bride's mother.'

And Ruma would only say, 'I wish "he" were alive to see this day.'

'He'—her husband—had passed on as peacefully and unobtrusively as he had lived. He had asked her to sit close to him one morning. She was tired and had several things to do, so she had said, 'Let me just finish with the grinding and I'll join you.'

She would always regret this because, as she ground her spices on the black stone slab, her thoughts wheeling freely around her, she could not hear him singing soulfully on his bed, 'Je raat, amore duaar guli, bhanglo jhodey'—The night my house was destroyed by the storm.

One part of her was irritated, she worked like a dog, morning to night, while he just ate, slept and sang. But she loved him in her own way. He was not like the rest. He could not pull a rickshaw, he could not sit long enough at a shop, he could not be a mason, he didn't know anything very much, except to sing and act. And here, at Rashbehari Avenue, there were no takers. So, he just sang to keep his soul together and that is what he was doing when his soul took leave of his body. By the time Ruma had finished her pounding and had cleaned up, splashed water on her face, in preparation for her little cosy time with her husband, he was dead.

But now there was no time to dwell on the dead. She was alive. She had five daughters and by God's grace, the eldest one was going to be married to the son of the house. What more could a poor woman ask for? Juhibaby hung on to every word she could hear. She knew what sarees had been bought and stored in the steel trunk. She knew the details of the trousseau that their mother had been painstakingly collecting for her firstborn. She knew about the loans, the debts, the bartering. She was the unofficial bearer of news from the Small House to the Big House.

Till date, people talk of Chhayamoni's wedding to Benu sahib with hushed awe. A servant girl so beautiful and accomplished was a rare combination. She got approval from all quarters as she sat bedecked, head hung low, her red bridal veil covering half her face. But the person who never left her for a second was Juhibaby. She clung to her sister with a desperation that came from a soul unfed and unwanted by her biological mother, the principal actor of her undesired birth. Ruma was too busy running around organizing the rituals, in between showing off her newly found status, to bother about her youngest child. The only time she had reacted strongly was when Juhi refused to let go of her sister during the circumambulations around the sacred fire. Then Ruma had marched in and in one stroke had dragged the wailing Juhibaby and unceremoniously dumped her in the corner.

'Now you just shut up and behave yourself! You are not a baby anymore,' she had hissed.

Juhi had cried herself to sleep, exhausted, abandoned, a forlorn figure in a crumpled crepé silk outfit and fake jewellery.

With Chhayamoni married and busy in the newly renovated side of the house, Juhibaby was not encouraged to walk in and out as freely as she had earlier. Now, whenever she came to the Big House, the servants would make up stories and put her off. On one occasion Mrs Mitra too managed to mumble something about 'leaving newlyweds alone.'

Juhibaby was very curious to know what the newlyweds were up to, what was it that kept her beautiful Mamoni away from her? Once she had cajoled her way to the new extension and had chanced to see her sister's face smeared with vermillion as she came out of Benu sahib's embrace. Juhi had turned red with shame and had run back to the Small House. But when she shared the information with her sisters, in the presence of Ruma, all she got from her was a resounding slap.

'Silly girl! Don't forget our status. We can't keep wandering in and out of the mansion now. We are the girl's family and must keep our place.' Poor logic as far as Juhibaby was concerned.

Ruma now turned her attention to the task of marrying

off her other daughters who were growing up faster than she could cope with, which left Juhibaby mostly ignored, as if she did not exist.

Until the year Juhi celebrated her sixteenth birthday. Nobody had thought that this last child would turn out to be such a beauty. 'She has beaten Chhayamoni hollow,' was the common refrain. Juhi did not appreciate such comparisons because deep down Mamoni was her only mother, her companion, her soulmate.

With great difficulty and many hospitalizations later, Mamoni had recently given birth to a son and the 'annaprashan' ceremony, when the baby is fed his first morsel at the age of six months, had been spread over a whole week. And it was on this occasion that Ruma was pleasantly surprised to get an offer for none other than Juhibaby's hand.

She had protested, 'Why don't you see my other daughters? Juhi is too young.'

But the marriage mediator had insisted that the boy's family was interested only in Juhi.And thus at the tender age of sixteen, Juhibaby was married off to a person she had not set her eyes on, becoming part of a family she did not know and sent off to a city she had never known even existed...

Chhayamoni could not attend the wedding. Her little child was suffering from a mild attack of chickenpox and the Mitras were loath to expose their newly begotten grandchild to the slightest risk.

✦

In her black and white wedding snaps, Juhi looks beautiful and distant, as if this were something happening to someone else. Her three unmarried sisters standing around her are looking glum and Ruma is wearing an apologetic smile. Juhi does not smile.

Yet, she is happy to be away from her mother and her sisters. She is happy to be away from the school which she had hated.

As the flower-bedecked hired car, bearing the newlyweds, rolls out of 156, Rashbehari Avenue, Juhibaby glances desperately for one last glimpse of Chhayamoni.

2
Pandara Road

In all her sixteen years, Juhibaby had never sat on a train. Born unwanted in a wagon and raised somewhat apologetically in 156, Rashbehari Avenue, Juhibaby had never had any reason to travel by train until now. Her earliest memories had been of that jolting wagon lumbering over undulating roads that carried them to the next small village where they would stop and perform.

So when Juhibaby sat for the first time in a train at Calcutta's loud and bustling Howrah station, she was numb with shock. Tired out by countless rituals, her body frozen with fear of making contact with her new husband, who sat equally frozen next to her, the only thing that Juhibaby could think of was food. She was paralyzed with hunger, petrified that the growling sounds in her stomach would be amplified for all to hear. She had been awakened at dawn to bathe in a turmeric and cream paste which had been rubbed over her entire body as a preamble to being prettied and decorated, officially served up to her husband, a beautiful virgin. She had enjoyed the attention as many gentle hands had fawned and fussed over her, remarking on her tender skin and smooth contours. The day had been full of excitement and surprises.

Chhayamoni had been wedded in the lilac and blue mansion, the Big House. But for her own wedding, a local wedding hall had been hired. Chhayamoni and her husband had paid extra money to decorate it with special lights and flowers and the band had played film songs raucously throughout the day. Juhibaby felt hot and sweaty, dazzled by the gifts that they had received. She had never before been the centre of attention and was awkward and confused. The three older sisters were doing their duty sullenly, darting envious glances at her. Juhibaby knew that they felt cheated . They could not understand how Juhibaby, the youngest of all the sisters, was getting married before them. Juhibaby felt angry with them. It was not like she had wanted to get married before them. And it was not like their mother had had much of a choice. Left with four daughters to marry off, how could beggars be choosers? And if Juhibaby got herself a good family then their position in the social ladder would improve the prospects of the three remaining sisters.

✦

And now as the train pulled out of Howrah station, the last-minute teary farewells over, Juhibaby realized just how famished she was. Coyly, she glanced at the tiffin box containing an elaborate nuptial feast. It was a copper dabba with five compartments gleaming under the yellow bulb, swaying slightly as the train picked up speed. Juhibaby tried to imagine what the container held. Though she was told about the wedding lunch menu, she had been too excited to bother with such details. She was the bride! She had to have her hair done up in tiny ringlets, her hands and feet had to be soaked in borax water and scrubbed with a pumice stone and Cutex nail polish applied on her fingernails and toenails. She also had to check the fittings of her petticoat and blouse for any last-minute glitches and to supervise the trunk, which would carry her meagre trousseau all the way to another corner of the world where her new home awaited her. All this was truly intoxicating for the sixteen-year-old, ravishingly beautiful Juhibaby.

She glanced surreptitiously at the pair of trousers sitting motionless next to her. They were a grey tweed, formal but not very expensive. She had seen really expensive suiting worn by the Mitra scion, her brother-in-law, Benu sahib, at his marriage. That smelt of class, of subdued elegance. But the trousers sitting next to her were shiny, sparkling and fragile. And suddenly she felt a terrific attraction, rising from within her. This was to be one of many such sensations that she would experience as a new bride but this first time sent a powerful shock right through her body.

She quivered slightly. As if on cue, the trouser moved a bit and a hand, square-shaped with nice round neat cuticles, came and self-consciously rested in the air, an inch above her knees. She stared at the hand, curious and excited. It did not touch her, merely hovered over her knee uncertainly. The gold band, the wedding ring which she had slipped onto his finger just a few hours earlier, looked distinctly uncomfortable in its new perch. As Juhibaby sat there, head bowed, shoulders revolting against the strain of keeping her veil and saree pallu pinned tightly across her shoulders, the second hand swooped down and picked up the tiffin box. She stared in fascination as the hands opened the boxes and arranged the bowls of food in the space between her and the trousers. Head bent demurely, now in her field of vision were two hands, a pair of trousers and six bowls of food from which delicious smells arose. Her heart beat loudly with hunger... or maybe it was her stomach? Then, the two hands delved into a cloth bag and emerged with two steel plates, two smaller bowls with curved rims, and two steel tumblers. Dinner set, the hands now went back to meet the trousers and rest on them. No words were spoken. Juhibaby grew anxious. Was this her cue? Was she supposed to ask her new husband to eat before her? Did she have to serve him? She eyed the delectable fish preparation desperately.

Fish had always been her weakness. Though her sisters preferred chicken and the rare treat of mutton, Juhibaby herself craved fish in any form. When she had been growing up in 156, Rashbehari Avenue, she would be drawn towards the kitchen in the Big House, where Shonama, the head cook, would drop turmeric-slathered pieces of fish into a cauldron popping with hot mustard oil. Juhibaby would stand near the door, desperate for a small piece of the shimmering fry, only to be rudely shooed away. Sometimes, she would bully or charm her way to Chhayamoni's wing and get a big piece of fish. Her mother barely had money to keep a basic kitchen running in the Small House. Subsisting mostly on cheap rice and vegetables from her patch of garden, fish was a luxury. It was only much after her sister had been married into the Big House, that Mr Mitra, Chhayamoni's ex-employer-turned-father-in-law, had made arrangements with Amar, the fish vendor, to leave five pieces of fish, mostly the secondary head and tail, daily at the Small House. So when Juhibaby was growing up, there was only one tiny piece of fish for each member. You could take time to savour it, smell it, gobble it, chew on it for hours till no trace of the fish remained on the plate, but one piece was all you got. You could never ask for more.

Suddenly Juhibaby could wait no longer. She dipped her

fingers into the bowl of fish and scooped out two portions and dropped them on the two waiting plates. The hands resting on the trousers next to her did not move and so she impulsively took a plate and placed it on the nervous lap. She heard a soft deep laugh and glanced up to see a most handsome young man smiling shyly at her. Her heart skipped a beat. Was this good-looking stranger really her husband? Just as quickly, she averted her eyes and fixed her attention on the oil-laden gravy, which was threatening to separate itself from the chunky piece of fish. Then one of the hands reached towards her plate, plucked out a portion of fish, deboned it gently and then proceeded to slide it into her mouth. Embarrassed but ravenous, Juhibaby delicately parted her lips. Then she opened her mouth wide and surrendered to the sheer joy of eating fish. As morsel after morsel went down her throat, she began to feel satiated and drowsy. Suddenly she was jolted into reality when she glanced at the hand, which was now streaked with the bright yellow curry and small grains of rice. She had been eating so quickly and hungrily that she had forgotten that the hand going into her mouth was not hers, but his. Mortified, she stopped eating. The hand, unperturbed, nonchalantly served itself some rice and proceeded to eat quietly. Meanwhile the train rumbled into the night, thundering over rickety bridges, boasting its presence through loud horns, overlapped by the louder horns of passing trains.

✦

Juhibaby could not remember when she actually connected with her husband in a real way. There was no thunder and lightning, no moment when she saw stars. It was as if they had always known each other, as if he would always be around to feed her. Juhibaby's first marital home was A-181, Pandara Road, New Delhi. When the newlyweds reached the house, after a full twenty-four hours of being on a train, Juhibaby distinctly remembered the beautiful alpanas, floral patterns made from powdered rice, decorating the portal. Pink lotuses surrounded by delicately designed conch shells in purple and green. She had never seen anything so exquisite, so symmetrical, so harmonious. Eyes downcast, she went through all the rituals accompanying a bride's official entry into her husband's home. She did not look up at the faces of the women who were performing the rituals. Again all she could see were hands.

One pair of hands, oldish and bare of ornaments, led her inside the house. A younger pair of hands, mocha-complexioned, wearing a thin bracelet guided her to tip with her right toe the vessel containing rice, symbolizing the bride's auspicious entry into her new household. There were numerous other hands, with dazzling bracelets, armlets, rings, and bangles, swirling around in many-hued silk sarees. Still Juhibaby did not dare to look up. There was no one from her side of the family there. Her mother-in-law had easily convinced a much-relieved Ruma that henceforth Juhibaby would be like a daughter and therefore, Ruma should not take on the added expenditure of sending an escort. So here was Juhibaby in a foreign land surrounded by an army of people whom she had never before set her eyes on. The pair of trousers was next to her throughout, joined to her with his angvastra tied to the end of her saree pallu, signifying ritually that henceforth they were one. A lot of bantering and laughter accompanied them as they moved from one ritual to another, till finally she found herself seated on a colourful mat on the floor, in front of what seemed like an altar. Quietly she lifted her gaze to see a tiny room. It was about four feet by four feet in size, stacked with tins, big cartons, boxes and bottles of all shapes and sizes. The lower half of the space was converted into a makeshift altar where Lord Shiva jostled with Lord Ram gazing benignly at Lord Krishna's photograph that tilted precariously over a tin box. Beautiful marigolds and roses were arranged in front of each deity and the air was thick with the sweet and slightly overwhelming smell of incense.

Now the aged arms lifted her veil and a face peered into her face. This was the official 'mukhe dekha', the bride-viewing ceremony where the mother-in-law officially saw the face of her son's bride and blessed her by gifting her an ornament, traditionally a gold one. Even the poorest of the poor normally squirrelled away one such gold token to be given during this ritual.

Juhibaby gazed at her mother-in-law for the first time and was instantly struck by the strong resemblance to her husband, the same aquiline features and honest deep brown eyes, brimming with a sweet compassion. Juhibaby quickly looked down as her mother-in-law wiped a tear and pressed a red velvet box into her hands. After that several hands lifted her veil, looked at her, praised her beauty, pressed a gift into her lap and gave way to the next inspector. Juhibaby was dying to see the gifts and felt extremely concerned that the pair of mocha arms was systematically syphoning each one into a large cloth bag. Finally the ceremony was over and everyone exhorted the sister-in-law to be the last one to see the bride's face. With that the mocha arms disengaged from stuffing the cloth bag and lifted her veil. Their eyes met and Juhibaby had a strong feeling that they had met before, but where? Juhibaby saw a dark-complexioned girl of uncertain age, with a high brow and bulbous nose. But the eyes were the same, a liquid brown like her husband's and his mother's, full of understanding and compassion. A brief flicker of a shy smile passed like a current between them and the veil was dropped back into place.

Fifty years later, one would die in the other's arms in a taxi. A substitute for the sacred water, Gangajal, ritualistically poured into the mouth of the departing soul, would be provided by a flustered Sikh taxi driver in the form of a plastic bottle of tap water.

✦

The first night had been smooth. Though Ruma had not discharged her maternal duties and given explicit instructions on what was expected of a new bride when she confronted her husband on their first night together, Juhibaby kind of knew about the birds and bees. The memory of seeing her beautiful Mamoni hurriedly breaking out of Benu sahib's embrace when she had barged into their room as a six-year-old, still remained. Her clothes were askew and there was a lot of vermillion sindoor smeared on her forehead. Her sister had giggled in embarrassment but her brother-in-law, the rich and fancy Limping Man, had flailed his arms and neighed like a horse. Appalled though she was, some innate sixth sense told Juhi of the intimacy she had interrupted.

The government flat at A-181, Pandara Road had two small bedrooms, one sitting room, also decorously referred to as the 'drawing room', one back verandah, converted into a dining area, a kitchen and that tiny storeroom which housed the family altar. There was also a verandah in the front of the house, which, partly covered by bamboo chicks, made a compact bedsitter, with a table and chair. This was the room of her elder brother-in-law, Rajeshwar. He was a bachelor and like her husband, a government servant. All this information she had garnered from the continuous flow of chatter and revelry that had engulfed her since she had entered her new home. Juhibaby and her husband, Brijeshwar, were given the last room, which opened into a tiny backyard. Here, according to the information helpfully offered by one of the faceless saree-clad guests, her mother-in-law had planted her tulsi, the holy basil plant, and her brother-in-law, an ardent nature lover, had his pocket-size garden consisting of a collection of flowering bushes, roses, arcadia and the regal rajnigandha, the night queen.

Juhibaby had once seen a film in Calcutta's Menaka Talkies, on the lane adjacent to156, Rashbehari Avenue, in which the bridal room had been decorated with rajnigandha flowers hanging from the bedstead, and the groom, drunk on the local brew, had staggered in, pulling at the flower strands till he had collapsed in a heap on the floor, at the feet of his bewildered bride. The image had been imprinted into her young mind and so, when Juhibaby and her husband were, in accordance with the ritual of 'phool sojjer raat', the first night, shoved into the bridal room by giggling relatives and the door dramatically shut behind them, she was surprised to find it decorated with sweet-smelling flowers arranged in lovely floral patterns around the bed. There were no strands of rajnigandhas hanging from the bedpost, no dim lights, no nuptial music, or the mandatory shehnai. A naked bulb, a flower-strewn bed, a bedspread converted into a curtain, was all that met her eye.

Her husband had changed into a fawn-coloured silk kurta worn over white pajamas. In a way, it reminded her of her father, and she started to relax. Her father too invariably wore a kurta-pajama while sitting in the pit to sing his soulful songs to heckling audiences. Vaguely she wondered how he was in the other world he had gone to. She could see a turmeric stain on her brand new husband's pajamas, near the knee, and she smiled inwardly at the memory of the meal on the train. She stood stock-still near the bed, hardly daring to breathe. Moments passed. Neither said a word. They could hear muted sounds outside the closed door. From the backyard sounds of utensils being washed and the rhythmic sounds of 'shish-shish', tamarind rind over copper vessels, overlapped with her mother-in-law's soft laughter. Somebody was shutting windows and the rattle of heavy keys came very near their back door, causing her to freeze for a moment. Some wedding guests, who were bedding down in the 'drawing room' on mattresses and blankets hired from the local tentwalla, had started to sing and Juhibaby was suddenly and powerfully transported back in time. She remembered with a fierce intensity how she would nod off to the sound of distant singing by members of the jatra troupe her parents had been a part of.

Suddenly she found a pair of hands thrusting something into her mouth. Perpetually underfed and starved for attention as a child, habit kicked in and Juhibaby opened her mouth wide. Holy God! It was fish! And not just any fish, her favourite fish, the silvery white hilsa of the ocean. It had been deboned and she chewed voraciously on its succulent flesh that had been curried to perfection. Eyes closed, she ate her fill till she heard a soft familiar laugh. Juhibaby opened her eyes to find her husband feeding her fish, big drops of mustard oil dripping freely onto his pajamas. They both laughed heartily and instantly hushed up for fear of being heard. But still they stared into each other's eyes bright with laughter, a finger on their lips as though they were sharing a secret. That was how Juhibaby and Brijeshwar or 'Shono', metaphorically and literally translated as 'listen', as traditional women were not encouraged to call their husbands by their name, spent the first night together, feeding each other, looking at each other from opposite sides of the double bed and basking in each other's presence. They did not sleep all night but as it turned towards dawn, Juhibaby dozed off and saw herself in a tunnel. She was locked in the dark, she could not see, she could not breathe, but from somewhere a hand came and slipped a piece of fish in her mouth. She screamed in terror, just once, but slowly succumbed to the comfort of the food melting on her tongue as her Shono, her husband, watched her from his side of the bed. His beautiful bride was sitting upright, fast asleep, chewing peacefully, her rosebud mouth moving up and down, clamping over the non-existent fish. He sighed contentedly and noiselessly shut the tiffin box containing the fish, which he had sneaked in from the kitchen earlier in the evening. Only then did he try to pat clean the turmeric and oil stains on his pajamas, a shy smile lighting up his face.

✦

The days after her marriage whizzed past in a whirl. Juhibaby was now officially named 'bourani', queen of brides, and indeed she was a bewitchingly beautiful bride. Gently guided to wake up at dawn, Juhibaby had to complete her ablutions and bath before entering the room with the family altar. Here she had to help her mother-in-law select flowers, fruits and leaves for the morning worship. Actually this was only a ritual because the real work had already been done by Beenarani, her sister-in-law, who awoke at the crack of dawn and readied the basic lunch preparation of rice, lentils and vegetables, prior to leaving for school. She was a teacher at a Montessori school and drew a salary of four hundred rupees a month, a sum she handed over to her mother who in turn gave it to her as and when required. By the time Juhibaby emerged from the puja room, Beenarani was dressed, her saree pallu pinned neatly on her shoulder, a folded hanky tucked in at the waist and a rexine purse under her arm, ready to leave for school.

Juhibaby was left with the official duty of preparing the fish. Fish was considered auspicious in Bengali families and often eulogized as a 'fruit of the ocean'. The simple Brahmin family she had been married into also held this view. In the days before refrigerators became a necessary and integral part of every household, fish had to be inspected, prodded around the ears to test for freshness and consumed as soon as possible. Then Juhibaby would grind the herbs, just the way she had seen her mother and sisters doing, hunched over the sil-batta, the shiny black grinding stone found in every kitchen. She would place the ginger, green chillies, mustard and poppy seeds and grind it all together into one aromatic, pungent tasty mass. How she loved the fresh aroma of the ground herbs! She was the one who had to serve the meal to her husband and his brother as they sat at opposite ends of the rickety second-hand dining table, eating a full-bellied lunch of fish and rice at nine-thirty in the morning before leaving for work.

Between then and their own lunchtime, Juhibaby had nothing much to do. She discovered quickly enough that her husband, his siblings and their mother were self-sufficient islands. They made their own beds, washed their own clothes, hung them up, ironed them using a copper coal iron and kept all their personal belongings meticulously. Sometimes she had seen her husband fold his trousers and place them under their mattress, so that they would be automatically ironed out by morning and they could save the expense of coal. In the Small House where she grew up, things were not so organized, for Ruma was too occupied with earning enough to feed four daughters to pay much heed to neatness and cleanliness.A trifle nervous, Juhibaby tried to keep their sparse room as neat as possible. She placed her steel trunk on top of the wooden chest, which housed the ancestral copper and brass vessels, only brought out on rare occasions. She covered the trunk with a small embroidered tablecloth, given to her by Beenarani who was a gifted seamstress and was forever knitting and sewing after lunch. It was in one such bag stitched and embroidered by Beenarani that Juhibaby's presents had been kept during her 'mukhe dekha' ceremony. With the excitement and greed of a deprived teenager, Juhibaby had panicked about her precious gifts, even imagining that they would be taken away from her. She was awash with relief when, at the conclusion of the functions, Beenarani came to her room and not only handed over each and every gift, but also gave her a list that she had made, marking each gift with the name of the giver. Along with that she had brought the embroidered tablecloth, which bore her name and that of her husband on a pale yellow background. It was an exquisite cross-stitch design that spelt out the message: 'For Dada and Boudi, my beloved elder brother and my sister-in-law'.

This had been placed on Juhibaby's trousseau trunk. Years later this same cloth would create trouble between her daughter Meehika and her.

✦

In the early years of her marriage, Juhibaby did not know a word of Hindi. Which was fine because she stayed indoors and had little interaction with the outside world. Most of the visitors were their Bengali neighbours and she had got accustomed to the rhythm of frequent visitors like Oshima di, Neela di and Opoor Ma. The flat next door was occupied by the quintessentially Punjabi Seth family comprising of Mr and Mrs Seth and their two obese sons, Bittoo and Billoo. Mr Seth rode a blue Lambretta, a two-wheeler scooter, to work and Juhibaby never failed to marvel at the ease with which Mrs Seth would ride pillion, her tiny choli unable to win the war against modesty, revealing mounds of quaking flabby flesh. When Mrs Seth visited them for the first time after the wedding, Juhibaby was gifted a grand sum of five rupees with which she could get a good synthetic saree. She accepted the money gracefully and stood there quietly, beautiful and dumb. Her mother-in-law spoke Hindi like a native and had been chatting with Mrs Sethi for a while when the vegetable vendor came to the door. Her mother-in-law picked up a green bottle gourd, which in Hindi was also referred to as 'ghia', and quietly murmured 'ghia' to herself. This prompted Juhibaby to go to the kitchen and come back with a pot containing ghee, clarified butter, and primly announce 'ghia'. Mrs Seth burst into gales of laughter and for several months to come friends and neighbours teased Juhibaby about her 'ghee 'and 'ghia' episode.

When Juhibaby sang, which was quite often in those early years, she filled the tiny government flat with vibrations so charged that everyone who heard her, would momentarily stop whatever they were doing and just bask in the purity of her melodious voice. She would hum while cooking, standing in the cramped and humid kitchen, unconcerned about the strong smell of garlic or the sputtering of the spices as she stirred the gravy. Sometimes her mother-in-law would smilingly request her to sing a particular favourite, a

Rabindrosangeet, composed by Rabindranath Tagore. This was a passion shared by most Bengalis who also loved fish and rosogullas with equal fervour. Promptly Juhibaby's veil of shyness would evaporate as she stepped into her childhood world of performance and dance. Strong visuals of Ruma and her frail father would seep into her consciousness and her mind would go back to 156, Rashbehari Avenue. How was Chhayamoni? Did she miss her?

The postal delivery system in the late fifties was governed by several factors, including inclement weather, the health of the postman's wife and what the postman ate for dinner the night before. Letters were few and far between and a very precious commodity. The sky blue rectangular envelope, its flaps clumsily stuck together by the swish of a wet tongue, had to be gingerly opened from both sides in case a single precious sentence got torn by a rough hand. Juhibaby had received two letters from Chhayamoni in all this time. Since neither had a sparkling education, the news was always basic and crisp: 'All well. A lot of load-shedding these days, so we are all hot and sweaty. Babooshona, your nephew, got a prize in the school competition for carrying the best egg on a spoon. Ma's gout has worsened. Your brother-in-law well. Hope all okay with you. Give my pranams, salutations to your elders, love, Your Didi Chhayamoni.'

It was one of those days when everything seemed to be moving at a snail's pace. It was mid-morning and Brijeshwar, Rajeshwar and Beenarani were all at work. Juhi's mother-in-law was sitting cross-legged in her puja room, pounding small betel nuts which would go into her mid-morning quota of paan, to help her digestion. Juhibaby was hunched inside the kaal kothri, the coal cellar, a dark box-like cave in the wall. In 156, Rashbehari Avenue, she had rarely ventured into the kitchenette in the Small House and so had no idea, in the beginning, how to light a coal stove. Her mother-in-law always smiled whenever she saw Juhibaby's milky white arms sprayed with black coal powder. Today she was hunched over a pile of coal, carefully sifting it for the evening meal when she felt a sharp dizziness stab her body. Had she been standing, she would surely have fallen. She shook her head as the walls started swirling around her. She must have cried out 'Mamoni', because the next thing she knew was that it was late in the night, and her mother-in-law was sitting next to her fanning her with a bamboo hand fan. When Juhibaby finally opened her eyes, she just smiled and told her, 'You'll be a mother soon.'

Who? What? Juhibaby could not comprehend what her mother-in-law was saying. How did she know? The six hours before her blackout had been completely erased from her memory. She had vomited copiously, had reacted violently to the lingering smell of betel leaves on her mother-in-law's fingers and had a small knot, three fingers wide, under the right side of her belly, enough signals for an experienced dai, a midwife and caregiver like her mother-in-law, to know that she would be a grandmother soon.

Juhibaby's eyes scanned the room for her husband. No sign of him. Just then, as if on cue, he entered, parting the two pieces of cloth that served as a curtain to the door. He quickly glanced at his mother, refraining from showing any signs of affection to Juhibaby. He was carrying a doctor's prescription and a few silvery packets of 'English', as allopathic medicines were referred to. His mother murmured an excuse and left them, silently pulling the curtain shut. Juhibaby looked expectantly at her husband. He looked shy, a little nonplussed. She noticed the crease on his shirt and her heart melted with love for him. He must have come back from office, rushed to get the lady doctor from the government-sponsored dispensary and then walked all the way to Khan Market, a good twenty minutes away, to get the medicine. He went to the bedside and gently held her hand. She locked her fingers with his tightly, murmuring anxiously, 'You won't leave me, will you?' Her voice was a misty whisper.

He looked at her quizzically and just as quietly mumbled, 'No.'

Even though his voice was full of gruff tenderness, Juhibaby started to panic. She tried to open her eyes but something was holding on to her, pulling her down. Whatever it was, it was taking her away from him. 'Help! Help!' she tried to scream but no words came out of her mouth.

No, no. She must keep her eyes wide open. A deep warm laughter broke through her panic, calming her. She knew that laugh! Finally, she managed to open her eyes and looked straight into Brijeshwar's smiling, strong gaze. Suddenly everything was still, all sounds stopped. She was aware only of his eyes locked into hers. He was hers. She was safe. Nothing else mattered. He held her gently, rocking her as she clung to his shoulder and in a few minutes she was fast asleep, her mouth slightly open as she breathed out a sigh.

✦

When Juhibaby 's firstborn, Dada, as Meehika was later taught to call him, was born, the entire family rejoiced for days. Juhibaby had just turned seventeen and had not the faintest idea of what was happening to her. Everything had turned around so rapidly within a year of her first stepping onto a train that had dropped her at the doorstep of her new destination thousands of miles away from her home that she was unsure if this was real. But the pain along with the baby that was making heroic attempts to leave her body was definitely real. And excruciating. But what calmed and soothed her during the traumatic experience was the unconditional love and empathy of her new family—her husband, his siblings and their mother. No amount of pampering was enough for Juhibaby. She was the fair and beautiful queen, whose only job was to bequeath the largesse of her smile upon them and all other matters, big or small, were attended to by the family. Her husband fed her the medicines himself, hovering around her till she delicately swallowed them, turning up her pert nose so gracefully that all he wanted to do was take her in his arms. Beenarani would bathe Juhibaby, lugging the heavy iron bucket filled with piping hot water mixed with an assortment of herbs meticulously hand-ground by her mother. Soon the house was criss-crossed with ropes hung with a variety of homemade nappies, vests and a beautiful array of patchwork duvets and quilts, all hand-crafted by Beenarani. It was a very busy time for the family as neighbours and friends kept dropping by to greet the newborn.

But Juhibaby was tired and listless. Though only seventeen, she felt like a middle-aged woman. Her body ached, her thighs trembled with the memory of her child hurtling out bloody and waxy into the able hands of her mother-in-law, the official midwife. She was too numb to even feel wonder at this little creature to whom she had given birth. Most of the time, she would take her medicine and sleep. Occasionally the infant would be put to her breast and then she would feel a slight sense of connection between them. But on the whole she mostly dozed and let the others take care of her and the baby as well.

When Khokon, alias Dada, was born, Brijeshwar had

sent the mandatory telegram to 156, Rashbehari Avenue. 'Shoo-khobor... Good news. Son born. Mother and son well.'

In reply, Chhayamoni's husband had sent a money order of fifty-one rupees, on which Chhayamoni had scrawled in illegible writing, 'This is for you to buy his first vest from his maternal side.'

Chhayamoni had not forgotten the custom of 'mamar badi', donning the infant with his first vest that came from his mother's maiden home. Ruma, on the other hand, had not called once. Juhibaby kept waiting for Chhayamoni's phone call. Anxiously she had asked Brijeshwar if he had remembered to write the telephone number of their neighbour, Mr Seth, who was the only one in that part of the colony who had the privilege of owning a telephone. Mrs Seth was kind enough to call the family if the matter was urgent but overall she had made it clear that the phone business had to be on a 'very urgent basis only', otherwise she was not going to ferry messages to and fro.

Khokon's first birthday was a grand affair. All the relatives and neighbours were jam-packed in the Pandara Road flat, jostling elbow-to-elbow, knee-to-knee, as the delicious aroma of freshly fried samosas and stuffed kachoris wafted over them. Forty-five people turned up and when the family sat down to do the post-mortem of the function later, they counted six silver glasses, three silver kajaldanis for the kajal or kohl that would be smeared on the infant's eyes to keep away bad spirits, eleven pairs of clothing and sixty-three rupees in cash, apart from the eighteen sugary rosogullas and twenty-six kachoris that had not been consumed.

One spring afternoon, Khokon was toddling all over the room, Juhi's mother-in-law was napping on a chair, her mouth slightly parted, snoring gently, and Beenarani was knitting a crochet cap for Khokon. She kept going up to him to measure his head and the distance between his ears and he kept fighting her off with his chubby little hands. Both aunt and nephew were playfully engrossed with each other when suddenly they were startled to hear a scream and a thud. They looked stunned as they saw Juhibaby crumpled on the floor in a heap. The old lady was the first to react. She rushed to Juhibaby and held her up in her arms while checking her pulse. Beenarani tucked little Khokon on her hip and ran to fetch water. Within seconds Juhibaby's eyes turned blue and her eyeballs rolled upwards. Without wasting a minute, her mother-in-law pulled out a blanket, rolled Juhibaby into it and tucked her up tightly. Then she instructed Beenarani to wet a small towel and place it on Juhibaby's head. This done, she waited expectantly. Sure enough, within minutes Juhibaby opened her eyes, turned and smiled, 'Is it tea time?'

'No, it's another baby time,' her mother-in-law said, smiling faintly.

Juhibaby blinked uncomprehendingly as both women helped her out of the blanket with Khokon toddling around them, wondering perhaps why his mother was emerging like a gift from inside a gift wrapper!

✦

Meehika was born exactly a year and five months after Khokon Dada's birth. She grew up hearing the story that she had almost died at birth and taken her mother with her. This though came from her maternal aunts, Juhibaby's three spinster aunts who were maliciously jealous of the success of their youngest sibling. Whenever Mee confronted Juhibaby on this issue, all she got was a feeble denial, which upset the young Meehika even more.

What Juhibaby remembered of that horrid rainy August evening, was the same dreadful gut-wrenching contractions that she had survived in the recent past. Beyond that she remembered briefly that the hospital she was trundled into was in the throes of some kind of epidemic, because nobody attended to them let alone gave them a room. With great difficulty, Brijeshwar and Rajeshwar had managed to cajole a very busy nurse into loaning them a mattress, which they spread out on the open corridor, outside one of the wards. By then Juhibaby was in the middle of her terrible contractions and she could barely keep the end of her saree pallu on her head to show the customary mark of respect in the presence of her husbands' older brother. All she recalled was that the pain was so intense that she wanted to die. She lay on the floor in horror, as dozens of feet and legs flew past her, doctors and nurses in dirty white coats and uniforms, screechy wheelchairs, stretchers on wobbly wheels and a steady stream of anxious relatives almost trampling over her to get to their loved ones. Juhibaby had never been admitted to a hospital before. Khokon had been born at home, midwifed by his grandmother. But Mee, all ready to enter the world, had several prenatal complications and so the family had thought it best to have the delivery in the hospital. Juhibaby had several visitors while lying on that mattress in Sucheta Kripalani Hospital in the heart of New Delhi. Maya di and Oshima di had come to visit Juhibaby and had huddled next to her on the floor, stroking her feet and hands, murmuring words of encouragement and womanly sympathy.

Juhibaby must have zoned out between her erratic contractions, for when she came to the sunlight was slanting down and the corridor looked eerie with strange elongated shadows. With a supreme effort she managed to lift her ungainly body off the mattress and desperately started to look for a familiar face. Beenarani and her mother-in-law would only come by late evening with her supper, but where was her husband? She lumbered down the corridor and at the far end she spotted him walking towards the entrance with Maya di and Oshima di. She ran after them, clutching her large ripe belly and calling out to them as loudly as she could, but they would not listen. She lost sight of them and in panic she turned into another corridor, trying to follow them but only to see them even further away. They were laughing and chatting merrily, walking with a speed that Juhibaby in her condition could not hope to match. She kept calling out to her husband, 'Shono! Shono! Listen, listen.'

But it seemed to her that Shono was in no mood to listen and was basking in the attention of the two ladies. He was leaving her forever. Did he just smile and wave at her in a gesture of 'goodbye forever'? Doggedly she followed them as they entered the maze. She on one side and they on the other. The maze grew deeper and darker and suddenly there loomed a wall. She veered around and saw another wall in front of her and then two more walls on either side of her. A cul-de-sac. She was trapped! She couldn't come out. This place was small and terrifyingly dark and she was having trouble breathing. She kept yelling, 'Shono! Shono,' but all she heard was an eerie reverberation of her beloved's name, mocking her 'Shon...o! Shon...o! Shon...o!'

Meanwhile, Brijeshwar had returned after politely escorting the ladies to a bus and had found to his utter shock that his beloved Juhibaby was missing. Quickly he searched in the delivery room area crammed wall-to-wall with moaning women and scanned the filthy canteen and reception area that now resembled a war zone. But Juhibaby was nowhere to be seen. In an epidemic situation when hundreds are dying, nobody was unduly concerned about a missing pregnant patient. It was only a couple of hours later that a woman came bursting down the corridor shouting that there was a woman in labour under the stairwell of the new wing that was under construction. There they found Juhibaby, almost dead with exhaustion, the baby's head partially out. Because of the crisis, senior doctors and nurses who were on round-the-clock duty quickly cordoned off the area with bed sheets and curtains and assisted Juhibaby to give birth to a bonny little girl, who let out a blood-curdling shriek of complaint as if to say, 'What's wrong with you people, couldn't you hurry up considering I was half out!'

And that is how Meehika turned out to be... A pusher, a survivor for she had pushed herself out of her mother's half-dead body, to seek out the bright world after the terror of the claustrophobic womb.

3

Bhaanga Kashore

When Mee turned sixteen, she decided she wanted to celebrate her birthday with her friends, without Juhibaby, Dada or any other family members around. Juhibaby had made a big noise about sponsoring her daughter's party and so acrimonious was the spat between the mother and daughter that the normally reticent Brijeshwar was forced to intervene. A sum of seventy-five rupees was negotiated and Mee victoriously threw a party with this princely amount. She designed her own ensemble: a deep blue, double-breasted coat with epaulettes, worn over matching bell bottoms. She brushed her long silky hair to one side, jabbed and smudged some lipstick over her lips and cheeks and liked what she saw. They felt so grown-up, the gang, partying on the terrace of the house, smoking, and gorging on deep-fried salty snacks. It was the first time that she had tasted alcohol, which had been siphoned off by Ritika from her father's well-stocked bar. One of them kept guard as the whisky was poured into a steel glass and then passed around. It smelt and tasted horrible but hey, after two rounds it actually felt good. Mee was beginning to glow. She felt at her best here, amidst her peers who complimented her on her taste in clothes and who solicited her advice on their personal problems. No Juhibaby here to continuously nag her, 'You will amount to nothing, hobnobbing with this group of silly friends.'

Mee shut out Juhibaby's voice and concentrated on the moment. Suddenly, Pratyusha, who was guarding the terrace door, yelped a warning, 'Khokon coming.'

In a trice the party turned sober and girly, cigarettes were stubbed and flung over the parapet, the bottle of whisky was stuffed into the water tank and all the girls started singing a popular Hindi movie song in a high-pitched falsetto.

'O aaj mausam, bada beimaan hai,
Bada beimaan hai, aaj mausam...'

Khokon, who had come up to spy on his sister and pass on the information to his mother, was momentarily stumped. He had expected to catch her with some of the callow colony youths who roamed around combing their hair with thin combs tucked in their hip pockets. Instead he was hugely disappointed to see a group of rather silly girls having fun by themselves. He left, but not without casually checking all the nooks and corners for any lurking boys. He went down to report to his mother who grunted again, 'This girl will not amount to anything.'

Granny, who was lying on a sagging bamboo cot in the corner, winced a wee bit. 'What has happened to our fairy, our dear Juhibaby? Why does she not smile and laugh anymore? Why is she always after Meehika, after all, she is only sixteen?'

And then Granny remembered that by the time she was not much older than sixteen, she was already the mother of Rajeshwar, Brijeshwar and Beenarani. She remembered her husband, who had TB, with remote compassion and as she drifted into a reverie of the time they had spent in their home in Simla, her heart warmed. The days of terrible hardship, when all she had wanted was the next meal for her children. And then when the eldest, Rajeshwar, grew up and got his first job, the thrill she had felt on holding the money he had pressed into her trembling hands. It was Brijeshwar though who had to climb up three steep hills in the snow without a coat to get to school, and so she had saved penny by vanishing penny to buy him the greatcoat, which he still wore to this day when the weather turned chilly. For Beenarani she always imagined a wedding, maybe not a grand one, but a simple boy would be enough for her simple daughter. Alas! Beenarani was plain and dark-complexioned and in that colour-conscious society, nobody asked for her hand. In frustration and humiliation, Rajeshwar, as the patriarch and surrogate father, declared to the world that he would marry only after his sister. And so it was left to the middle sibling, Brijeshwar, to marry and carry forward the family name.

Granny was stoic, strong-willed with an over-developed conscience. Even when she prayed to all her colourful gods, tucked inside her tiny puja room, her prayers were mostly 'take, take', rather than 'give, give'. She would often whisper to Lord Shiva, 'Hai, Bam Bol, hai Mahadev, please take my anger, my pride, my greed... take everything.'

But one day, she heard herself whispering to him, 'Give... give... give me a good wife for my Brijeshwar.'

Lord Shiva must have heard her prayers because the next thing she knew was that they had found a sixteen-year-old Brahmin girl in Calcutta, whose mother could not afford a dowry and was therefore willing to send her daughter to a distant city. Also, according to the marriage broker, the girl was extraordinarily beautiful. Juhibaby, her beautiful daughter-in-law, looked as though she had descended from heaven itself, with her adorable features and milky white complexion. And the way she sang, Granny could not ask for more. Now, she wondered sadly, why is she so agitated of late? She either sleeps for hours on end or else leaps up and starts doing several tasks all at once.

But Granny left before her world could crumble. One autumn morning as the family moved about doing their chores, she felt herself dissolving. Juhibaby was in the kitchen, serving the men their morning meal, Beenarani was having a bath, Khokon was in the backyard, hitting a ball 'tuk-tuk' against the wall and Mee was preening about in the latest dress that she had designed for herself, a red ghagra with a tight-fitting black choli top. As she ran towards Granny, flaunting her youth and beauty, expecting the usual endearments, she paused midway. Granny, though smiling at her, was also clutching her heart. For a brief second Mee thought Granny was playing with her—they had evolved a little game where one would enact a scene, silently, only with gestures and facial expressions, and the other would guess the action—but this time Granny's eyes looked strange. As if she was not there. And seconds later, as Meehika was later to see in movies, the old woman collapsed into herself in slow motion. Mee caught her seconds before she hit the floor.

This was the first time that Mee had met death and she was inconsolable. After all, Granny was the one person who loved her unconditionally, just as she was. She also believed in her. Mee remained in solitary mourning, even as the household roused itself back into a limping normality. Even Ritika and Pratyusha could not get her to join them for cigarettes or the occasional pilfered beer. Juhibaby emerged from her cycle of sleep and hyperactivity, to conduct the post-death rituals with great efficiency. Everyone commented on the daughter-in-law of the departed soul, as she went about gracefully conducting all the ceremonies and attending to all the guests with dignified courtesy. She not only had to see to the cooking but also be a pillar of strength for her husband and his siblings, who were bereft by the loss of their mother.

It was around this time that the husband of the principal of the school where Beenarani taught, came to the house to offer Meehika the main role in a play that would be performed during the annual Durga Puja celebrations. It was an immensely popular play, 'Nati Binodini': the stirring story of one of India's first prostitute actresses, for whom one of her clients had built the famed Star theatre. After being blessed by the sage Ramakrishna Paramahamsa, the actress relinquished the arc lights forever. Mee was thrilled to be offered the role. In any case, she had six months free before she joined college next summer, after passing the ICSC board exams.

Though not fluent in Bengali, her mother tongue, Mee worked hard to do justice to the role. Imagine her consternation when towards the end of a tedious month of rehearsals, the director introduced her to a beautiful film actress saying, 'Sorry, but you are too immature to play this role. We have decided she will play this part.' The 'she' in question, a fair damsel with a generous bosom, smiled distractedly at Mee.

Mee's world shook but she had her Granny's blood. She hung around the rehearsals as if nothing had happened, gritting her teeth to hold back her tears, but on the way back home via the andheri gali, their familiar lonely, dark, smokers' alley, she tore each and every page of the script and howled her heart out to the winds and the stray lovers embracing in the shadows. But something happened when she saw her ravaged face in a shop window: the rejection and defeat made her determined to never let her guard down again.

'Who are these silly people to throw me out? I will show them who the real actress is!'

When she told her family that she had been replaced, everyone had something to say. From Juhibaby it was a tart, 'Good, now that you know you can't act, concentrate on your studies instead.'

Only her father's eyes welled up momentarily and he abruptly left the room. Through her unshed tears, Mee caught a glimpse of him pulling out his ragged diary. Later, he would gift her this prized possession.

Mee was desolate without Granny and only too glad to slink back to her friends. But with the casual cruelty of youth, her friends had changed and no longer seemed to want to include her in their group. So, with three months still to go for college, she joined an English drama group, very famous at the time, dictatorially governed by an English director with corn blue eyes. They rehearsed in Mandi House, on top of a very large building that was being constructed by a culture-loving industrialist to serve as a hub for the arts.

The ceiling was very high and the pillars, solemn and intimidating, stretched across the vast floor at equal intervals. It was in and around these pillars that a lot of activity happened, both back and front stage. Mee had been cast in the crowd scenes of the play they were rehearsing, with two small individual scenes of four lines each. For the rest, she had to be part of the crowd who formed the human backdrop of the set. She was placed opposite a callow youth and they had to thrust their pelvises against each other and on cue, chant:

'What's the point of a revolution,
Without general...
general copulation
copulation
copulation.'

Mee was aghast and red-faced with shame, when she eventually understood the meaning of what she was reciting. How on earth could she do these vulgar movements in front of her parents who would certainly come to see her perform? Tears filled her eyes as she tried to protest. The lead actor and the director exchanged a snide smile. Then the latter, with exaggerated sweetness, reminded her that it was she who had approached him for the role and not the other way around. Mee was silenced. She remembered her first audition with the drama group. There, amongst the tall daunting cement pillars, she had been asked to perform, sing, dance, do anything... Her knowledge of theatre had been restricted to English plays performed in her girl's convent school, where marks were given to the person who spoke in the best British accent. She had mastered the art of rolling her tongue and breathing between pauses to get herself many awards in elocution in front of her bathroom mirror. Her rendition of Sylvia Plath's 'Daddy' (a fascinating poem she had sneaked from the Class 12 head girl who always won the inter-school elocution contests), held her spellbound when she saw her mirror image recite in a cultivated, sonorous voice,

'Dahddy...you basturd...I'm thhhhhhru!'

Of course, it was all quick and hush-hush, as the entire family shared a single bathroom.

So, confidently, she decided to experiment with an American accent which she believed she had mastered after hours of listening to American pop songs on 'In the Groove' and 'A Date with You' on the small transistor radio that she was forced to share with Dada. On the day of the audition, she had worn her only pair of Levi jeans, which she worshipped, over which she pulled a tight orange skivvy, ignoring Juhibaby's pointed frown at her budding breasts.

When Meehika's turn came, she stood up and, in front of a large crowd of anxious competitors, contorted her lithe body into what she thought were the latest American dance moves, and sang with a studied American drawl:

'Putta nother nikkle in,
In the nikkle odeon
An all I wanna
Is lovin'you 'n
Mew-sic...mew-sic...mew-sic...'

It was only her enthusiasm and self-confidence that saved the day for she had sounded ridiculous. But she got to be a part of the crowd scenes.

Seniors in the theatre group saw Meehika as a very good-looking, fair-complexioned girl with shiny black hair, interestingly attired, sitting apart from all the others, cigarette in hand, immersed in a book. In reality, Mee was dying to be with everyone but did not know how to make contact with them. She was terrified that they might laugh at her. Who knew, supposing Juhibaby was right, supposing she really was not a good actress? So with eyes on her book, both cigarette and heart in her mouth, and her entire being focused on what the others were doing, Mee had spent that entire summer vacation.

✦

Mee joined Miranda House to do her graduation in English Honours. She was the only girl in the Ladies' Special bus who wore thick eyeshadow and tucked her hair into a fashionable bandana that matched her outfit. The meagre pocket money that she wrested from Juhibaby at the beginning of every month went on lipsticks and eye colour from a fancy shop in Khan Market.

Though Khokon went to a boys' college, their timings matched and invariably they left home together. While he sat at the dining table, peacefully tucking into his staple breakfast of sizzling 'loochi-aloo chechki', Mee would be busy arguing with Juhibaby about money, or the dress she was wearing, or the time she intended to be back. Khokon cast disapproving looks at her flamboyance and haughty self-confidence. But Mee was too self-absorbed to even notice her brother. Their karma, waiting in the wings, would engulf them one day.

In college, Mee was a star. She represented her college in drama, elocution and debates, winning trophies and awards. She was popular and attractive. People like to copy her style, which was exuberant, edgy, funky. Yet she was also studious and her peers and professors gravitated to her. It was here that Sudanshree and Meehika bonded over Camus and pani poories.

It was then that she met the old man at a theatre workshop at Mandi House.

She, at nineteen, was in the second year of her graduation and he, at sixty-two, was a doyen of the magical world of drama, a globetrotter, a refined aesthete who had worked with the crème-de-la-crème of European stage actors. He fell in love with her, suddenly and swiftly. On her part she was clueless, having never experienced romantic love before. Juhibaby, never one to encourage personal conversation, would mutter, 'Don't ask me such questions! I never asked my mother and neither should you ask me.'

This would turn Mee mutinous with rage. 'That's because you were from a different generation,' she would hurl and storm off, leaving Juhibaby missing Chhayamoni, her sister-cum-foster mother.

She rarely thought of her own mother Ruma, and needless

to say, Ruma made no attempt to reach out to her daughter either. Both decided that the other was 'happy and busy', and thus absolved themselves of the difficult task of unravelling the tangled skeins of their past.

Meehika could feel the old man's immense sexuality and developed the art of manipulating him. She would purposely choose clothes that accentuated her waif-like quality. She wore powder pinks and virgin whites with maddening necklines which plunged down to hide unknown delights. She left home demurely covered in Dada's frayed man-sized jacket, which she would take pains to languorously remove when she was sure that she was being watched. Because she was learning the ropes of acting from a professional, she took each role very seriously and would give it her best shot. Slowly she emerged as the best actress in the group.

Mee had always loved to sing and Granny would say that she had inherited it from her mother. But if Mee asked her to sing, Juhibaby would shrug her off, 'Don't be silly, is this the time to sing? I have so many things to do.'

And Mee would march off resentfully. She recalled the time when as a child of nine or ten she had wanted to learn the harmonium. Ritika, whose father was a well-to-do businessman, had employed a special music teacher to coach his tuneless daughter and many afternoons found Mee learning more from the music teacher than Ritika, who was busy raiding the refrigerator for leftovers. Thus, when Mee asked her mother if she could officially have a music teacher to teach her the harmonium, Juhibaby had categorically refused. 'Your voice is like a bhaanga kashore. It's far better you concentrate on your studies instead.'

Mee had turned hot with shame at her mother's harsh words. Juhibaby too had turned hot with helplessness and remorse. Helpless, because with her husband's meagre government salary, how could she afford one hundred and fifty rupees a month, for something as non-essential as music? Remorse, because she knew that Mee like her, flew on the wings of music. But Juhibaby also knew that because she was a bird without wings, she could not help her child to fly. Conflicting emotions raced through her as she brusquely wiped her eyes of the tears that were threatening to pour out.

Juhibaby vividly remembered the time that she had been pushed onto the stage at the age of four to replace someone's gig. No one had taught her anything. She had been painfully thin, undernourished, wearing one of her sisters' faded hand-me-downs, when suddenly she found herself facing a sea of leering faces. She, who knew all the songs by heart, had just stood there trembling in fright while some strange sounds escaped from her shivering lips.

Only when some drunk voice from the audience had yelled, 'Teach this little bhaanga kashore first, before she kills us with her music' to a tittering audience, did Ruma grab her roughly and shove her backstage. Juhibaby, trembling from the memory, now turned around to stroke her daughter, her heart melting with love. But as her hand tentatively reached out, she recoiled at the aura of profound rage surrounding her daughter.

'You mean creature!' Mee spat out the words, long venomous serpents clinging to each syllable. 'I'll show you one day...the world will know that I am not a bhaanga kashore. How dare you...You think my voice sounds like a bloody broken cymbal?'

And with that Mee had stormed out of the house and had not returned till late in the evening. She felt a pathetic rage and a sense of deep isolation, 'Who is there for me?' she thought,

'I don't want to be like Ma, nose to the kitchen grind, day in and day out... fish and rice...fish and lentils... fish cutlets and fish fillet... Surely there is a world outside of all this?'

And then on her way out she had bumped into nosy Dada who looked positively gleeful. 'What happened? What happened?' he chirped curiously.

Mee turned her head high and in a voice choking with emotion declared, 'Ma is jealous of me because I happen to sing better than her.'

And then, as an afterthought, 'And oh! By the way, I have been selected to be the lead singer in the drama we are doing.' Her desperate lie was concealed under layers of studied casualness.

Dada's face twisted with envy, as he tried to hide the animosity he felt towards his 'fair and beautiful' sibling.

Mee stared at him for a full minute. 'God,' she thought, 'he hates me so much now. If I were to be successful in life, how much more would he hate me?'

She turned abruptly and walked off, forgetting to change her clothes, forgetting to take her wallet which always had just enough cash to take an autorickshaw if the need arose. She walked all the way from Pandara Road to Mandi House, the humid air and the blaring of horns caressing her wounded spirit.

'How does it matter if no one loves me? This big shot Old Man director eats out of my hand...'

Years later, she was to tell Pratyusha that the Old Man, besides giving her a passion for theatre, also opened her eyes towards her own power. She told her friend, 'Those days I was a maddening little minx with the self-esteem of a dead rat! Ugh!'

✦

Mee graduated with honours and the family insisted she do a Master's in English Literature. After all, Dada too was well qualified. After his Master's in science (double promotion and all), he had got a walk-in admission at the Birla Institute of Technology at Pilani, where he was studying to be a mechanical engineer.

So here she was, straddling two worlds: one, of a college student, the other, theatre. Mornings would find her changing two buses to reach the university, where she sat in drab lecture rooms listening to crisp saree-clad lecturers droning on about 'Paradise Lost' and 'Paradise Found'.

She was not quite sure where her paradise lay but one thing she did know was that she loved to go for theatre workshops in the evenings, where she was part of a group who hung around Mandi House, smoking, drinking endless cups of tea and discussing in minute detail, every aspect of the theatrical production they were mounting. Currently, the group had jointly improvised a script called 'Kadduram ki anokhi dastaan', the tale of a pumpkin, where she was playing the lead role of the pumpkin. These were little vignettes, street plays, that the group performed in the JJ colonies, the jhuggi-jhopdi hutments, of the rapidly developing eastern corridor of Delhi. They were heady days, there was purpose in the air (they were definitely going to change the sordid establishment and usher in the revolution) and very little money in one's purse. The troupe sang, danced, gave impassioned performances on social issues, passed the hat around at the end, and with the meagre pickings, ate a frugal meal at the Refugee Market which catered to the poor and jobless, all the while doing an animated post-mortem of the performance, dissecting it for mistakes and further improvement. Afterwards, everyone was meticulously handed over bus fare, and the little money left over was put aside for the next performance.

Miranda House, situated in the centre of the university campus, was a college to reckon with in the late seventies. But when Meehika found herself in its hallowed precincts, she was not really involved. Her mind was in theatre. Though she did make a few friends and had the mandatory 'scrambled egg on toast' at the famous cafe of the even more famous St Stephen's College down the road, she did not build any close, lasting friendships. Hence, in her later years, when she really needed friends, there were none.

She would finish her classes, clamber on to a crowded DTC bus full of frustrated sex-starved men who had mastered the art of 'grab-stroke-pinch', that is, molesting young girls like her. So she devised her own ingenious way of staving off her maulers: she would carry two jholas, cotton cloth bags, instead of one, and during peak hours, would frustrate many a grab-stroke-pincher by placing one bag in front, protecting her crotch, one bag at the back, protecting her bottom, cover her breasts by pressing both elbows together and her face, nose down, with her palms. In this way this one-woman army steered her boat on rough public transport. Mee boasted to her friends that she had started a trend which many a young girl travelling on local buses would follow for years to come.

One day, one of the theatre group members had come on to her. He was from Mauritius and had come to study in India. He was smitten by the fair-skinned, beautiful Mee, and whenever he got an opportunity, he would sidle up to her and clasp her hand. Mee was not particularly perturbed. She quite enjoyed being desired.

All this went on for a while, because in the theatre community of which she was a part, physical displays of affection were not frowned upon. But one day when he grabbed her too long and too hard and she could feel his repulsive breath, she casually strolled over to another member of the group, Kishore Bohitdar, and whispered to him, 'Hold me!'

Kishore was dumbstruck. He had been simultaneously attracted to three girls in the group and every night before going to bed, he fantasized about the one who had given him maximum attention through the day. Coming from a small town in Orissa, where his father taught at the local college and his mother whiled away a part of her time at an NGO, this plethora of girls in tantalizing ghagras, puffing away at cigarettes, quite open to hugging and being hugged in return, was like a fantasy coming true. He had never been attracted to the girls he had met at his local college in Orissa. For one, they were staid, they came on bicycles, wearing salwar kurtas or sarees which covered every inch of them except their timid faces and some even called him 'bhaiyyo', brother. So when Meehika whispered to him, 'Tighter, hold me tighter!' he could scarcely breathe in his excitement.

In fact, it had been Meehika who he had fantasized about last night and now here she was in reality, virtually begging him to embrace her. With a palpitating heart, he held her, hoping against hope that his stupid body would not expose him. Though he tried to be as casual as possible, he could feel his erection, bursting from his pants. This went on endlessly till, suddenly, she let go.

'Thanks! Actually, Kallu,' she pointed at the Mauritian, 'was trying too hard...I wanted to put him off. Thanks again,' she whispered and walked away. He stood there for a while, nursing his wounds.

That was how it started. Once bitten, twice shy is a common adage, but what Kishore Bohitdar was experiencing was 'once stroked, forever yearning'. He had never come so close to a girl before, if one discounted the awkward hit-and-miss groping that happened one afternoon when he was in the final year of his Master's. But that had been as stupid as it was forgettable. This one was real. So he waited in the wings, quietly, patiently, strategically. In his heart of hearts, he knew she would be his one day.

But that was not the way Mee had either seen it or planned it. He was a regular guy, a nice guy, although a bit of a vernacular who loved shiny vernacular clothes and always smelled of onions. He was also too short, dark and intense. But he was dependable, a follower, slave material who seemed to be very attracted to her.

At home, things were most uncomfortable. The government flat of A-181, Pandara Road, was too small to house her unmarried uncle and aunt, along with her own parents and the ever-irritating Dada who had his own history. In his last year at the engineering college at Pilani, he had choked on a piece of mutton and had to be hospitalized. So panicky had Juhibaby become, that she all but forced him to return to Delhi, where he was now studying for a Master's in philosophy. Not only that, he had also won the affection of Miss Cuckoo Chowdhury, a wealthy Brahmin girl. Understandably, he was over the moon. At that time, Mee was struggling to find her feet, and worried sick that now that she had completed her postgraduation, her parents would start the hunt for a bridegroom.

Mee distinctly remembered the day when Saraswati, goddess of learning, deserted her. It was the day before her last Master's exams. She was in an autorickshaw, laden with textbooks, returning home after a quick rehearsal, to do a last-minute cram before her final exam. Chaucer, Spenser, Keats and Milton were names and numbers jostling in her mind at random as she chugged along Lytton Road. Suddenly the rickshaw driver swerved violently and as he applied his brakes, all her books tumbled out of the rickshaw and spilled on the road in injured disarray. Stunned, she stooped down to retrieve them, and saw the fracas that the driver was having with a group of young people who till a second ago were like a herd of lazy cattle crossing the road, only to break into a run just as their auto neared them. The autorickshaw driver had had to slam on his brakes to avoid a collision and was now cursing mutinously under his breath.

It took her only a second to recognize the heartthrob of Delhi theatre. Tall, slender, with a stunning face and glowing skin, Meera Raichand exuded an inborn charm and dignity that set hundreds of hearts on fire. Meehika was no exception. She had saved money to watch three of her plays at the hallowed National School of Drama on Bhagwan Das Road. One was Maxim Gorky's play 'Mother', where Meera Raichand's performance as the mother of a jailed convict was so brilliant that Mee had gone home and almost hugged an alarmed Juhibaby. Well, almost. And had stopped short. Juhibaby had given her a puzzled glance and carried on with her work. And now, there was Meera Raichand right in front of her. She was even more dazzling without make-up, casually standing on the kerb, wearing a brilliant orange kurta with a rainbow-coloured dupatta. Mee was transported to a world of theatre performances, the arc lights, the fade out of the conversation and rustle of clothes as the third bell announced the play's opening and silence fell. And then the slow fade in of music and spotlights as the actors in their costumes materialized like magic, into the spaces between light and dark. And at that point in Mee's fantasizing, Goddess Saraswati had deserted her. She leapt off her lap and slid onto the kerb and waited for several years till Mee begged for forgiveness and cajoled her back into her life.

In the meanwhile, Mee finished her MA. She had stood fourth in the university when she did her BA, not a mean task for a girl who spent most of her time applying eyeshadow, dodging eve-teasers and looking for opportunities to have a sly smoke. Now she ranked sixteenth in the university in her postgraduation. Juhibaby was relentless in her nagging: 'Prepare for the IAS...prepare for the IAS...If you don't, you will not amount to much else.'

The Indian Administrative Service was a national deity whose favour was widely sought, especially by the middle class. Besides, Chhayamoni's only son had also appeared for the exams. Thrice. So Juhibaby was naturally keen that her daughter should follow in the footsteps of her nephew. Mee did not have particularly happy memories of her Calcutta cousin or the summer holidays spent in 156, Rashbehari Avenue, when as children, Dada and she were taken along to visit Juhibaby's maternal home. So every time Juhibaby would bring up the IAS exam, Meehika would flounce off.

It was Kishore Bohitdar who one day casually introduced Mee to the three-year diploma course at the National School of Drama. He had applied the year before, and though he had passed the written exam, he had, to everyone's surprise, failed the interview. Subsequently, he changed course and applied and got admission at the famous JJ School of Art in Bombay. But he was besotted by Mee and through her, theatre, and so he helped Mee quietly fill in the form and apply for the course. Because she was yet not smart or shrewd enough to give a false address, the letter asking her to appear for the written exam, arrived at A-181, Pandara Road, with the bold 'National School of Drama', Bahawalpur House,

Mandi House, emblem on the envelope. It was Dada who, at Juhibaby's bidding, tore open the envelope and declared war on Mee's intentions. 'Has she lost her mind? After doing a postgraduation in literature, she wants to do "nachon-kodon", singing and dancing for a living?'

Little did he know that in the years to come, Meehika would win several awards and accolades for just that...singing and dancing.

Juhibaby was equally caustic. 'Is that why we raised her, depriving ourselves of all pleasures, for her to spoil our family's good name?'

Rajeshwar, Big Uncle, was unequivocal in his disapproval, 'What is the future of doing drama? What kind of job will she get? Nothing doing, she must sit for the IAS.'

Beenarani, her good aunt, tried to intervene by convincing her brother, 'Dada, give her a chance, she is an intelligent girl who knows her mind.'

The whole family pounced on her with so much venom that she was forced to make a tactical retreat which left only Mee's father. Now, Brijeshwar, the gentle soul, spent most of his time in his room studying foreign languages, browsing through his modest collection of Russian and Chinese prose. After work, post-tea, he could be found hunched over a game of chess with the elderly Ghosh babu who lived in A 174, Pandara Road. He had left most matters of home and hearth in the hands of his able older brother. So Rajeshwar was the one to sign Dada's and Meehika's school report cards. But now Brijeshwar was in a dilemma—he could not quietly sit on the fence, hide behind the cover of his beloved books, puffing on his pipe stuffed with juicy Capstan tobacco. He had to make a choice. So, unknown to the others, he quietly gestured to Mee to come to his room. He was standing in front of his open cupboard, looking for something. Sensing her, he turned around, his eyes calm pools, and handed her his aging diary which she was so familiar with.

'For you, Meethuma...For whatever it means.' He always addressed his only daughter by this special name.

Gingerly, she opened it and saw page after yellow page of poetry. The right-hand page was written in the Bengali script, and on the left side was the translation in different letters and characters which Mee vaguely thought could be Spanish or Russian. As she stared at the fraying, leather-bound diary that smelt of tobacco, she had a brief glimpse of her father's youth: the changing handwriting, the thin yellowing starchy pages, the undefined doodles, as if it were a comma or a question mark indicating his state of mind, the stray blob of ink dropped and then clumsily blotted away, the smell of yesterday.

'Good luck for the National School of Drama. Remember that life can be full of adversity. Always face it squarely. I will always be there for you,' he whispered to her as he closed the cupboard door, thereby indicating to Mee that his blessings were with her and their quiet rendezvous was over.

✦

Mee stood first in the written exam as well as in the interview. Just fresh from her Master's degree in literature from Miranda House, she floored the interviewers with her knowledge of Western drama, literature and poetry.

For the interview she had to prepare a small solo performance. What could be more apt than the piece from the play she had rehearsed one whole summer, not so long ago, a soliloquy from 'Nati -Binodini'? That time she was humiliated. This time she would come out with flying colours, she vowed to herself. There was a reason for failure. Her desire to win was coloured by an avenging streak.

She got the piece translated from Bengali to Hindi by Kishore Bohitdar, who by dint of being from Orissa, which shared a border with Bengal, had a fair knowledge of Bengali. The two spent several hours in a disciplined frenzy, as time was short. Mee's piece de resistance was Nati Binodini's last song, as she bade good-bye to her beloved theatre:

'Aami bhobey aeka,
Dao re dekha.'
O lord of all worlds,
Grant me a vision
I am desolate on this earth.

Dwivediji , professor of music, was so spellbound by Mee's voice modulation and soulful rendering, that forgetting he was an interviewer, he stood up and clapped for her. Though the other interviewers were restrained and promptly requested Professor Dwivediji to calm down and control himself, they nevertheless conferred amongst themselves, and Meehika was welcomed to the prestigious school with a handsome scholarship of three hundred and fifty rupees a month.

All in all, there were twenty-three boys and girls in the class. The Government of India had decided that there should be one student from each state, so Mee represented the Delhi seat of the national integration programme.

The first year was the worst. Mee's knowledge of Hindi was restricted to bus conducters and rickshaw drivers, and 'Bhaiya, kitna paisa?' At home, she was forced to speak Bengali and right through college it had been English all the way. So when she was cast as the village belle, Mallika, in Kalidas' epic play 'Ashad ka Ek Din', she spoke the Hindi dialogues with such a marked English accent, that the seniors hooted her off the stage. Mee was heartbroken. Never in her life had she been so mortified, if one did not count the rejection she faced after being removed from 'Nati Binodini'. Poor soul! Born a Bengali, she could genuinely not understand the difference of genders in Hindi, the national language. Though she excelled in the Western Drama classes, sometimes forcing the very young, recently employed teacher, Miss Sita Kumar, to beg her not to show off her vast knowledge of English Literature, she hopelessly lagged behind in Hindi speech and diction. But she was determined not to lose her 'I-always-rank-first-in-my-class tag', so she borrowed piles of books by Hindi and Urdu writers from the well-stocked library and in the quiet of her room, read and reread the poems and prose of the great ones, till she improved her diction and confidence to a fair degree.

The girl's hostel had a total of ten rooms which accommodated the twenty-odd girl students. Mee felt she was fortunate to share her room, which was the largest in the block, with a wonderful girl from Karnataka, who was in her final year and spent most of her time in the boys' hostel down the road where her boyfriend lived. Though Mee got a regular stipend, she was perpetually broke because of her cigarette and tea habit, and was always at loggerheads with Juhibaby for extra cash. She would go on weekends to Pandara Road, getting Juhibaby to pay for the autorickshaw by pretending to be out of change. Every week she would leave her large bag of dirty laundry at home and go back with a fresh lot. Juhibaby muttered incessantly, 'Look at you...look how old you are...yet you can't wash and manage your clothes... I was raising the two of you when I was your age.'

'You were not doing it alone, dear mother. All your life you had our dear aunt Beenarani to do the major mothering.'

And with that hurtful barb she would leave the house and only return for dinner if she couldn't find a meal elsewhere.

Meanwhile, Kishore Bohitdar had completed his first year at JJ School in Bombay. He wrote her passionate letters about how much he loved her and missed her. In some uncanny way, she started missing him too. He seemed different, an intellectual, an artist, someone who would not scale her down and pin her into a small box marked 'Personal Property: Wife'. Something her mother was content to be. Meehika felt disgusted at the way she would plonk herself on her husband's two-wheeler... the way she cooked all day to serve her lord and master...her pati dev...her god-like-husband! Ugh!

But she was not like her mother. She would have a marriage based on equality and art. By the end of the following year, Mee and Kishore were married. Kishore Bohitdar had just started earning a stipend, working for an advertising firm in Bombay, after his classes got over. They had a quiet wedding in Delhi, followed by a rather noisy reception at the Constitution Club. Here Mee did everything that a bride was not expected to do: she kept disappearing periodically to catch a smoke, did not cover her hair with a veil, as a mark of respect to elders, could not keep her saree pallu pinned to her shoulder—it kept dropping any which way revealing her young cleavage—met her colleagues and friends from the National School of Drama with whooping yells and slobbery kisses, and on several occasions, hitched up her saree to squat on the floor for group photographs.

Juhibaby was angry and agitated. Meehika was once again pushing to do the unthinkable...getting married before her older brother...once again she had defied everyone to have her way! Her three spinster sisters who had come all the way from Calcutta to attend their niece's wedding, were thrilled to go back with suitcases full of gossip. All their lives they had been sick with envy for the golden life of their youngest sibling: handsome husband, devoted and loving in-laws, a son as well as a daughter. Now as cracks appeared in the happy family, they revelled in it.

After the wedding, Mee sauntered in to A-181, Pandara Road, and as quickly sauntered off, lugging a suitcase that she had haphazardly packed to visit her husband's home in Orissa. Even before Juhibaby could do the ritual of 'chaal bhaanga', Mee was off with a breezy 'Bye'. From the corner of her eyes, she saw the ludicrous sight of her mother standing with her three sisters, holding trays of lit lamps and mounds of rice, which as ritual demanded, she would have had to throw backwards into the house without a backward glance, signifying that from now on her karmic debt with her maiden house was over. The rice symbolized food, which henceforth would be provided by her husband. Mee was pleased with herself for managing to outwit her mother's archaic intentions. What she wanted most was a smoke and maybe a small drink to soothe her nerves.

Kishore Bohitdar too was facing his demons. Kicking himself for his sudden decision to marry Mee, he was nervous about taking her to meet his parents, who did not attend the Delhi wedding. Now the newlyweds were to take the Konarak Express, which would reach Cuttack after a gruelling thirty hours. From the railway station, their house was another hour away, and Mee would always remember with horror how they were met at the station by almost a hundred people, mostly enthusiastic students and staff from Kishore's university town, who first garlanded, next mounted them on an open-air jeep and led them in a noisy procession of drums, firecrackers and loud film music to the house of her husband's parents.

Mee fell in love with her mother-in-law instantly. Warm, sociable, broadminded, she welcomed her only daughter-in-law heartily. As the days went by, she not only made it clear that she was not expecting Mee to help in the cooking, but also declared that since she smoked anyway, she should do so in her presence, and not waste precious 'getting-to-know-each-other-time', by hiding and smoking in the toilet. Mee thanked her lucky stars. She had finally found a mother. Growing up in shame had made her very susceptible to guilt, and here she was made to feel honoured. But unknown to her, mother and son would discuss her quietly.

'Why don't you stop her smoking? It is so embarrassing. She smokes in front of everyone now.'

'But I thought you were the one who said it is okay?' Kishore asked, perplexed.

'Saying is one thing but don't you think she should be intelligent enough not to do it? What kind of sanskars, values, has her mother given her?'

Kishore Bohitdar did not protest.

Meehika went back to Delhi to finish her last year at the National School of Drama. Nothing had changed. She did not wear vermilion in her parting as a mark of a married woman, nor the red and white bangles of matrimony. She also did not add Bohitdar to her name. She continued to wade through the third year course, which was now taking a horrifically stifling turn. Kishore Bohitdar went back to Bombay and they continued to exchange passionate letters. Mee could not wait to join him in Bombay. She had been there once and was not overly fond of it, with its pungent ocean smells and the terrifying crowds she encountered in her foray into the local trains, but she yearned to get out of Delhi with its moribund culture. Moreover, Dada was going to be married soon and she sensed that from now on she would be even less welcome at Pandara Road. Besides, her stipend from the drama school was over.

Juhibaby packed a pressure cooker, some steel and aluminum vessels, a tea maker, a couple of assorted kitchen appliances and a white melaware dinner set with pink roses, in a large green hold-all, as Meehika prepared to make her new home in the city of Bombay. Mee energetically brushed her freshly washed silky black hair. Some droplets fell on Juhibaby as she bent to tie the hold-all. She averted her gaze. Both 'bhaanga kashores' were relieved.

4
Ghatkopar East

Kishore Bohitdar was in a state of panic. This was not the way he had planned or foreseen his life. He had grown used to living by himself, if one could discount the fact that just a fortnight ago, his world had changed completely. For three years he had been a 'good boy', working day in and day out at the JJ School of Art. He loved the environment at JJ, the mad and committed teachers, the old-world stone arches and delicate architecture, the fun-filled classes where they ran riot with colours, only to be sobered down to work with a single medium. He had lived in the hostel, had his share of fun with the boys swigging chilled beers at Leopold, when his parents sent him the extra funds for festivals, hung around with girls from Sophia College but despite all that, he missed Meehika and the brief but intense period that they had shared in Delhi. He missed her with a gnawing ache. Her letters were intellectual pronouncements about love, the way D.H. Lawrence saw love. She wrote poems and quoted T.S. Eliot and Sylvia Plath with a passion, as if to hide her vague and continued sense of desolation. His letters were more ordinary, mostly explaining at great length the reasons for his delayed response. Every letter had some reference to money, money gained, money lost, money spent, money needed.

She wrote to him about the new world of theatre and art, sometimes sending him brochures of films or plays she had seen through someone who was travelling to Bombay. He replied with a doomed sense of anxiety as if sensing that she was not there for him, and so he had to try with all his might to make her love him. But she was always in another zone. At one time, she was caught up translating a play with a very good-looking senior from Nepal. Why, he wondered, did she need to do all these extra-curricular activities? And why in the name of God did the Nepali monster have to be so good-looking? On another occasion, she seemed to be obsessed with a boy from an illustrious family and once even wrote to Kishore, stating frankly that she could not stop thinking about him. Kishore wanted to personally throttle seven generations of the bastard's lineage. His mother did not help much. In her weekly telephonic conversation, which they had in the hostel's common room, in full earshot of others also waiting for their calls, she never forgot to express her vague sadness at his choice of bride.

'Hmmmm...chalo...what's to be done, now that you are already married? By the way, have they increased your stipend?'

'No, Ma! Don't worry, she too has got her stipend so we are managing fine.'

'Humph! Managing fine, it seems...husband and wife in different cities...does it take time for these long-distance marriages to collapse?'

She should have held her tongue, Mee was to tell her friend Pratyusha, years later. 'That was precisely what she was hoping for but was too "educated" and too "cultured" to admit it. Obviously wanted a seedhi-saadhi, tame, Oriya bride, who would cook her maasbhaat.'

Pratyusha had laughed uproariously at Meehika's effortless rendition of her mother-in-law's Oriya accent.

Now mother dear's ominous prophecy had come true. Kishore Bohitdar, after three years of living a bachelor's life, had fallen in love...with his professor's wife.

✦

Meehika gazed out of the window of the third class compartment of the Bombay-bound deluxe train as it chugged along the dust bowl of central India. There was nothing to do: she had left Delhi, the place of her birth. Now in her early twenties, she was travelling alone to her marital home. She vaguely recalled Juhibaby's parting words, 'When I left my father's home, I had my husband, your father, by my side, but look at you, all togged up and off on your own! May God be with you!'

That was the closest she had come to expressing her love for Mee. Quickly, she had averted her eyes and moved away to once again tie up the leather straps of the army green multi-purpose hold-all that Mee was going to take with her. Mee had missed the moment. She was too busy trying to 'get the hell out of Pandara Road', as she was to say later.

The heat was unbearable and through the half-shuttered slats of the vestibule windows, hot dust was insidiously seeping onto the passengers, making them torpid and immobile. The pathetic whirring of the single ceiling fan, encased in a round cage, added only sound to the heat. The train was behind schedule. It kept halting at every station, leaving the passengers boiling in the midsummer heat. When the train moved there was at least some semblance of a breeze, but when it was a stationary it was unbearable. Mee glanced around and saw that most men were down to their undershirts and the women were lazily fanning themselves with folded newspapers or whatever else they could lay their hands on. Mee took a cautious sip of the now boiling hot water, which Beenarani had thoughtfully packed for her in an old school water bottle. She smiled mentally at the memory of herself as a little girl, marching off to school, proud possessor of a brand new red water bottle. How carefully her family preserved everything that their hard-earned money had bought! She tried to read but her mind was too active and her eyes drooping with the heat. She closed her eyes. Some of her friends had come to see her off at the station. The usual last-minute gush of love and panic of separation had filled them all when it finally hit them that from now on there would be no institutional support, no free hostels, no free meals at the canteen, no stipends for cigarettes, tea, movies, no loving professor to cajole you when you sulked, no seniors to protect you from the outside world. One was truly alone. Even parents had an air about them that stated this bald truth: 'Okay, so we have raised you, educated you and put up with all your nonsense over the years. Now here's what we offer you...a nice smart kick in the rear, the harder the better, which will land you in a place where you will, eventually, find yourself standing firmly on your own...yes, truly on your own.'

Mee finally dozed off.

✦

Kishore Bohitdar leapt out of bed and scrambled to grab his underpants which were lying on the floor. From the corner of his eyes, he watched Sunanda stir on the bed. In a moment she was up, reaching for a cigarette.

'What time is the train?'

Her voice was deep, mellifluous, sexy. A sexy woman's voice.

'Four-thirty.' Kishore's voice was a tense whisper.

'Relax, you'll make it. Come here and give me a kiss... don't know when I'll get another one again.'

He turned to her and grabbed her hard, and then, to his consternation, began to weep. Big hot tears rolled out of his eyes. He was not sure why he was crying. Was it the guilt of cheating on his wife or the fear that from now on meeting Sunanda would be very difficult? He was too tense and preoccupied to pressurize his mind for answers, so he gratefully accepted Sunanda's loving caresses accompanied by her sexy cooing: 'There, there, don't you worry...things will be fine. See, professor saab doesn't know a thing and neither will your wife... This is strictly between us.'

Kishore managed a grateful tear-streaked smile. They reached for each other again, she older by almost two decades, he a callow youth. Though he knew he must rush to the station and pick Meehika up, he found himself unable to move, chained to Sunanda's exotic smell. Oh! How he loved her smell, her feminine smells, mingling with the masculine smell of cigarettes. He remembered vividly the first time he had met her. She was the sexy wife of Dean Prakash Chand. That day she was wearing an embroidered red kurta with elaborate mirror work, and when an odd mirror sparkled, reflecting the sun's light, to Kishore Bohitdar it spelt magic. Though not beautiful, she had an arresting face with clear skin, a full mouth and large light brown eyes with amber tints. Between her eyebrows on the bridge of her rather stubby nose, she wore a coin-sized blazing red bindi. When she pushed back a strand of hair from her forehead, he had noticed small specks of silver grey hair dotting her temples. He had felt comforted as though she were his mother. She had smiled and welcomed him to their house where he had gone to personally hand over a late project to the Dean who was also their teacher of mechanical art. He had been grateful to her when she had offered him a glass of water, and had left the room quietly when the Dean had entered the room in his pajamas.

During the next two years, he hardly met her. Just occasionally when he would either bump into her in the library or at some college function. Then God knows how this happened! Especially at this juncture of his life when he was to settle down with the girl he had married. Not that he was dying to become a householder. He had enough of his parents' cozy intimacy. He was raring to experiment, to expand, to dare, to dream but he had been caught in a snare of his own making, and now the hunter was going to emerge from that train, stalk him, bind him and slowly devour him piecemeal.

Sunanda Sen was a dilettante, a free spirit, a product of the era of Protima Bedi and the flower children. She had studied at Calcutta's famous Jadavpur University, and could hold her own in any area. She herself remained vaguely puzzled as to how she came to be married to the dull and uninspiring Prakash Chand. The two redeeming factors in her insipid marriage was that, one, they did not have any children and, two, she came to Bombay and straightaway entered the art circuit which otherwise for a newcomer would have taken at least a decade. Her current life was a picnic, a paid holiday. Dean Prakash Chand paid for everything and gave his precious wife all the space and privileges she automatically assumed to be her birthright. The Dean worked hard to support her. Obviously there was no question of responsibility or obligations involved. After all, she had given him the privilege of marrying someone as fine as her. Currently, she was researching an obscure art form, practised by the tribals of Raisena, a remote hilly part of Madhya Pradesh. She did two or three hours of focused work at the Asiatic Library and then declared to herself that she had worked hard enough to earn herself a fresh guava juice or a chilled beer at Café Samovar in the Jahangir Art Gallery at the Kala Ghoda intersection.

It was just a fortnight ago that she had accidentally bumped into Kishore Bohitdar, as he stood on the pavement outside the gallery, with his art work. The Kala Ghoda art festival in South Bombay excited many an art institution, including JJ, to send their ace students there to learn the art of marketing their works and so it was that one hot afternoon, their paths criss-crossed. She was just about to hail a taxi and he was crossing over to use the toilet at Jahangir and was searching his pocket for a one-rupee coin needed to use the facility. Suddenly, he was startled by a husky female voice.

'So, young man, what finds you here?'

He looked up, and it took him almost a minute to recognize the Dean's wife. She was dressed in a cobalt blue skirt with a summery top, with a dipping neckline suited to the rising temperature. Kishore Bohitdar could not but help dart a furtive glance at her ample bosom. She had a multi-coloured stole thrown carelessly around her shoulders and what struck him as being both odd yet very exciting was the coin-sized bindi between her brows. A bindi with a skirt... how daring...how different...how utterly smart. He continued to stare at her, mesmerized.

'Don't you remember me? I am Sunanda.'

'Ma'am, of course ma'am...ummm I just...'

'It's hot...want a beer?'

Kishore forgot to pee. He nodded dumbly and followed her to a quiet lane behind the Taj Mahal Hotel where she led him through a small doorway which opened into a wide dimly lit room. In the smoke-soaked, quietly humming air-conditioned room, he saw exquisite decor, beautiful posters, bric-a-brac and eclectic murals, displayed in an artfully casual way. The ambience was definitely European. As they were led to a corner table by the shaded open glass window, he saw the ease with which she greeted several foreigners sitting at various tables. Obviously, she was a frequent visitor. He sat down, gawky, a little diffident as she took over, ordering their drinks and snacks. He was speechless but very excited to be near her. Vaguely confused, he wondered why.

He did not remember much of the afternoon or the sequence of events which found him in bed with her. Mercifully, it was not in the Dean's house. He had gotten really drunk with a reckless mix of vodka, whisky and beer. She was calm, in control, her blood red bindi sending quivering messages to his spine. One part of him was warning him, 'She is old enough to be your mother...What do you think you are doing? Is this some hidden Oedipal complex showing up?'

But before he could argue with his drunken, devastated mind, she had coolly put her hand on his forearm and trailed her stubby silver-ringed index finger up and down its length, sending high voltage currents down his spine. He gave up the fight even before it began.

✦

By the time Mee's train slowly lumbered into Bombay Central station, the dreaded monsoons of Bombay had arrived in full force. So, with the hold-all and pots and pans, the future that Juhibaby had hopefully envisaged for her, clattering about her feet as she lugged it along, she made a heroic attempt to drag herself out through a line of impatient irate passengers, all intent on being the first to alight. She hopped onto the wet, puddle-ridden station, searching for Kishore. She waited for over an hour on the now fairly deserted platform with her damp and soggy luggage. She couldn't believe that he hadn't come to fetch her. Though he had sounded pretty excited about her coming to Bombay when she had given him the train details, yet why had she had felt a tight knot in the pit of her stomach? And now as she waited for him she could feel the knot tightening again. 'Where could he be? Has there been an accident?'

Though she had had the foresight to scribble his address in her diary, she had never seen the place before. She could, of course, take a cab and get home but what if he came after she'd left and they missed each other? She grew angrier by the minute.

'The irresponsible bastard, is this the way one treats one's wife?' Her thoughts were mutinous.

After waiting for two hours she decided to find his house. He had moved out of the hostel and rented a one-bedroom flat in Ghatkopar East. He had managed to extract the deposit and three months' rent from his still-doting parents. The rest he would have to manage on his stipend.

Mercifully, finding an address in Bombay was far easier than finding one in Delhi. And people were polite and helpful. The taxi finally halted outside a dilapidated weather-beaten complex of tall shabby buildings, with peeling paint. Tiny box-like balconies jutted out in ugly symmetry, each carrying a tale of its inmates: toy cycle, upturned bucket, large water drum, lingerie on ropes hung from the ceiling. Through the din of the incessant downpour, wet to the bone, Mee dragged her pathetic luggage to the dank, dark lobby which housed a cranky elevator which would take her to the fifth floor. Where she hoped to meet her husband.

Outside Flat No. 502, she searched for the doorbell. She pressed it several times, but nothing happened . She knocked. Again, nothing. Now Mee was getting really alarmed, the knot in her stomach pressing hard. What was she to do now? She knew no one in Bombay. Where on earth was Kishore?

The door to the right opened a crack and a face peered out and then just as quickly retreated, slamming the door shut. Mee was thirsty and more than that needed to use the toilet urgently. She tentatively rang the bell of the shut door. A simple wooden nameplate stated 'Shetty'. This time the door opened wider, revealing a large lady with a homely face.

'Kya chahiye? Who do you want?'

'Err... Merein pati. My husband... he stays next door... but it seems he is not in.'

'You are married to that dariyal...the bearded man? Accha? How sweet, he didn't look married. Then where were you all this while?'

'Err, Aunty, if you don't mind, may I come in and use your toilet? And if you permit, may I wait here for my husband? I'm new to the city and I don't know why my husband didn't come to the station to pick me up.' Mee tried bravely to hide her panic.

'Okay, baba, come in but leave the wet luggage outside. We'll keep the door ajar so we can keep an eye on it...anyway which mad person will come here in this pouring rain? Come... come inside.'

Mee gratefully entered the tiny flat, stuffed with the large furniture of bygone times. It smelt of coffee, an aroma that seemed to rise above the musty smell of wet clothes and shoes. The afternoon downpour was incessant.

By the time Kishore Bohitdar reached Bombay Central, the train had left for the yard. He stood for a while nonplussed, and then made a mandatory search for Meehika. He was feeling strange, not exactly remorseful but sort of irritated. He really was not ready to have Meehika move here. His body and mind were with Sunanda Sen. One part of him wanted to take a cab and go right back into her arms, the other part thought it better to go back home and check if Meehika had somehow managed to find a cab and reach home.

It was nearly nine at night when he peeped into the Shetty household to find Mee sitting primly on a sofa, drinking coffee with Mr and Mrs Shetty. For a second his heart melted. How could he do this to her? She looked so forlorn and dejected, despite her body language projecting a suave confidence. Then he saw her stony eyes filled with anger and he rushed to drag her luggage into his flat, fumbling for his house keys.

Mee never forgot the first time she set eyes on her marital home. While the Shetty household was wholesome like an overstuffed toy, Kishore's flat was like a dirty and deflated baseball. There was an overpowering stench of pickled socks. As Kishore all but ran to open the window, Mee's gaze went to the one thin blue-striped mattress without a sheet, and a pillow, also without a cover, flung carelessly on top of it. All over the room, at irregular intervals were mismatched tumblers, cups and glasses in which cigarette stubs were floating in leftover tea. In the centre of the room, some half-wet jeans and T-shirts lay spreadeagled on soggy newspapers. The walls were painted a deep blue, lit by a single blue neon light. Mee gingerly stepped into the next room, a tiny bedroom, which housed two suitcases and a bedroll. There was no fan and no curtains anywhere. The adjoining kitchen had a kadappa stone slab, on which sat an incongruously brand new shiny gas stove. Dirty saucepans and kadhais were haphazardly piled up in the sink, and half a dozen eggshells were scattered all over. Near the door there was an open dustbin, bursting with stinking garbage and as Kishore hastily turned to cover it with a newspaper, a large bandicoot leapt out and scurried under the shelf. Mee screamed in shock while Kishore got into active mode, chasing the rodent out of the front door. Mee stepped into the bath cum toilet, and jumped out in one wide leap, horrified to find large cockroaches crawling all over.

'Oh Kishore, you know how scared I am of cockroaches! Couldn't you have cleaned the flat before I came?'

Utter silence followed this unplanned wail. Later, when his mother would ask him curiously, 'So how did she like your new flat?' he would quote her first line in her new home, 'Couldn't you have cleaned the flat before I came?'

But Sunanda, his Sunanda, would not have cared. She had been to the flat five times, mostly around midnight when the middle-class neighbours were not at their snoopiest best. She was perfectly comfortable lying down on the sheetless mattress, smoking, drinking endless cups of sweet tea, and using the cockroach-friendly bathroom noisily and unhygenically. He was so aroused by her presence in his humble life that he did not mind pouring mugs of water after she had left.

By the time Mee had managed to achieve some semblance of order in the room, and had unpacked her hold-all and stowed it away, it was past eleven o'clock. There had been no conversation, no hugs, and no explanations. Tentatively Kishore suggested that they drink some vodka to celebrate her first day in the new house. She agreed because she was tired and angry and just wanted to sleep it off. In any case his unkempt beard and sweaty shirt had put her off and she was in no mood for intimacy. On his part, he was desperate to talk to Sunanda, and hear her motherly reassuring words. He slunk off on the pretext of buying food.

While Kishore made his quick clandestine phone call from the corner STD booth, waiting to pick up their takeaway dinner order of Chinese hakka noodles with chillie chicken from the all-night street-food vendor, Meehika sat in the cockroach-infested, blue-walled, neon-lit room, waiting for her life to unfold.

✦

It did not take Mee long to get to know about Sunanda Sen's role in her husband's life. First she had found the packet of condoms tucked deep inside the folds of the hold-all in the bedroom. When confronted, Kishore had turned bland, his blandness a new experience for Mee.

'Does my wife need to know why I have got them?'

It was on the tip of her tongue to ask him, if there were just the two of them, what was the need to hide the packet in the bosom of a tightly rolled hold-all? But she held her tongue. And then shortly afterwards she had found a funky wooden bracelet, smeared with a blue-tinged soap, lodged between the grimy glass panes in the bathroom window, where she was gingerly checking for hidden cockroaches. This time Kishore sounded a little irritated.

'Meehika, I have rented this flat only recently.' And then, a trifle too dramatically, 'For our life together, in fact. Must have been left behind by the previous tenant. You don't expect me to check behind windowpanes, do you?' Thereby subtly implying that Mee was a snoop.

Surprisingly, when the moment of truth finally arrived, Mee was calm and composed. She had just finished cooking a pot of khichdi, carefully measuring out the exact proportion of rice, lentils and water. It was one of the few things she had learnt to cook, because she was petrified of the pressure cooker bursting and so always stuck to low heat dum cooking. Since they did not own a refrigerator, she clumsily watered down some curd to make a semblance of raita, to keep cool in Mrs Shetty's fridge. Kishore would not be home before ten at night. So she decided to soak the dirty clothes and be done with the washing before he returned. And that is where she discovered Sunanda's note. It read, in a beautiful, free-flowing handwriting, 'Kishore, my darling! Hang in there! She couldn't be so bad. As for me, I pine for you day and night.' There was a smiley and a sketch of lips, pursed in a kiss. It was signed 'Sunanda' in a stylish flourish.

Mee stared at the pink card which she had found in the front pocket of Kishore's jeans. At first her cheeks began to burn and her heart started pounding. This was not the life she had seen for herself. She was not sure about how much she loved Kishore but he was all she had. And then slowly all the bits and pieces started falling into place: his self-serving passionless love-making, his energetic exit from the house in the mornings and his slow, dragging-the-feet entry late at night, his evasive silences, his cranky mood swings and the general pall of gloom surrounding him, especially on weekends. Suddenly she remembered that once she had even plucked a short strand of brownish, grey hair from his shirt collar, and had not realized at that moment, that the hair was not hers. Instinctively, she ran a finger over her long, jet black hair. So Sunanda, whoever she was, had short greying brown hair.

A sob rose in her chest...and then the tears gushed forth. Oh! So this is it? That is why he did not pick me up from the station...that is why he does not take me out...that is why he does not introduce me to any friends. That is why he has isolated me in this tiny flat, not even trusting me to go down to buy provisions? With each tumbling realization, more tears rolled down, as she wallowed in the weeping that went hand in hand with deep self-pity.

Then, as though yanked by a chain, her tears and self-pity stopped as abruptly as they had started. Suddenly she felt very composed, as though with this shock, this kick in her rear, she knew she would be propelled into something grander, something brilliant, on par with what she expected from life. She almost smiled at the vision of herself, hunched up in the tiny dirty bathroom of suburban Ghatkopar East, washing her cheating husband's dirty jeans, cooking khichdi for him and sitting in the airless musty house, waiting for his return.

'They're gonna put me in the movies,
They're gonna make a big star out of me
The biggest thing that ever hit the big times,
And all I have to do is, act naturally.'

Out of nowhere her mind picked up this ditty, as she decided to first dry and then hide the soggy card. This would be the proof of his infidelity. She wouldn't let on that she knew, till the right moment came. Oh! The game!

'They're gonna put me in the movies...'

In that phase of her life, all Meehika wanted was to do world-class theatre. She had decided to never compromise her ideals by doing cheap commercial movies, with their stereotyped stories and bump and grind routine, yet she never missed a chance to travel to Odeon or Regal in Connaught Place to catch the 11 a.m. shows which had cheaper tickets. This love-hate relationship with the movies had something to do with Juhibaby's parochialism. Her mother looked down upon anyone who was a 'Hindustani', which in her lexicon was everyone who was not Bengali. So virtually all of north India, except West Bengal, was labelled 'Hindustani' and subject to Juhibaby's quiet derision. Mee's childhood best friends, Ritika and Pratyusha, were Hindustani, Kishore Bohitdar, her son-in-law, though hailing from Orissa, a state virtually next to West Bengal, was still a 'Hindustani'. So without question Hindi movies and film stars were totally and inexorably 'Hindustani'.

Yet, there was one exception to this rule. Ma was crazy about the superstar Rajesh Khanna. Mee remembered one outing when Juhibaby had quietly taken her off to the dilapidated Stadium cinema house. There, when the charismatic heartthrob of the millions broke into song, 'Yeh shaam mastaani, madhosh kiye jaa, meri dore koi kheechey, teri ore, liye jaa...' even the diehard parochial Juhibaby had forgiven Rajesh Khanna, for being 'Hindustani'.

Of course Meehika never told her family that she used to quietly sneak out at eight-thirty on Wednesdays to watch 'Chitrahaar' in Ritika's house, which was the only house then to have a TV. She would sneak back by 9 p.m. just in time to see Juhibaby and Beenarani stirring to serve dinner to the men. They would have been horrified to know that Mee had been sneaking out to watch those stupid heroes and heroines dancing around a tree in those ghastly 'Hindustani' commercial movies.

'They're gonna put me in the movies...'

Mee had managed to dry and hide the card in a small zip case, waiting for the day she could dramatically expose her rotten husband. The clothes had been wrung and hung out in the matchbox balcony. She had not carried the raita to be refrigerated next door and so it lay sour and curdling next to the pot of cold congealed khichdi on the kitchen slab. And now she waited for her errant husband to return.

He came in at midnight. She awoke instantly when she

heard the by now familiar sound of the key turning in the lock, but pretended to be asleep. She sensed him glance at her as she lay on the mattress on the floor, an upturned novel on her chest, in a well-orchestrated pose. After a few minutes she cautiously opened an eye and saw him scowling, very busy as he removed his tie, shirt, watch and wallet. Before removing his jeans he glanced at her again but she quickly shut her eyes. She heard him remove his jeans in the next room. By now she was getting more and more agitated and was dying to rush to him, pound his chest mercilessly and abuse him in the choicest language. But she held her counsel. Emotions could wait for another day. After all, everyone had a right to fall in love with anyone they wished. This came from a deep part of her heart, a knowledge so complete that many years later Pratyusha would ask how she could take such a huge slap on her face with so much understanding. Even Mee sometimes wondered whether she was pretending to be understanding or was she really so. Though she knew it intellectually, felt it emotionally, believed in it strongly, yet she could not help but be deeply hurt by his choice. In her logical mind, she knew it was futile and stupid to be hurt by the free choice of another individual. Wasn't life all about free choice and the ebb and flow of relationships? That was what she believed yet here she was feeling totally confused and betrayed. She was caught between the ideals of love that she saw in her heroes, D.H. Lawrence, Simone de Beauvoir, Doris Lessing, and her own fragile response. She had never loved herself deep down so how could she love anybody else including poor Kishore Bohitdar?

She suddenly thought of Juhibaby. How would she react to this news? Would she gloat? Would she say, 'I told you so?' Or would she say, 'This is retribution. This is what happens when you hurt your parents and take misguided decisions?' She could hear Juhibaby's nagging tone, the one Mee swore was reserved only for her.

She heard the flush of the toilet followed by the sound of him having a bucket bath. After a while he came out wearing a fresh white kurta pajama, smelling very male, very sensual. Ordinarily, by the time he finished bathing, Mee would have had the dinner hot and ready on the floor, spread out over the previous day's newspaper. Today she continued to lie down, feigning sleep. Kishore did not wake her. He went off to the kitchen, and Mee heard him serve himself and a few minutes later, dump the plate in the sink with an annoying clatter.

'Bastard!' Her mind started churning again. 'Can't he even ask if I have eaten?'

The rain was incessant. Drumming all around them, mysterious, frightening. Kishore switched off the tubelight and the room plunged into darkness.

✦

Unknown to him, it was Kishore Bohitdar who once again was instrumental in catapulting Mee to her next path. Late one evening, he had come home excitedly and told her about the ad campaign.

'We'll make a quick buck...all you have to do is get your portfolio done. I have already spoken to Suresh Morly. He does all our soft ads, so he won't charge much.'

And with that, Mee had become an overnight sensation. Sick of her own inner turmoil, lonely and stifled in that tiny flat in suburban Bombay, she was ready to fly... to act, to create, to dream. It was no surprise therefore that when the camera clicked, she was transformed. She had arrived at the studio earlier than the time given to her, in an autorickshaw which she had stopped well before the main gate. In her Delhi-style cotton kurti with budget dark glasses, she cut a very middle class, just-off-the-local-train figure. Till her make-up and hair were complete. And then, Mee herself let out an embarrassed gasp, as if wondering how it was possible to be thus transformed.

She became a mini hit. A single shampoo ad had somehow caught the imagination of the middle class. The ad itself was directed by the famous South Indian film director who was rumoured to charge by the hour. Mee, with her silky, jet black waist-length hair, had been the perfect choice. Within weeks she found herself being sought after and invited to parties as more job offers came her way. Kishore Bohitdar stayed distant and aloof as though he were not part of her success.

After an exciting, glamorous day of shooting in big expensive studios where she, as a principal actor, could order anything to eat and drink, coming back home in a rickety autorickshaw to cook for a missing philandering husband was a let-down. But Mrs Shetty next door was a real help. She would often keep her door ajar, so that she could drag in a grateful Meehika for a cup of coffee in exchange for gossip from the 'shooting line' as she referred to the entertainment industry. For Mee it was a breathing space, a no-man's land between her two opposite lives.

The young people she met in the studios were mostly ex-students from prestigious South Bombay colleges. They used to hang around the advertising world in their casually chic attire, and young assistant directors would drive off home in chauffeur-driven cars, while she, the 'star', had to slink off into the shadows to find a conveyance back home. Naturally, she couldn't dream of inviting anyone to her home in Ghatkopar East, though her second cheque had managed to buy them some cushions, chatais for the floor, potted plants and cane mooras from an ethnic store in Juhu that she had seen featured in a glossy magazine at the studio. Still, the apartment reeked of isolation, struggle and deprivation, stale food, damp newspapers, and the particularly nauseous smell of rat droppings.

After a couple of months she was cast in a hair oil commercial, which required the unit to shoot for three days in Delhi. The money was good and she would get to fly, her first time in an airplane. But Mee was not overly excited. In fact, she was rather jittery. The thought of herself locked in a metal tube, thousands of miles above the sea, was terrifying. Her fear also came from meeting her family in Delhi. What was she to tell them about Kishore Bohitdar and the state of their marriage? Juhibaby would surely smell that something was amiss. So Mee decided to surprise her family by not announcing her arrival in advance.

Meehika felt a tight knot in her stomach all morning as she carefully packed for the journey to Delhi. She was resentful of the fact that Kishore Bohitdar had not only gone off without his fake, hug-and-bye routine but had left the flat in a worse condition than on most days: a pair of jeans unsure whether it needed a wash or a place in the dustbin, was draped on the window grill, a wet towel thrown majestically on the crumpled unmade bed, lay soaking up the cotton mattress, cups of tea and stubs of half-smoked cigarettes were in every possible place, a squeezed toothpaste tube from which snaked out an inch-long frothy paste, lay abandoned on the corner table without its cap. As Mee started to put things back in place and clear the kitchen, folding and tidying the bed sheets, running a cautious 'Laxman-Rekha' tube around the bathroom, mentally thanking the inventors of this miraculous cockroach deterrent, she felt the knot forming in her stomach. She ran her hand gently over it and for one strange moment, panicked. Could she have conceived? Then instinctively she knew she could never have. Kishore Bohitdar was no Romeo, in fact he was more of a shy, gawky boy-man, a mama's single child, who felt obliged to satisfy the carnal libido of two women. So with her it was always a panicky reaction, as if saying, 'I am satisfied and God help you if you are not.'

And with that would end any, by now almost rare encounter, that they would have. So obviously the strange stabs in her lower abdomen were not an indication of a little Kishore or Kishori waiting in the galaxy to choose her as its mother.

By the time she had organized the flat, made the food arrangements for three days with the part-time help, handed over the keys to Mrs Shetty, because as usual Kishore had forgotten to keep his set, she was running very late and just made it to the airport in the nick of time.

'Welcome, ma'am, seat number 27C, at the rear please.'

Mee tried to match the air hostess's plastic smile with a suave, 'Yes, I know, thank you.'

The interior of the plane was delightfully cool and smelt strongly of a sweet air freshner. As she was late, most people were already seated, and as she walked through the narrow aisle, she heard a child whisper loudly to her mother, 'Look, Mummy, the shampoo ad girl!'

Mee pretended not to hear. All she wanted was to find her seat and sink into it. As it was she was in a foul mood because the autorickshaw driver had overcharged her for luggage, the cheat.

As she was about to move beyond the curtained first-class section towards the more congested rear, she suddenly came face to face with the person just ahead of her who was putting his hand luggage in the overhead locker. As he turned, she realized with a sense of shocked awe that it was none other than the famous South Indian director, who had directed her in her first ad film. Despite his dark glasses, he mesmerized her with his intense masculinity and strangely wet and shining lips.

'I'll have you ubb-graded. Sit nexd to me. First class is yempty.'

The command in his voice thrilled her as much as his sexy masculine perfume and the heavy South Indian accent that she found strangely endearing.

'No sir, I will be fine...'

He ignored her and within minutes, she found herself sitting next to this powerful mogul from the world of films and advertising.

The take off was reasonably all right. She tried to hide her nervousness as the huge plane careened on the runway and with an explosive shriek lifted its belly against the earth's pull, by casually flipping through the safety instruction card in the pocket in front of her. That done, she closed her eyes and tried not to be drawn by the magical waves that were emanating from the man sitting next to her. On his part, he had not said much, yet she could sense the animal attraction between them.

Nageshwar Babu, for that was the name of the demigod sitting next to Mee, was to whisper to her later in his charming Telugu accent, 'My Gawd, you jusst pani-gged! You clluunn-gged on to me, beg-gging me to let you off the airoplane.'

And then he had kissed her sensuously, 'Darling, itt iz naat a trine, that I can pull the chine, is it?'

And that was Mee's first encounter with claustrophobia. And her first encounter with what would turn out to be a torrid affair. Two major firsts on one day in one airplane leading her to her first family... her home in Delhi.

5

Fame

It was just past midnight on the third day of her ad shoot in Delhi that she knocked on the door of A-181, Pandara Road. She knew the rules. Normally, everyone slept early as they had to go to work the next morning but tonight would be an exception. Startled and a little grumpy at first, everyone slowly woke up and gathered for the married-daughter-comes-home-ritual. Beenarani quickly did the 'thakoor-phool'. Mee had to open her mouth and gulp some old flower petals which had been retrieved from the feet of the family deity, the kul dev. That done, everyone trooped into the parlour where Mee self-consciously handed out the gifts that she had picked up from Linking Road in Bandra: chappals for Ma and Beenarani; wallets for her father and Big Uncle. Sensing the hostility emanating from Dada, she almost chose to ignore him but as an afterthought handed him the pen she had chosen for him, a cobalt blue body fitted with a shining revolving star which the hawker, a young boy, had practically forced into her hand. This done, the conversation naturally veered around to Kishore Bohitdar. Juhi was the first to remark, 'What is this? You don't look married at all... Where is the sindoor in your parting?'

It was with great difficulty that Mee managed not to explode. One part wanted to weep and reveal the story of her sordid life in Bombay, a life with a weak, cheating bastard. The other part quieted her down. No, this was not the right time. My secret of pain should be kept in its place, my bosom. So keeping her tone casual, she said, 'Ma, in Bombay it is not necessary to broadcast one's marital status. As an actress, I don't want people to give me only one kind of role, you see...' She tapered off.

'So what kind of work are you doing?' This one was from Rajeshwar.

'Well, quite a bit actually, haven't they been showing the shampoo ad in Delhi?' Then, with an airy wave of her hand, 'In Bombay it is in every corner!'

Then without taking a breath, Mee rattled off all the commercials and shoots she had done, including all the failed auditions and the rejections, confident that they would never know the truth. When it came to the part of her five-star stay in Delhi, they were really impressed. So she must have done pretty well for herself, to take an airplane to Delhi and stay in such a grand hotel. But Dada had more questions.

'Who is directing the ad? What is the name of the company? How much are they paying you?'

Mee was dying to tell Dada that the person who was directing the ad was none other than 'the' Nageshwar Babu, whose professional fees for one project could keep their family going for a year. She was also dying to tell him that his silly, middle-class sister, wife of a philandering cheater, daughter of fearful law-abiding parents, had actually made an inroad into the 'scanning range' of a powerful movie mogul. Though she felt energized and confident at the thought of being noticed by Nageshwar Babu, she held her tongue. How could she tell her brother how dangerously close she had come to succumbing to him.

She did remember that at some point inside the aircraft, she had clung to him desperately, begging him to take her off the metal monster which, like layer upon layer of a black veil, was closing in upon her. There was no exit. Everyone was sitting like strapped robots, facing two sour-faced middle-aged air hostesses wearing morose red-bordered sarees. She wanted to jump out, she couldn't breathe, darkness was enveloping her...exit...exit...where is the exit? At the back of her mind the words 'panic and emptiness', 'panic and emptiness' kept reverberating like some superb audio jugglery that foreign films specialized in. Later, luxuriating in the foamy bathtub in her hotel room, her first tub bath, it suddenly dawned on her that the lines were from the novel, *A Passage to India,* where the protagonist, an Englishman, had got some kind of panic attack, auguring his spiritual quest, in the middle of a dark cave in India.

The warm bath had soothed her nerves, and as she stepped out of the tub, daintily clad in the white cotton bathrobe which she found hanging on the doorknob, she felt as though she had stepped out of the skin of poor middle-class Meehika from Ghatkopar East, into that of an affluent Meehika, born to luxury. As she gazed down on the sparkling blue swimming pool several floors below, she realized she was starving. Recklessly, she ordered mutton korma, paneer shaslik, Kashmiri pilaf, and topped it with a delicious banana sundae. She knew that everything was on the house. She kept the bathroom light on all night and slept fitfully. Towards dawn, she entered a metal tunnel which kept sliding downwards every time she put her foot on it. Just as she was about to fall into the bottomless pit, she woke with a thudding heart and was hugely relieved to find herself in a warm sunny room with large bay windows, the soft purring of the air conditioner making her want to snuggle right back into the buttery soft duvet that covered the length and breadth of the spongy double bed.

✦

The shoot had gone well. At work Nageshwar Babu was a tyrant, as she found out soon enough. His every command would reduce the unit to a quaking mass. At first she too had been nervous and out of form. The brief intimacy that they had shared on the airplane had removed her mask and exposed her vulnerability. But being a trained actress and a good one, had helped her stay focused on the product, the oil, which went by the name of Narayan Kalp. Mee loved it, believed in it, merged into it, so much so that when Nageshwar Babu shouted, 'Cut,' everyone believed that Mee and Narayan Kalp had become synonymous, oiliness dripped out of her.

The second night, the production person had made her share her room with the choreographer, a sprightly girl with hoarse infectious laughter. Sometime post midnight the phone next to her bed had beeped. Sleepily, she answered it. It was Nageshwar Babu. She was suddenly wide awake.

'Sorry amma, eim too late, will yuo jine me for a caafi?'

'Err, sir...okay,' Mee's heart was thumping. 'Where, sir?'

'Come to my room on the fourteenth floor, Room 1402. I am waanting to disguss some pra-ject, ma.'

'Sure sir, I will be there in five minutes.'

She put down the phone and looked towards the choreographer sleeping in the next bed. What if she woke up and found Mee missing? After all, she was a married woman, whatever the state of the marriage. She was torn in two. One part wanted to spite Kishore Bohitdar. Yet, the thought itself filled her with remorse. He was a pathetic struggler, desperate to shed his small-town identity, desperate to taste the wine of freedom and success. She understood because she too was like him. The only difference was that they had two different scripts, about the same subject.

Mee tiptoed out but not before applying a rationed dab of the imported perfume that she had indulged in at a sale last month. But if she thought it was a personal rendezvous, she was wrong. There were four or five people in the room, chatting and drinking. There was also the young female assistant director with a striking face on an obese body, holding a glass of whisky and ice. Mee refused the offer of alcohol and asked for hot chocolate instead. A silence followed as everyone filtered her pronouncement. Nageshwar Babu praised Mee for her performance and everyone agreed. Mee basked in it all: expensive hotel stay, big director, cozy bed, free food and a neat sum in her pocket at the end of the day.

She was told that there would be a photo shoot the next day, the print ad as it was called, and she should be ready by eight in the morning.

Next morning she kept an anxious eye out for Nageshwar Babu but he did not come to the set. The print ad was the work of the still photographer, Mee was informed. All through the morning, she had to keep changing costumes and suitably glowing expressions, as she held and caressed the precious product, Narayan Kalp, which would see them through all the bills for the next three months, considering Kishore always had a good reason to back off when the time came to cough up his share of the expenses.

Mee did not like the photographer or the make-up man. They probably did not like her either. 'Too much attitude' said the quick look that passed between the two men.

'Make-up dada, are you sure I should use a pink lipstick? I feel a lighter one is better.'

Mee's tone was sharp. She was not to know that one did not address a make-up artist as 'make-up dada'. Just 'dada' was enough.

The make-up seemed to take hours to apply, and the intense lights and the strain of remembering her lines, made Mee irritable and edgy. Before each shot, she yelled imperiously, 'Make-up', as if the make-up palette would just swim up to her and dab her face. She had cut herself off from the person, the human being, the make-up artist who was given the job of beautifying her. She did not know at that point, that in earlier days, the top heroines would touch the feet of the make-up artists before they sat down for their make-up.After all, a major part of their careers depended on the talent of the make-up artist. But this novice from Delhi just yelled 'make-up', sending quiet ripples of hostility around the set.

She ruffled the photographer as well. They were shooting in an expensive bungalow in South Delhi's Vasant Vihar. Mee did not know a thing about lenses or lights or angles, but so haughty was her approach that the photographer (he later received a Padma Bhushan for his excellent work) did not turn up after lunch and sent his third assistant instead. Of course, Mee had no idea that she had caused any offence and went through the shoot just as before: imperious, grumbling, snooty, her eyes and heart hungering for a glimpse of Nageshwar Babu.

They finally met in the lobby. She was stepping out to meet her family and he was coming in from a meeting. He proposed that he drop her in his car. Though she was grateful for the offer, knowing the dangers of travelling in

Delhi in the dark, she still pretended to demur, 'No really, sir, I'll manage.'

'What, ma, I am simbly sayying that the car will be with you, Dilli is naat safe. You meet yure fambly and then we will have din-ner together.'

Suddenly Mee felt wanted, loved, sought after, a sense of great power swept over her, as she unconsciously ran her fingers through her hair, twisting a strand around one finger.

'Sir, I may have to spend the night there,' she lied.

He looked disappointed. She felt elated, powerful. Then fear overtook her. She should not play too hard to get.

'Sir, why don't we have a quick dinner at the restaurant, and then I can leave?'

As they sat opposite each other in the Haveli, the hotel's Indian restaurant, a noisy bunch of unit members came down to eat the buffet dinner, which was part of the production arrangement. They stopped short on seeing them, bowed, scraped and bolted. Mee smiled an internal smile of victory, the corners of her mouth turning up charmingly. Strangely, she was not overly thrilled by Nageshwar Babu's offer of playing the heroine in his forthcoming Hindi blockbuster and she wondered why. Any girl in her place would have done anything to get such an offer, then why did she feel so distant and detached?

He glanced at her sideways. It was this waif-like 'touch-me-not but protect me with your manhood' air about her, that was maddening him. But he would go slow. She was not one of those one-night starlets who threw themselves at his feet with regularity. He just had to give one look, and the girl would be arranged. But this one was an educated girl with middle-class values. Sadly, he remembered his tramp of a wife and his heart squeezed momentarily. So beautiful, despite her recent weight gain, talented and yet so wayward. What did he lack, what was it that he could not give her that made her succumb to any male, be it his brother, best friend, or the newest driver in his entourage? And yet, her days as a chorus dancer would not let her forget their lightning trajectory into fame and money, so she pursued him relentlessly, keeping a hawk-like vigil, lest she lose him and plummet back to poverty.

By the time Juhibaby had packed a kurta pajama for Kishore Bohitdar, as the 'jamai shoshti', thanksgiving for one's son-in-law, it was almost two a.m. As Mee held the gift to her chest, a wave of guilt swept through her. Her mother must have had to stint a bit to save up money to buy this gift for her cheating, indifferent husband, but she held her tongue. As she stylishly got into Nageshwar Babu's chauffeur-driven car, her heart went out, very briefly, to her family, as they stood in a line, waving clumsily till they faded from her vision.

✦

'Violet Movies' was the production company which had been calling and leaving their number at the local STD booth. Mee had set up a deal with Singhji, happily also from Delhi's Karol Bagh, who charged her five rupees for delivering a message. Mee was a little wary whenever she heard of film producers. She remembered Juhibaby's dislike of 'Hindustani' eccentricities and 'filmy' people. To her, a film producer was a pot-bellied, fat man who wore a loud animal-printed shirt, revealing a hairy chest studded with thick, obnoxious gold chains. When, after a good deal of prodding from Mrs Shetty, Mee agreed to meet the producer, she was in for a pleasant surprise. Raj Tandon was, in appearance, the exact opposite of what her fearful mind had conjured. He was lean, dressed in jeans and a T-shirt, soft-spoken and appeared to be a thorough gentleman. She agreed to do the film. Of course, it was only in the second meeting that she came to know that she was to play the second lead. The main lead was an older actress with a colourful reputation.

They were to shoot in Darjeeling, where they would film two songs on her. By now, Mee was becoming a seasoned traveller. Her new light blue VIP suitcase, a wedding present from Ritika and Pratyusha, was always packed and ready with two sets of clothes, shoes, purse, lingerie, and a basic make-up kit. Kishore Bohitdar was a relieved man. To find his silly wife busy with her silly career, was comforting. At least he did not have to face the guilt of deserting her, as he got busy climbing the ladder of corporate success with a little help from lovers like Sunanda Sen who had a flourishing circle of friends, lovers, ex-lovers, hangers-on, dilettantes, poets, painters, actors, and even a prominent South Bombay politician. She had mastered the art of social behaviour: she was everywhere, at all major city functions, exhibitions, inaugurations, book releases, ribbon-cuttings, nobody could miss the presence of the Dean's liberated wife, in her funky clothes and coin-sized bindi. Close by but not too close would be Kishore Bohitdar, trying not to be overwhelmed by all that was happening in his young life.

Mee and Kishore now barely spoke to each other. Mee did not ask him any questions and Kishore did not volunteer any answers. But Mee took some pleasure in noting that Kishore was a little curious about her detachment. Could he smell that her life was taking her to another course?

Within a couple of years of their married life they had become like two strangers in a train compartment, who by dint of circumstances are forced to sit facing each other for hours on end. Kishore filled up his void with Sunanda. Mee filled up hers by thoughts of Nageshwar Babu and her shooting schedule.

✦

When she first met the heroine in Darjeeling, Mee felt a pang of envy. Tall, buxom, sensual, this lady knew how to madden men, and that is exactly what she did. Already the mother of a young boy, a well-kept secret, she got involved with the much-married leading man and the entire unit had to wait endlessly till the couple would remember to take a break from their impassioned lovemaking and emerge to give their shots.

Darjeeling was hilly, cold, windswept and quite desolate. Mee had been allotted a large room with a high ceiling, stuffed with frayed old-fashioned furniture, next to the room reserved for the main lead. Most nights she could hear strange thudding sounds which shook the old wooden structure. One night on a chance visit to the heroine's room, she found her sprawled in bed at a strange angle, talking on the telephone, banging the wall next to the bed with her legs. Seconds later, Mee heard a similar rhythmic banging from the other side of the wall: someone was replying to this leg Morse code. It took her a moment to realize that the adjoining room was the hero's. At least it solved the mystery of the thudding walls, when finally she understood the elaborate code signal of the lead pair, before one slipped into the other's room.

But the heroine was loving and warm-hearted, and had a sweet contempt for Mee's utter seriousness regarding her role.

'Don't be silly, darling! This is not your theatre, that you have to work so hard and not have a little fun.'

Mee did not pay heed to her advice, as she continued to be aloof and totally absorbed in her role, making her look like an over-serious schoolgirl. But what Mee did pay heed to, was the heroine's wardrobe: her array of costumes, shoes, bags, wigs, watches, costume jewellery, which were stacked neatly in different cupboards specially installed in her room. Her bathroom had candles around the ancient chinaware bathtub, and hanging from newly hammered knobs on the wall, were baskets of colour-coordinated lingerie. She, who cared so little about acting, cared deeply for all the extraneous things that went into its making. Sadly for Mee, it was quite the reverse.

Nageshwar Babu was in Hyderabad, making pre-production arrangements for his new film which was to be shot next month. His production people had been in touch with Mee about the dates and other contractual matters. This time she had got a substantial raise in remuneration and had planned to buy a griller-toaster for the family in Pandara Road, and silk Pochampalli Hyderabadi sarees for her mother and aunt. But it was for the man himself that she pined. She tried his number on the phone but hung up quickly when a female voice said 'hellooo', in a husky drawl. Though at that point, nothing much had really happened between her and Nageshwar Babu, she knew in her heart that something would happen in a matter of minutes when they met again. She imagined that she was in love. She needed to be in love. She wanted approval and to be perceived as the perennial 'Miss Virgin Goody Two-Shoes.' She was not brave enough to follow her heart and certainly not brave enough to face its consequences. So she hid inside her 'baby doll' persona and played her waif card, the poor baby lost in the woods. He will come, my prince in shining armour, my olive-skinned South Indian 'Hindustani' movie mogul with the wet and shining lips, will come and take me away into a world where,

'They're gonna put me in the movies

They're gonna make a big star out of me
The biggest thing that's ever hit the big time ,
And all I have to do, is act naturally.'

✦

Hyderabad in the early eighties was an insufferably hot city. Built on stony terrain where grass and thorny bushes peeked reluctantly from the parched earth, the whole city seemed sweaty and breathless. This was Mee's first visit, and though she was given a luxurious suite, the difference of temperature inside and outside the hotel was so stark, that it required willpower to step out. At the back of her mind, she knew why she was given this grand room: actually there were two rooms, separated by a curved wall, broken by grills in an art deco design. She recognized it from her art classes at the drama school. The giant king-size bed with its cushioned headrest and colour-coordinated bed linen, was a bit daunting. The outer room was smaller and had a nice seating arrangement, including a couch. Mee smiled to herself. A casting couch? She was not in the least bit alarmed. She was ready to play the game. By now she had convinced herself she was in love with Nageshwar Babu. Was it the power that he exuded or the naked look of passion in his eyes...? She hummed contentedly as she unpacked her blue VIP suitcase and started to hang her clothes inside the wardrobe, which smelt strongly of napthelene balls. The month-long schedule, she knew, would need strict discipline, so she decided to put out her clothes, bags, jewellery, shoes, stoles, neatly in advance so as not to waste time. At least she had picked this up from the senior heroine from the Darjeeling schedule.

Ding-dong! Ding-dong! Ding-dong!

The musical bell was rung with authority and she knew

who it was. Heart racing, she ran her palm over her hair, dabbed some perfume and sauntered forth to open the door, lady-like, delicate, making sure that she wore an expression of surprise on her face. He was standing there, one arm on the doorframe, a shiny gift-wrapped package under the other. He smelt of cigarettes, Old Spice and a wisp of perspiration, enough for Mee to feel weak in the knees.

'Hello, amma!' His voice was soft and persuasive.

That was when a tornado struck her life. As she was to confess to Pratyusha later, she did not remember the sequence of events. It was so fast and so jumbled that funnily, all she could recall intensely were smells: the smell of his underarm, its curly, wiry hair tickling her face as she lay there, the smell of his breath, cigaretty, warm, sweet, the intimate smells of their bodies as they thrashed about passionately on the snooty king-size bed; the pungent smell of hot, spicy sambar-dosa that they had ordered from room service afterwards. And of course, when with sweaty palms she had opened the wrapper of the gift that he had brought for her, she had inhaled deeply into the exquisite mother-of-pearl box which contained deliciously perfumed incense sticks.

'Most famous in Hyderabad.'

'And most expensive,' giggled Mee's mind.

Heady days followed. Nageshwar Babu was the king of the South Indian movie industry and at night she was his queen. He pampered her no end, her tiniest wish was his command. He took great pains with the lighting and angle of his shots to present her in the best possible light. As soon as she entered the set, she knew she was special, the chosen one. Everyone bowed and scraped before her, second only to Nageshwar Babu. One scene required her to sing a song for the hero. Mee loved to sing, but she was so unsure about her singing abilities, that she spent a good two hours arguing with

Nageshwar Babu to record it playback instead of making her sing. He tried to convince her that in this new wave kind of cinema, the raw, uneven quality of the heroine's voice would be far more effective than playback, but Mee was at her pouty best. One part of her was shamelessly taking advantage of his affections, but deep inside she was battling Juhibaby's voice, 'You can't sing. Your voice is like a bhaanga kashore.'

She tried desperately to keep her mother's sharp retort out of her mind. And suddenly it happened.

'Lights...camera...rolling...action.'

Mee transformed into her character, Savitri. Her being sank into something soft, something indefinable and from a place deep inside her, beautiful notes started emanating. She wafted outside herself and saw Savitri singing mellifluously to the hero. Her whole being vibrated as she became one with the moment, everything else ceased to exist. The set was electrified. Everyone was spellbound, even Moorthy, the noisy tea boy stood stockstill, his tea caddy swaying gently. The spell was broken by a thunderous applause, which jolted her back inside herself with a throbbing thud. Vaguely she could sense the beaming face of her lover and the entire unit, smiling and cheering. Before she could bask in the applause, Juhibaby again made her entry, 'Bhaanga kashore!'

And Mee instantly retreated into her shell. Somebody who sounded just like herself, was whispering into her ear, 'Don't get carried away...this is because you are the boss' current obsession.'

From the corner of her eyes, she saw the pained look of her co-artist, as she noiselessly slipped away into the make-up room, ostensibly to get a touch up done, but actually to dry her tears of anger and envy. Nageshwar Babu winked at Mee conspiratorially.

✦

Time flew by, carrying Mee on its supersonic wings as days, weeks, months, dates, diaries got chock-a-block with her personal schedule. Now she barely slept in her flat in Ghatkopar East. It was far away in the suburbs, besides being downmarket. As she was working virtually round the clock, doing three shifts at a time, most of the people she was working for, were happy to put her up in hotels near their sets. Mrs Shetty would wait vigilantly to catch hold of Mee, on her rare visits home, to get the latest gossip about the stars she pored over in *Filmfare* and *Stardust*. Kishore was hardly around, spending most of his time travelling, ostensibly on work. So it was dear Mrs Shetty who could be woken up any time of day or night, as she was the self-appointed caretaker of their house keys. Mee was also fortunate to get the services of a secretary, the good old angel, Mishraji, who advised her most soundly to book a flat in the fast-developing locality of Versova beach, where the mangrove jungles were being ruthlessly cut to be replaced by concrete ones. It would be expeditious to buy now, when the prices were lowest and the carpet area highest. So Mee invested in an apartment which would be ready the following year.

Embarrassed by his heroine coming to his sets in an autorickshaw, one of her producers made a down payment on a new car. Mee was thrilled to go to Ashish motor training school for a four-week driving course. As she cruised along with her trainer, she laughed confidently as the morning breeze lifted her hair and her spirits. Her first car. When she had called A-181, Pandara Road to give them the news, she was met with a noisy silence, a silence rippling with questions.

'A car, within such a short time, in a city like Bombay?'

'A new car?'

'A second-hand car?'

'How come we have never owned a car?'

Beenarani was the first to ask, 'What model is it?'

'It's a beautiful white Fiat, Premier Padmini, and it is brand new.'

She did not want to tell them about the instalments, because the concept was new and scary. She was yet to be part of the later generation whose lives rotated around fancy homes, cars, appliances and EMIs: Equated Monthly Instalments.

Every now and then, she would coax the trainer to let her drive all the way to Versova, to see how the luxury building was coming up. Two floors, three floors and then majestically, the twelfth floor. Hers was the only apartment building on Versova beach which was twelve storeys high. Though she hated the overpowering smell of dried fish that knocked one over as one turned into Versova, yet Mee loved the sounds of the earth-movers, the big heavy machines that were used for building houses. She loved their steady roar as they dumped cement from their large elliptical rotating bellies onto the pavements. She was also mesmerized by the sound of workers pulling at heavy steel cables, shouting in unison, 'Dum laga ke...haiyysha.' They were migrants from distant Uttar Pradesh and Bihar, here to build homes for the rich.

Sitting in her car, parked under the shade of a tree, hiding behind designer sunglasses, Mee watched her dream apartment being constructed.

✦

It was time for Mee's first trip abroad. She was to be part of a film stage show in Dubai, where she had been assigned two songs and a solo dance. Mishraji had been very prudent in taking all the money in advance, and sending it smoothly towards the new apartment. She was working hard and at a dizzying speed, so she left all monetary matters in Mishraji's able hands. Fifty percent of the money she earned was in 'black', cash payment without a written record, which suited her perfectly, because housing in Bombay was a parallel black economy and even the prime minister could not hope to buy a flat through bank cheques alone.

After evenings of hectic rehearsals, costume, hair and make-up trials, Mee was ready for her first foreign sojourn. She was in two minds, actually three. One part was afraid of the metal monster, the aeroplane, the second part was thrilled to be the only one in the immediate family to call herself 'foreign returned', a healthy prefix for the middle class in the eighties, but the third part was really ecstatic, because in Dubai, they would be joined by Nageshwar Babu.

This time, the flight was not as frightening as the first time. Besides which she had remembered to swallow generous amounts of Kaliphos, the tiny white homeopathic pills which Beenarani used to dole out before every exam, vouching for its efficacy to calm nerves. Since she was travelling first class and feeling calm and poised, she did not think it necessary to refuse a nice glass of wine to help her stay that way.

She was overawed by the luxurious life of Dubai. Though the hotel that they were staying at was large, there were still other larger and grander structures dotting the cityscape. She was fascinated by Al-Ghurair, a ten-storey shopping mall with an escalator, one of the first in the so-called civilized world. She shopped recklessly with the dirhams she had been given for her local expenses: a mixed bag of kitchen utilities, handbags, a shirt for Kishore, shoes for herself and assorted souvenirs for the family at Pandara Road. The city reeked of abundance as skyscrapers made of chrome and glass reflected back the sun's dazzling heat. Its public relations department left no stone unturned to proclaim that the garden city, made by the tremendous energy of human beings, was crafted out of a barren desert. The wide roads, dotted with palm trees, turned into ribbons of lights at night, as plush cars whizzed past noiselessly.

The hall in which the show was held was smaller than she had expected, but the programme was a success. The audience was mostly Indians, Gujaratis, Sindhis, Marwaris, with a smattering of Arabs with their burqa-clad women. After the show they had been invited to a dinner party at the mansion of a wealthy Arab sheikh, and it was here that Nageshwar Babu had promised to meet her. Mee was in high spirits the whole day.

The mansion was like a mini palace. There were turbaned durbans and security men with walkie-talkies, manning every corner, reminding the awed, giggling group of guests of a Hollywood gangster movie set. The sheikh was old, charming, spoke fluent English, and airily introduced a gaggle of bejewelled women as 'my wives'. They instantly went into active mode, playing hostess to the guests. The dinner was laid out in a centrally air-conditioned durbar-like hall with a high ceiling and intricately inlaid arches. The mahogany dinner table could accommodate forty-two chairs, with intelligent recesses in between for better service. Mee knew, because she had mentally counted. Twenty-four... thirty-six...forty-two, and back again to reconfirm one...six...twelve...Large cooked animals were served with aplomb. While the rest of the cast thoroughly enjoyed the free banquet, Mee kept herself from gagging by repeating the number of chairs... Eight, twenty... forty-two...Besides she was getting butterflies in her stomach waiting for Nageshwar Babu.

As if on cue, he was ushered in with fanfare by the

organizers of the show, followed by the gun-toting security men. Mee floated up to meet him but stopped short as she saw a woman right behind him, clutching on to his arm.She was short, plump, fair-skinned, with sharp bright eyes and a huge gold necklace, a mangalsutra, which bobbed on her chest, screaming for attention.

'Helloo,' she said.

Mee's world stopped spinning. She knew it was his wife. She knew it from the ostentatious mangalsutra and also because she had heard that voice before, the same 'Helloo'.

Nageshwar Babu stood there stoically, no expression crossed his face. The host came forward smilingly and led them to their seats which were diagonally opposite to where Mee was seated. The entire unit was happy to have the movie mogul in their midst and much bantering and chatting followed: they had all been polishing off the expensive liquor with alarming speed. Mrs Nageshwar Babu was obviously known to many and Mee could feel the sly gaze of people on her as she stood, awkward, stumped, defeated.

Close to midnight, Nageshwar Babu rang the doorbell of her hotel room. She had been waiting. He shut the door behind him and opened his arms wide. She melted into them. No conversation, no explanations, just the two of them fitting into each other naturally.

'Like hand-in-glove,' Mee was to tell Pratyusha later.

'Yeah, hand-in-glove all right! You guys were sneaking around behind his wife's fat backside.' Pratyusha, who was on her third vodka-tonic, had giggled uncontrollably.

✦

Bollywood, 1988. A star was born. She was the new sun on the horizon. Three of her five movies were, in filmy parlance, 'super-duper hits', two in the South Indian and one in the Bombay film industry. At the award functions, she glittered, as journalists clamoured to ask her questions, photographers jostled to take her pictures. Her Ghatkopar East flat had turned into a transit camp. Kishore Bohitdar continued to be busy checking out weekend getaway places with Sunanda Sen, sponsored by the poor unsuspecting Dean Prakash Chand. Mrs Shetty continued to be the official keeper of their flat keys. Mee continued to drop in, drinking delectable home-ground coffee in tacit exchange for gossip about the stars, their 'andar ki baat', making up stories of their intimate life, as her mood dictated.

Mee was wearing her long green silk skirt with a matching top on the day her name was announced as the winner in the 'Best Actor, Female Category'. To a thunderous ovation, she waltzed her way to the stage, where to her utmost chagrin, the award was given away by her lover-mentor, Nageshwar Babu.

Was this a fake award? Had he engineered it?

She became tongue-tied when asked to speak, all her elocution and debating skills deserting her. All she could manage was a hoarse, 'Not used to speeches, I am speechless. Thank you everyone,' as she made a stumbling exit.

Three awards in such a short span would have made anyone ecstatic, but Mee felt nothing.

She plonked the much-coveted award next to the two earlier ones, on the top shelf of the rickety cane shoe stand. Its lower shelves were overflowing with footwear in various styles and colours. She made a quick mental note to tell her interior designer, a young girl just out of design school, that she needed colour-coordinated shoe racks in her walk-in cupboard in her new apartment. The Ghaktkopar flat was in a mess, as always, a smelly blur of unwashed jeans, underwear, wet towels and cigarette butts. Kishore had left word through Mrs Shetty that he had some important project work over the weekend and would be back on Monday. She felt too tired to begin from the beginning, Operation Clean-up Behind the Husband, but she was well acquainted with her own malaise. Whenever she saw a mess of any kind, some switch within her went into 'auto mode', as she turned into a human vacuum cleaner, dusting, swabbing, cleaning till she brought cleanliness and order back into her life, without which she was paralyzed.

The month of May was the worst in Bombay, just prior to the onset of the monsoon. While Delhi's heat was dry and cutting, Bombay's heat was wet and enveloping. The hired air-conditioner was not at its optimum and Mee felt choked inside the tiny fifth floor flat. She listlessly wondered at the speed of time and events: it seemed just the other day that she had landed in this flat on a monsoon-flooded day.

She must have dozed off because the next thing she heard was the strident knocking on the front door. What was the time? Who could it be? Woozily she opened the door to find Mrs Shetty standing with a bunch of letters, along with the building electrician.

'What, baba? Your front doorbell has not been working for so many days... I even told your husband...he also didn't say anything, toh mai socha, I will ask Kamble to fix it.'

'Thank you, Mrs Shetty, what would I do without you, Auntyji?'

The last was soft, grateful. Mee had never called her 'aunty' before. Mrs Shetty, mother of two married daughters, quick to observe the frail, frazzled newborn star, rushed off to her flat and returned minutes later with a bowl covered by a newspaper.

As Kamble fussed around with wires and switchboards,

Mee quietly ate neer dosa with spicy coconut chutney under the vigilant gaze of Mrs Shetty. Then she spent the next two hours trying to hide her déjà vu as she described the award functions, the colour of the saree worn by Mrs Shetty's favourite heroine, Rekha, and the private life of the current heartthrob of the fickle nation. She snapped to attention when Mrs Shetty, her eyes shining innocently, remarked, 'Do you think it is true? I read in the South Indian magazine that Nageshwar Babu has a young girl in his life! They interviewed his wife, you know.'

To stall any suspicions, because Mrs Shetty knew that she too had worked with him, Mee pretended to be very curious and interested, though she didn't have the guts to ask what his wife knew or had said. She quickly deflected Mrs Shetty's attention from the topic by holding out her hand for the stack of fan mail which the latter was still clutching on to possessively.

'My God, who gives them my address?'

'Them' were her ardent fans who had sent her postcards, hand-painted cards, letters from all over India. Some were from remote villages in Bengal, written in illegible Bengali—Noar hati, Ultto danga, Belgharia, Sunderbans. Some were from different states of South India, where according to one of the fan letters, a fan club had been formed for her. Mrs Shetty was thrilled to bits.

'What, ma? I am living next door to a star...I am so lucky. Next time my brother calls from Australia, you will say hello to him?'

Mee nodded graciously, distractedly tossing the entire bunch of fan mail into the already overflowing wastepaper basket.

'Next week I shift to my new home. Where can I carry all this clutter?'

And then, as a shaft of fear ripped through her: 'You will come and visit me, wont you?'

Mrs Shetty's wrinkled sagging cheeks quivered slightly and her eyes moistened. She shook her head sadly and stood up. 'How beta, where is Ghatkopar East and where is Versova? I don't even know the bus number.'

'I will send the car for you,Auntyji.'

A tenderness enveloped Mee. This was the woman who had stood by her like a rock in these past tumultuous years. She never judged, complained or made any demands, if one could discount her need for starry tales. Mee thought of Juhibaby and shuddered.

It was on another day that Mee had to sit Mrs Shetty down and gently explain to her that her marriage with Kishore Bohitdar was not working out and that she was moving to her new flat, alone. Though initially alarmed, Mrs Shetty soon warmed up to the idea that in modern times people did make these choices.

'If Chikki was earning like you, then even she could leave that rogue, Sudhakar. How much he tortures her with drink and cheap women.'

Chikki was the younger of her two daughters, whose bad marriage was a constant source of tension in the Shetty household.

'Don't worry, I will get Rukmani bai to clean the flat daily after your husband goes to work.'

'Thank you, Auntyji.'

It was not so easy to break the news to Kishore Bohitdar about her decision to move out alone. For weeks Mee had been preparing herself for the big day when she could finally announce to him that her body, mind and soul had had a conversation, and had decided to make a bid for freedom and a new life, without him.

Picking the right moment was difficult. Dada was to be married two months hence and Juhibaby had made it amply clear that she should not come alone. It was mandatory that she come with her husband Kishore Bohitdar, the strong unsaid undercurrent being, 'Hindustani groom of your choice'. She had also given instructions that Mee should dryclean and wear the same Benarasi saree that she had worn on her own wedding, along with the five pieces of mismatched jewellery that had been gifted to her by various members of her family.

'No need to dress like a hippie. This is going to be a formal occasion, involving the girl's side, I don't want them to think you are odd,' Juhibaby had warned Mee.

The problem before Mee was that if she moved out of Ghatkopar East before the wedding, then it was certain that Kishore Bohitdar would not attend the function and Juhibaby's wrath would descend on her head. If she allowed him to move out with her, it was equally certain that it would need a lot of skilful manipulation for her to evict him from the new apartment. After all, who in his right senses would return to a dump in Ghatkopar East when he, as her lawfully wedded husband, had a right to stay in a fancy flat in Versova?

As it turned out, Kishore himself came up with the solution. He had been behaving even more oddly of late, and just before Dada's wedding, announced that he was going to the beautiful Kangra valley for a workshop in ceramics, and would join her in Delhi for half a day.

'To register his presence in the family album of photographs, no doubt,' sneered Mee's mind.

She felt almost sorry to have to witness his thinly veiled lies. As for her, it was an ideal situation. While he was away she would quickly move into the new apartment, and after the wedding was over, she would confront him face to face with her carefully hidden proof, the pink lipstick-kissed card. If he chose Sunanda Sen, then obviously it would be quits forever but if by some remote chance he chose her, like the 'unlikely event of a plane landing on water', giggled Mee's silly mind, well then, 'we'll see', is what she told herself.

Mee's 'to-do' lists were endless. In keeping with her fastidious nature, she would save scripts from her shoots, cut them and stitch them into little notepads, which she would then place in strategic corners, including the windowsill of the toilet. The notepad would be tied to a pen so even ablution time was used well as she jotted away. Her clothes had to be washed, ironed, packed. Jewellery, shoes, bag, books, utensils, bric-a-brac, stationery, laundry, curtains, bed sheets, photographs, all had to be segregated for the convenience of the packers...And then the question, what should she leave behind for Kishore Bohitdar? She made a mental inventory: the fridge, the cooking gas stove with the cylinder, the three pieces of eclectic furniture which comprised her sitting area, the two coffee tables, the wobbly cane shelf, the double bed and the hand-me-down, ugly steel Godrej cupboard. She gazed at all the items she had handpicked with care during her days of struggle when every penny saved would be added, calculated and stored in the old blue tin biscuit box which she hid between her stack of clothes, in the steel wardrobe. Mee had always hated her mother's parlour in A-181, Pandara Road: three stuffy sofas in a depressing rust and fawn combination, one centre table covered with a lace crochet tablecloth, a closet whose open shelves housed her father's gramophone records, neatly classified into 'Rabindra sangeet', 'Shyama sangeet', 'Modern' and on which ceremoniously stood the podgy Grundig record player, with its proud 'Made in Germany' label. Every door and window had long printed curtains, which never quite matched the colour or texture of the room, which horror of horrors, had been painted a rose pink by enthusiastic Big Uncle, Rajeshwar. Mee's taste was a complete reaction to Juhibaby's unimaginative middle-class one, as she strolled off alone to the congested side lanes of Jogeshwar, to marvel at the sight of exquisite tables with marble tops, old-fashioned round 'chakkies', used for grinding wheat in earlier days, now used as centre tables, wardrobes and beds made of Burma teak and rosewood by Muslim craftsmen, mirror-encrusted side tables. After much internal debate, calculations and haggling, she would narrow down to buying one piece at a time. She wanted a home, a family, a place to return to, but all she got was a dirty flat filled with the litter of an errant husband. It was only much later that the truth would hit her, that what you want, is what you create, and not what you expect the other to fulfil for you.

In the meanwhile, shifting to the new apartment had coincided perfectly with Dada's wedding. The packers arrived to move everything that had once been her home, into her new swanky high-rise flat. The griha-puja had to be performed. A pandit had to be found, who would conduct this ritual for her auspicious entry into her new home for a reasonable fee. This was ably handled by Mishraji who slyly offered his services as the officiating priest, playing on his Brahmin card, which gave him scriptural authority to conjoin Mee's earthly wire with the wire of divinity. Or so he thought.

A separate suitcase had to be packed for the wedding which would contain her clothes in the matching order of ceremonies: a salwar kameez for the morning ritual, a lehenga for the evening 'ai budo bhaat', the bachelor's party, a moderately glamorous saree for the next morning, followed finally by the wedding itself, where she would wear her own wedding saree. Mee packed the different sets of clothes in separate polythene bags, within which were smaller bags of matching footwear and jewellery. Each bag was neatly numbered with a black marker pen in the order in which it was to be used.

After almost two years of waiting to move out of Ghatkopar East, the big day was a bit of an anti-climax. Versova beach that Monday morning was in a stinking mood as it ignored yet another entrant into its smelly fold. The tide which washed ashore shells, dead fish, broken crabs, an unfortunate swollen, out of shape sandal in search of its owner, also swept with it, its salty, balmy green-blue fickleness. Standing on her twelfth floor balcony overlooking the Arabian Sea, Mee felt tall and victorious. Not bad for someone who had a very small run in the Bombay film industry. Yet she knew she was alone and felt an aching desolation, two strong contradictory emotions. A crow swooped past her, cawing loudly. She remembered how, as a child, she would watch Granny feeding the crows. 'Whenever some important event happens in one's life, ancestors visit us on earth in the form of crows.' Could it be Granny who was checking out her new house? Mee started to feel reassured. After all, Granny was the only one who believed in her. 'This one will amount to something some day,' she would say.

The puja havan fire had cooled down, the sweets distributed and eaten, the neighbours had been gifted small boxes of sweets as a gesture of ingratiation.

'Love thy neighbours like thyself.'

Mee smiled wanly. Now was the difficult task ahead: the family wedding.

Post the Dubai trip, Nageshwar Babu had distanced himself imperceptibly. Though she still throbbed at the memory of his touch and spent hours fantasizing about him, as a woman she could sense that she was on her way out. After snide reports by a certain section of the media, Nageshwar Babu's wife had become more suspicious and clingy than ever, so making calls to his residence was dangerous. This information was obliquely conveyed to her by her make-up man, who wanted to be in her good books. In any case she had no choice, considering the landline in her new apartment would take at least a week to instal. Though she ached to kiss his cigarette-scented wet and shiny lips, she had worn her strong suit: defence against hurt. She could not bear the thought of being neglected by both the men in her life so she decided to do the rejection, even though it meant that her heart would dissolve into a snotty, teary puddle of grief. The last time she had made an attempt to call Nageshwar Babu was on the eve of her shifting out, when she had been desperate for some reassurance of his love.

'Helloo???'...the suspicious voice of his wife had answered.

Mee had hung up but not before she heard Nageshwar Babu's voice, a tinge of anger in it, as he spoke in rapid Telugu and then the line had gone dead.

Was he angry with his wife for picking up the phone? Did he think it could be her? Did he pine for her the way she was pining for him?

The questions shimmered cobweb-like, unanswered, in the humid Bombay air.

✦

As the taxi drove past the grey squat structure which was the prestigious Modern School, Mee could see A-181,Pandara Road, wearing a rather busy look. All the doors and windows were wide open, and as she neared the house, she could see groups of people walking in and out, talking animatedly, all of them doing some chore or the other. As she paid off the taxi, she stole a glance at the sight of Oshima pishima, Maya pishima, Neeru's ma, carrying large buckets of vegetables to the shade of a cloth pandal outside the house where a group of chattering ladies squatted on the floor in front of mounds of fresh vegetables, bantering with each other, while another group was busy in front of a stove on which sat a giant kadhai, sizzling with a strong aroma: mustard fish, Juhibaby's favourite.

Mee slunk in from the back door. She did not feel like hobnobbing with her parents' extended family of expatriate Bengalis as they cheerfully rallied around for Dada's wedding. As she turned the corner, she stopped short: on the stoop facing the backyard, huddled very close to each other, sat her three spinster aunts on low cane moodhas, wearing identical expressions of envy and malice, matching their crisp, bordered sarees, as they whispered into each other's ears.

A quick flash of Macbeth's three witches crossed her mind, but her aunts were too real to even evoke a smirk. They fell silent, whispered sentences cut-off in mid-air as they stared at Mee who dutifully bent down and touched their feet.

The house was full of children in shiny clothes, screaming and chasing one another as elders tried to navigate their way past them, women chattering and laughing, yet despite the air of festivity, the house wore a pall of gloom.

'Am I projecting my anxiety into this scenario?' The thought resounded in Mee's mind.

She peeped into her parents' bedroom. Her beautiful aunt Chhayamoni was sitting on the bed with Juhibaby. Her aunt had aged gracefully and her silvery white hair framing her serene features made her look more like a grandmother than an aunt. Aunt and mother stared at her without smiling. As she entered the room she sensed someone behind her. She wheeled around to face a sniggering Dada, holding on to the arm of none other than Kishore Bohitdar. Her spoilt cousin from Calcutta, Chhayamoni's son, stood behind them, a leering shadow. Mee was stumped. How did Kishore manage to reach earlier than her? And why was Dada holding him in a vice-like grip? Why were her mother and aunt staring at her so coldly?

Before she could compose herself, Dada blurted out, 'So you are having an affair with that South Indian producer?'

Mee's ears grew hot and her heart skipped a beat.

'What? What nonsense is this?' Something like a croak escaped her throat.

Juhibaby's eyes were steely as she handed over a bunch of papers to Mee, who glanced at them and froze. They were bills of Hotel Ashoka in Hyderabad where she had spent a blissful month with Nageshwar Babu. In every food bill that had been delivered to her room, 627, was Nageshwar Babu's signature.

'What? How? What?' This time her voice was more like the yelp of a stoned mongrel.

'His wife got all the details and contacted Kishore. She is going to the press.'

Kishore stood there expressionless, except for his two sneaky eyes which kept darting off towards the ceiling or diving deep under the floor.

Suddenly Mee was swept by a huge tide of rage. 'Kishore Bohitdar...how dare you come to my house...? Shall I tell them about you and...?'

Before she could complete her sentence, Juhibaby lunged at her and tadaak! The sharp crack of a slap made Mee lose her balance and she fell in a heap in front of Kishore Bohitdar.

'You have brought us nothing but shame,' Juhibaby

hissed. 'Did you think you could win us over with your fancy apartment and car... Now I see how you got everything so quickly...You are nothing but a whore!'

'Whore! Whore! Whore!'

Mee's face stung with shame and hot tears of anger.

She looked into her mother's smouldering eyes and with a supreme effort, spat out, 'I hate you. I don't ever want to call you Ma.' And then she passed out.

6
Trapped

A wedding, a funeral and a deadly disease.

This is what the residents of A-181, Pandara Road experienced rapidly in that order, in the course of a few months from that fateful day in May when Juhibaby slapped Meehika on Dada's wedding day.

The wedding had gone as planned and the unsuspecting neighbours, friends, relatives and other guests came each evening in full finery. The core family, numb with shock after Kishore Bohitdar's startling exposure of his wife's infidelity, were only too happy to let the show go on, so that the focus of attention was firmly on food, jewellery, car rentals, lighting arrangements, the purchase of return gifts, and not on the antics of the wayward Meehika. The three spinster aunts tried their utmost to ferret out what had transpired inside Juhibaby's bedroom but they were tactfully deflected by Chhayamoni.

'Meehika has low blood pressure, so she needs to rest. She is tired after the long journey.'

This was the excuse they had unaninmously agreed upon for Mee's passing out.

Beenarani, her loving aunt, who only had a vague idea of what had happened because Khokon had whispered to her conspiratorially, 'Just take care of her, and see to it that she does not blab...Kishore is taking the first flight out and I don't want anyone from Cuckoo's family to know about all this', refrained from asking questions. Silently she went about tending to Mee, just as she had done all her life.

Having never married or known men, Beenarani's life revolved around the children of her brother and his wife, Khokon and Meehika. Now, as she looked at the tear-streaked, ravaged face of her beautiful niece, she felt a tear trickle down her own cheek. Just as quickly she remembered that she had to put the final touches to the 'tautto', the series of trays filled with gifts that go from the boy's house to the girl's house, this ritual being a high point of excitement in traditional Bengali weddings. Beenarani remembered Juhibaby's wedding thirty years ago. She had been young then and had made every single arrangement, even personally drawing the floral-patterned alpanas in front of all the doors. Their mother had been alive then. How nice if she were to see her only grandson getting married to the girl of his choice.

Cuckoo Chowdhury, Khokon's choice, was at that precise moment getting hysterical. Her wedding blouse did not fit her. She was standing in the middle of her bedroom in a petticoat, screaming into her bosom which had been squeezed into flat pancakes by the tight-fitting blouse. Her mother, Mrs Mimi Chowdhury, was trying to adjust her daughter's blouse by an act of wilful pushing and pulling which only resulted in a quivering dance of her fat, fleshy upper arms that rolled out from a low-cut sleeveless blouse, and more screaming from her daughter.

'What the hell has the tailor done? I'll have Baba sue him...'

Baba being her father, the softspoken, shrewd lawyer, the venerable Mr Arjun K. Chowdhury BA, LLB.

'Ki hocchay ta ki? Stay calm... Please...you are getting married...stop screaming!'

But Cuckoo was adamant. She wanted another blouse made...this very instant. Now!

In the meanwhile circumstance or fate, call it what you will, had quite another agenda. Mee had passed out after the stinging slap dealt to her by her mother, only to fall into a deep fever which raged relentlessly for two days, reducing her to a quivering, shivering mass of sweaty flesh. As she lay in the darkened corner of her brightly lit parental home, she could hear the sound of festivities. Sometimes the sounds seemed to come from very far, muted, dull. At other times, she barely had strength to squeeze her ear against the pillow, to deaden the deafening sounds of conch shells, tinkling bells and the bursting of fireworks. As the ladies performed the traditional 'eeloo' ritual in a shrill crescendo, wagging their tongues rapidly against their palates in supplication to the female deity for peace and prosperity, Mee knew that her brother had finally brought home his bride. She passed out again.

Cuckoo made her entry into A-181, Pandara Road as the official daughter-in-law. Though in her heart of hearts she knew she was making a mistake, her stubborn streak would not allow her to admit it. Khokon, though dark-skinned, was not bad-looking, having inherited something of his mother's good looks. Cuckoo was short, reef-thin with eminently forgettable features, her only saving grace her father's money. Besides she and Khokon shared a secret: two abortions. Thus, she was determined to charm her husband away to a separate house.

'We will live in Pandara Road for some time, and I will do my good daughter-in-law stuff, and then we will shift to the house in Vasant Vihar which Bapi has bought for us as a wedding gift...' This she had confided to Khokon three days after the wedding. Her father had invested a sizeable chunk of his ill-gotten wealth in this property.

Most days she woke up late, came out of her room in pajamas, hair tousled, sindoor carelessly smearing her forhead, and proceeded to chat loudly with her mother on the telephone placed on the meat-safe that stood in the centre of the dining area. Everyone could hear the conversation between the new bride and her card-playing mother.

As always, Beenarani and Juhibaby took turns to cook elaborate meals for the family. They were both in their mid-fifties now, older, slower but worked as a team in perfect unison. Cuckoo never offered to help them and they never asked for it. Suddenly she found herself elevated to Meehika's position, the place from which her sister-in-law had been unceremoniously ousted on account of her cardinal sin, the affair. Now Cuckoo became the daughter of the house, not the daughter-in-law.

At this point Juhibaby too made a cardinal mistake. When the neighbours and relatives started to drop by to wish the newlyweds or invite them home, Juhibaby would insist that Cuckoo wear jeans and leave her hair loose. With Meehika it had been different. She was her daughter. Juhibaby had to prove a point to Mee's in-laws that she had raised her daughter with traditional values, with sanskaras. With her daughter-in-law it was the reverse. Juhibaby wanted the world to view her as the perfect modern mother-in-law.

Within a couple of months, Juhi started sensing that things were not right. Khokon had started drinking, something new, and the stale smell of cigarettes lingered in their room. She tried not to hear the muted sounds of heated arguments followed by chilling silences. Khokon had stopped spending time with the family and barked out orders for food and drinks, according to his moods. Beenarani and she had chosen to play the role of servants to the whimsy of the newlyweds. Juhibaby's heart went out to her son. 'How thin he has become,' she moaned silently. He came in from work, gaunt, unsmiling, and headed straight for his room, the room vacated by Beenarani who now slept on a couch in the living room. The newlyweds did not eat with the rest of the family and most days expected their food to be served to them in their room.

Khokon declared, 'Cuckoo comes from a wealthy family, you know that, don't you? As it is the poor thing is cooped up in our tiny flat. It will take a while for her to get used to our rickety dining table.'

'And rickety in-laws as well,' Juhibaby's mind had murmured as she hurriedly hobbled towards the kitchen to rustle up a piping hot snack for them.

Juhibaby was still furious with Meehika and had not spoken to her since she had left the house, a week after the wedding. Like a condemned prisoner, head bowed, aggressively ignored by Juhibaby, Dada and Cuckoo, Meehika had got a surreptitious hug from Beenarani and a loving gaze from her father before she had gratefully slunk into the back seat of the cavernous black and yellow taxi which would take her to the airport and back to her empty life in Bombay.

✦

Death came swiftly and without warning. There was no ominous crashing of glass, crows cawing in the doorway, owls staring through the window in broad daylight, pet fish dying mysteriously in the fish tank. The heavens gave no sign, if one could discount the humble ant. An army of ants was spotted on the bathroom floor leading to the drain, thousands of them feeding on the oversweet urine of Juhibaby who lay sprawled on the floor in a world of her own. Juhibaby had been diagnosed with diabetes some time ago, and sugar was strictly off limits. She had managed to hoodwink the normally vigilant Beenarani and had satisfied her intense sugar craving by stuffing her mouth with two large succulent chamchams, that had been sent as an exchange gift by one of the Bengali neighbours. She had suffered another attack of hyperglycaemia, her blood sugar had soared dangerously and then she was immune to the world. She lay there, breathing peacefully through her mouth like an infant.

When Brijeshwar first sighted the army of ants, moving from under his wife's body to the bathroom in deadly disciplined order, he knew the worst. His beautiful wife, his companion of thirty-two years, his soulmate, was going to be taken away from him. His heart squeezed in his chest. She looked almost like she had on the day of their wedding, in this very room, trusting, loving, innocent and totally oblivious to him. He tried gently to wake her. She was in a diabetic coma. He held on to her tight, willing her to respond. She was cold and lifeless. Suddenly he felt a strange and frightening sensation in his chest. It felt as if his heart was being hammered by several nails to his body, and was being tugged and pulled ferociously in different directions. The pain was excruciating, like nothing he had experienced before. He couldn't breathe, he couldn't shout, he tried to raise his voice but he could only hear the hollow sound of saliva in his gullet. He willed himself to breathe but he was getting sucked into a vortex from where he caught a glimpse of his mother's profile, in the prime of her youth as she swam past him.

It was Beenarani who found them a couple of hours later, locked in each other's arms. Her brother was very much dead, rigor mortis had set in, and Juhi was in such a critical state that it looked like she would soon follow her husband. It was left to Rajeshwar to perform the heart-rending ritual of mukh agni, lighting the funeral pyre of his younger brother. Beenarani and Rajeshwar were like ghosts in grief, one petal of their sibling triumvirate gone forever. Juhibaby was in a world of her own and slept deeply through her hospitalization. Nobody dared to tell her about her husband's sudden demise.

It was late that evening when Meehika got a call from Dada informing her of their father's death. He did not insist on her coming and just gave her the news formally as one would to a distant relative. Mee shoved some clothes into a small suitcase and pleaded with the manager at the Air India reservation counter to give her a seat. He recognized her from one of the films she had done and obliged her by giving her a ticket from the VIP quota. So, alone, teary-eyed, her heart aching with grief, she arrived at A-181, Pandara Road. No one greeted her or talked to her. Even Beenarani did not seem like her old loving self and seemed to have withdrawn into a shell of her own. It had happened too suddenly. No one had been prepared. Mee could not bear to face the vacuum left by her adored father. With an aching emptiness, she saw his unmade bed, his characteristic bush shirts hung neatly on the wooden hangers in the cupboard. On an impulse she drew a blue checked shirt to her face and smelt it. Yes, it was there, just as she remembered from childhood, the lingering smell of his Capstan tobacco.

At the hospital, Juhibaby, in her drug-induced state, did not recognize her.

Back in Bombay, her luxury apartment felt like a prison. Kishore Bohitdar had vanished from her radar and Mrs Shetty informed her that his flat had been locked ever since she left.

Her heart hardened against him. Not only was he cheating on her, he had also betrayed her cruelly in front of her family. Try as she might, she could not forgive him and the more she thought about him, the more she hated him. The world around her had become very fragile...dangerously so.

The press had not been kind to her. After all, she was just a five-film wonder with a career span of three years. How dare she come in the way of the happily married Nageshwar Babu and his devoted wife? Though the movie mogul's wife had not called a press conference, as she had threatened to do, she had used all her influence with the media to truss up Mee. The mighty South Indian press conglomerate collaborated together and titles like 'Fall of the Starlet' and 'The Desperate Divorcee' were flashed in all the Telugu, Tamil and Malayalam newspapers and magazines, tainting her image irrevocably. She was now looked upon as a cheap one-night stand, a pusher, a home-breaker without morals. The year was 1991 and for all intents and purposes, Mee's fling with stardom was over.

That was not her only worry. Her bank balance was diminishing at a rapid pace. Mishraji had vanished when the scandal first broke out, taking his account books and whatever he felt was his due with him. Since Mee had left everything in his hands, she had no clue how much she was owed, and from whom, much less the size of her bank balance. She simply encashed a cheque whenever she needed money. It was no surprise then that one day it all finished. Now there was no money and no work.

She tried listlessly to contact a few Bombay film producers but shied away from their tones. She was welcome to meet them in their bungalows and villas tucked away in the far suburbs. After all, she had been the mistress of 'the' Nageshwar Babu. But this was not the route that Mee had envisaged for herself. She had come to Bombay to get out of Delhi. She had followed her husband here hoping to lead a quiet respectable life and do theatre. She certainly did not want to compromise herself in order to get roles so she waited in her luxury apartment, lonely, troubled and haunted by ghosts.

Then she met Rashmi Pandey and her whole world changed. Rashmi was a young star-struck girl from Benaras who had escaped her stepmother's cruelty to try and make her living in the Bombay film industry. A familiar enough story. She had good features, fair skin, large hooded eyes, a well-shaped nose with a prominent cleft at the end, a wide mouth with thin lips, but somehow when put together no one could call her a beauty.

What she lacked in looks, she made up by her conversational skills. Mee was introduced to Rashmi by Happy Singh, a property dealer who ran Happy Rentals in one of the quieter lanes of Versova. She had got chatting with Happy Singh at Roman Store, where she went to buy groceries, and when he heard that she owned a two-bedroom apartment and lived alone, he had suggested that she keep a paying guest and had handed her his card.

With a bank balance big enough to last only a month, Mee was left with little choice but to take up his offer. To her surprise, she hit it off with Rashmi Pandey at their very first meeting. Rashmi walked in with a suitcase, stacked her things neatly in the second bedroom and proceeded to prepare a lavish dinner. Obviously she was a pro because by the time Mee had finished her tea and biscuits, Rashmi was almost ready with supper. She had lentils with finely chopped greens in a pressure cooker on one gas burner and on the other she was rapidly rolling out paper-thin, perfectly round chapattis. Her salad of tomatoes, cucumber, onions and coriander had been chopped and refrigerated. While she worked effortlessly, she spoke effervescently, darting from one end of the spacious, well-equipped kitchen to the other, like a seasoned dancer. Mee watched in relief as the comforting sounds of crockery and cutlery announced her new life: a warm kitchen-centric home.

Before long Rashmi Pandey became Mee's best friend and confidante. She was tender, caring and attentive to the needs of the senior actress. She knew Mee's timings and would be available for all chores, be it making numerous cups of masala chai at odd hours, or rustling up midnight snacks in a jiffy. She sensed her loneliness, her bruised relationship with her mother, and gave her the comfort and warmth she so badly needed.

When they first met, Rashmi was not comfortable conversing in English. 'I studied in a Hindi medium school in Benaras, because my parents wanted us children to get a traditional education,' she told Mee.

So Mee spoke to her in Hindi. When the Hindi newspaper *Amar Ujala*, replaced the regular English *Times of India*, Mee failed to react for she had not shaken off the mental stupor of the past few months, and let it pass. Slowly the tone, colour and texture of her house started to change. She would wake up to the smell of samosas being fried for breakfast. The egg, toast and coffee person that she had been was getting hooked on to eating poories, kachoris, parathas and sugary homemade mithais like malpuas and gujiyas. Each morning and evening Rashmi Pandey would ring her metal bell and light an oil lamp in front of a makeshift altar in the corridor outside her room. The cloying smell of cheap incense would linger all day, sometimes even seeping into the food she had cooked in the kitchen.

Rashmi rarely stepped out and when she did it was only to audition for small parts in movies. Mee never asked her how she paid her rent and nor did Rashmi volunteer the information. The money that Rashmi handed over to her on the fourth of every month, was meticulously counted several times over (tip of the index finger moistened by a flick of the tongue)and then the wad of cash was ceremoniously handed over to Meehika as though she were honouring her with a gift, and not her monthly rent.

Rashmi may not have studied in prestigious institutions like Mee but she could have held her own as a professor of psychology in any college. Adept at understanding human behaviour, she hid her true nature behind a carefully crafted persona. Abandoned by her lover and saddled with a child at sixteen, she had been thrown out of her house by her stepmother. Leaving her newborn baby on the steps of the ghats in Benares one freezing winter morning, she had taken a train to Bombay. After that her story was almost identical to the thousands of young women who flock to the 'maya nagri', the city of dreams. She had slept at the railway station, worked part-time as a maid, impressed the lady of the house and used her connections to get higher up on the social ladder. While she carefully observed the mannerisms and style of the memsahibs she encountered, she hooked up with touts, pimps and brokers, in fact anyone who could get her a quick job and quick money.

Rashmi's strategy with Mee was simple: praise her, cook for her, be available all the time, be alert to her moods and generally make her believe that she, Meehika, was the centre of her universe. Mee's universe was empty: no family, no work, no money, no husband, no lover, no joy, so it was the most natural thing in the world for her to walk blindly into the honey trap that Rashmi had expertly woven around her. Since she had slowly and surely gained admission to Mee's past, as well as her fragile inner core, it was easy for her to keep stoking Mee's fears. If Mee developed cold feet about meeting a film producer, Rashmi would confirm her fears by relating some horror story about the producer. It suited her if Mee remained confined to the house. If Mee got panicky or anxious in a crowded shop, it would be Rashmi who would be around to mop her forehead, offer her water and steer her back to the safety of their home. If Mee got a panic attack in the darkness of a movie theatre, again it was Rashmi who soothed her with reassuring words and quickly arranged for Mee to see movies on video cassettes at home.

As Mee sat on her twelfth floor balcony, staring unblinkingly at the placid ocean in an unconnected limbo, days turned into months. Then one day Rashmi gently informed her that she had hit rock-bottom, that there was no more money in the bank. She had managed to confuse Mee about her finances so completely that she now believed that she owed Rashmi money. This was Rashmi's game plan and she had succeeded in making Mee completely dependent and disoriented.

It was a hot sweltering afternoon. The air conditioner which had not been serviced due to lack of funds, was emitting puffs of hot air. The next EMI was due. With a heavy heart Mee realized that she was indeed bankrupt. She had been forced to sell off her beloved car to meet the last quarterly instalment but now there was nothing left to sell. Then Rashmi suggested that she put the flat on rent and move to a smaller place until her career got back on track. Once again Happy Singh was contacted and he found them a suitable tenant.

✦

MHADA housing colony, off the Four Bungalows intersection, was a grey, ugly set of identical double-storey cottages built around courtyards with open drainage. Thirty such cottages comprised a unit and several such units, interconnected by narrow one-car lanes, stretched for several miles, right under the nose of the noveau riche in the high-rises that bordered and frowned down on this squalid housing society. So tucked away was it from the main road, that Mee, who must have passed it every day on the way to her apartment in Versova, had never known it existed. Until they found themselves with their belongings in Sector 64, Deepmala Housing Society. The courtyard was littered with plastic wrappers, cigarette butts and animal droppings. Outside each small cottage stoodplastic garbage bins, some covered, others open-mouthed, buzzing with flies. Dozens of parked two-wheelers and bicycles leaned against each other in perfect gravity-defying symmetry as children whooshed around on tricycles, chasing each other, round and round the common courtyard.

Cottage Number 22 was long, dark, dingy and tunnel-like. The small, grimy windows did not allow much sunlight or fresh air to enter. The cement floors were an uneven dull grey, the walls a sickening green with mismatched wooden shelves sticking out like jutting teeth on a ravaged face, the bedrooms on the upper floor reached by climbing a rickety narrow iron staircase and the pitiful ceiling made of asbestos and aluminium sheets. Everything was ugly and the exact opposite of the beautiful apartment Mee had been forced to rent out.

Once they moved in, Rashmi took over. Younger, more agile, a survivor, she lost no time in organizing the house according to her own tastes. Quietly she took over the upstairs bedroom which faced the park by quickly placing her suitcase there, leaving Mee with the room overlooking the dirty courtyard teeming with screaming children. Since they did not have much furniture, except for two mirror-work Rajasthani coffee tables, a bookcase, a couple of durries and the mattresses on which they were to sleep, it did not take Rashmi long to set up their new home. By the time Mee had finished meandering around the rooms like a disoriented ghost, the house was swept and clean and their belongings, such as they were, arranged.

By the end of the day the bathroom tiles had been scrupulously scrubbed clean and buckets and mugs were in place. A large blue emergency water drum had been installed as there was limited water supply in the area. A couple of potted plants which Rashmi used to tend to assiduously in the Versova apartment, including a tulsi and a beer bottle containing the ubiquitous moneyplant, had been hung up at the entrance. With their garbage can placed outside the front door, they were now firmly settled in their new home.

But soon cracks began to appear in the asbestos sheet of the roof and with the first onset of the monsoon, the roof partially caved in, creating a mini pool in Mee's bedroom. With the landlord flatly refusing to repair the roof on the pretext that he was charging them a minuscule rent, they had no option but to shift downstairs with their damp mattresses and suitcases, and live bravely in the dripping, leaking house, tiptoeing past buckets and cans kept at strategic places to catch the rainwater pouring in through the ceiling.

It was Mee's worst nightmare. It was important for her to live in a neat space with her things kept in perfect symmetry. She had kept her two earlier homes, even the dismal Ghatkopar flat, as clean as possible, and despite her frequent bouts of depression she never tired of arranging and rearranging the furniture. She would add a painting here, an indoor plant there, straighten a rug with her toe if it were not in alignment; everything had to be visually pleasing and in order. Here Rashmi Pandey had no problem sleeping and eating on the same bed even if it were right next to the perennially stinking toilet. For her, food was the main agenda and somehow she had managed to weave her web of food around the hapless Mee, something that even her mother had been unable to do. She would enthral Mee with stories of her life in Benaras, and the humble potato curry, rasa alu, and tali hui tuvar dal, fried lentil soup, which in her mother's kitchen were considered the most ordinary everyday food items, would gain the status of gourmet cooking. Naïve and helpless, completely in Rashmi's control, Mee was being led like a lamb to the slaughter. And so it was that when she finally met Rashmi's friends, the 'bhayankar auratein', the Deadly Women as they liked to call themselves, she felt as if she had known them all her life.

Rashmi talked endlessly about Fatima and Sunetra, her two closest friends. Such an adept storyteller was she that soon Meehika was almost begging her to invite her friends home.

Fatima, tall, nearly five feet ten inches, obese, weighing a hundred and twenty kilos, was a hairdresser who worked in the film industry by day and made an extra buck at night by serving as companion to rich businessmen. Her broker, a rather respectable term for his job status, arranged the meetings and took his cut. Whatever else she agreed to do, was her own earning. It was an arrangement that suited all parties, including her clients who enjoyed being with this large, hearty woman who drank and cussed like a man, yet was full of feminine wiles. She was born Fatima Sheikh, in Bhendi Bazaar, a heartland of Muslims in Bombay. She had fallen in love and married a Hindu Brahmin from Benaras, a distant cousin of Rashmi Pandey, and though the marriage had not worked out, Rashmi and Fatima had kept in touch. Mee was fascinated by her zest for life and her candid sexuality.

'My burqa is my weapon, my "hatiyar"', she would declare grandly as soon as she was a couple of whiskies down. 'When I want to be pak, pure, I wear it and cover myself completely. All you can see are my eyes. Makes me more mysterious and desirable too.' She laughed her hearty laugh.

'And if not, what then?' Everyone was very curious to know.

'Then I come into my own...apni pe utar aati hoon.' She paused dramatically. 'And when I come into my own,' she leered, narrowing her eyes, 'I play the Hindu card, I become the typical working class woman, I curse, bhenchod... madarchod... and send the poor man running,' and then, with a sly wink, 'but not before I have emptied his pocket.'

Cheers of approval and peals of laughter would follow this declaration.

Then there was Sunetra, Rashmi's childhood friend from Benaras. Short, dusky, softspoken with an air of purity around her, Mee was instantly drawn to her. It took her a while to understand how she fitted into the gang of 'bhayankar auratein'. One late evening, around Diwali, after the rains had gone, leaving the trees and birds in an expansive mood and the courtyard outside awash with a fragrance of autumnal flowers, Mee had wandered upstairs to check out the condition of the ceiling and was startled to see someone huddled in a dark corner. Stifling a scream, she realized it was Sunetra. She was sitting on the floor in front of a steel-rimmed plate on which burnt a small camphor fire. Eyes closed, she was tossing something into the fire and chanting. Their eyes met.

Mee stood transfixed as Sunetra gestured for her to sit down. Like a robot, Mee sat down in front of Sunetra who drew a circle around her with ash collected from the fire. She then proceeded to rub some of it on her forehead and to Mee's utter horror, picked up two large bones and started to hit them together, rhythmically chanting all the while, 'Eeeooo... om...phat!'

This was not the Sunetra she knew, the one who would help in the kitchen, who would count out clothes to the istriwalla, or who would sweep and mop floors. This was a goddess-like figure with flaming eyes and streaming hair, invoking some dark forces. Mee was chilled to the bone. She had seen pujas and traditional invocations to the gods but never anything like this intense chanting and ritual by a fire in the dark. If Mee had seen the human skull that Sunetra had smoothly sneaked back into the cloth bag, then perhaps the story would have changed. Sunetra meanwhile heaved a sigh of relief. She was tired of doing the fire ritual as part of her daily sadhana, and it was only on the insistence of her partner, Chipku or Clinger as was he generally referred to, who was a practising aghori, a tantric practiser of the dark arts, that she continued with it. Frankly, she had never been enthused by the idea of sitting in a handpulled rickshaw in changing weather, snaking through the narrow, filthy lanes of Benaras to reach the far end of the deserted Manikarnika ghat, to swoop down on a corpse, and after downing a couple of neat whiskies, sit astride it and enter the world of deep, dark meditation, what he called shav sadhana.

Though it was Mee who paid the rent and took care of their expenses, it was Rashmi who was the undisupted leader. She managed the house and the accounts. Mee was like a figurehead that everyone bowed to, but the actual power was not with her. She felt dazed and groggy all the time, nothing seemed to register. She had no idea that she was being given ganja or charas by the 'bhayankar auratein' to keep her on a perpetual high so that she would blank out for hours. This allowed the others to do pretty much what they pleased. They would wake up at noon, tired out by the debauchery of the previous night, then eat a hearty oily brunch and doze off in each other's arms. It would be evening by the time they got up and had copious amounts of tea before getting dressed. All day they hung around in cheap floral nighties in an unkempt, disorderly cottage, filling their lives with food and drink.

It was therefore no surprise that Meehika gained eighteen kilos at the end of that year. Since she could not understand why her clothes did not fit her any more, she innocently accepted Rashmi's suggestion of wearing a loose nightie the whole day, which the latter picked up from Manish market. At the back of her mind she knew that sooner or later, Mee's fancy clothes would be hers one day. All she had to do was to wait patiently. Her frantic need to collect beautiful things was her way of assuaging the guilt she felt on having abandoned her little girl. She envied Mee her beauty, her education, her smart English accent, which she noted with satisfaction was very rare now, and her deepest desire was to become her. To be 'like her' was a natural impulse but to 'be her', was a journey into darkness, for to become Mee, Mee the original had to be annihilated and Rashmi Pandey had no scruples about killing the hand that was feeding her. But that could wait. Today she wielded full control over the once successful actress.

Once in a while Mee's thoughts would trail in a diffused, dislocated way towards her family. She was still very angry with Juhibaby. How dare she slap her in public? But it was a cold, detached, indifferent anger which people normally reserve for bitter enemies. As for her family, everyone at A-181, Pandara Road had distanced themselves from her, except Beenarani who was the only one who answered the telephone. From her hurried, hushed conversations she got news of Juhibaby's erratic behaviour, her disturbed sleep patterns and the disorientation caused by her diabetic condition. Dada did not think it necessary to consult a psychiatrist. 'Bipolar conditions cannot be cured. We have to learn to live with it,' he pronounced.

Well, he was certainly not living with it. He was living in his own delusional world of make-believe. His father-in-law, the venerable Arjun K. Chowdhury, BA, LLB, had used his contacts to get him a job in one of the smaller multinational companies waiting to invade the Indian economy. Khokon's job was a far cry from his original interest, research in atomic physics. Currently his job description was to service clients and sell them heavy-duty products which he knew were bogus. The stress was showing on him: three-piece suits to work, car and driver courtesy his father-in-law's bounty at his doorstep, satisfying the demands of his garrulous wife, Cuckoo, and his mother's unexpressed but implicit sorrow.

Whenever Mee tried to contact her brother or his wife, she was cold-shouldered. She had done the unthinkable: she had committed adultery and they were not in a mood to forgive her. But more importantly, Khokon's father-in-law had strategically brought it to his notice that a new legislation was soon going to be passed in Parliament, which would ensure that the girl child too could be a legal inheritor of parental property. So it was in his interest to keep his stupid married sister as far away as possible. Not that their father had left them a fortune. He had put his savings from his meagre government salary into a small plot of land in the fast developing eastern corridor of Delhi, on the other side of the river Jamuna, which Arjun Chowdhury was determined to keep safe for his only offspring and her husband. He had sent his people to snoop around the area and had discovered that an airport was coming up two kilometres away, so if they held on to the plot, they would be in a very favourable position to negotiate a jackpot. So it was important to keep the sister at bay.

Not so Rashmi Pandey. From her vantage position as ringmaster to this motley circus of pathetic players, coinhabitants of Cottage 22, MHADA, she wielded a firm whip. It was she who decided the menu of the day, allotted jobs and responsibilities, fixed meetings and was the front face of all their activities. She was the one who arranged for the bhang and ganja from the drug dealer, Gafoor bhai, tucking it deep inside her blouse, slipping it out as and when required. By now she had total control over Mee's wallet which contained the rent money from the Versova flat, which she personally collected every month in cash. Though she still pandered to Mee and made a show of fawning and fussing over her, deep down she knew the game was over. Mee was in a drugged stupor most of the time. Vaguely she wondered why she hated her so much. Mee had never harmed her; on the contrary she was like a tame kitten, so where was this malevolence coming from? Rashmi Pandey shrugged off the question and got busy with the task of preparing the house for Diwali. This was a festival she had dreaded since childhood. When the neighbourhood was busy spring cleaning, shopping for new clothes, sweets and fireworks, Rashmi's childhood was spent in their tiny one-room hovel in Benaras, cooking and toiling for her stepmother. But now it was payback time. Her stepmother had reconciled with her after the death of her father and was going to come to Bombay to spend a few weeks with them. Rashmi had not asked Mee's permission but had merely informed her in passing that her mother would be coming and that she would be escorted by her son. Needless to say Mee agreed without demur.

Didi, for that was what Rashmi called her stepmother, was a faded beauty who still dressed like a film heroine of the 1970s: low-cut blouses with string-backs, georgette sarees worn several inches below the navel, spilling out layer upon layer of uncontained fat, hair cut in a fringe with side bangs framing her middle-aged jowls, and wrists full of matching glass bangles. With her was Rashmi's half-brother Kuldeepak, a good-looking but brash lout who wore a checked shirt with the collar turned up and tight, crotch-hugging, shiny brand new jeans. The guests made themselves comfortable, stacking their suitcases neatly on newspapers and spreading their sheets and mattresses territorially on the most comfortable space that they could find. Soon Mee found that her mattress had been shifted to the upstairs bedroom, this time on the garden side.

'This will be more comfortable for you,' Rashmi Pandey had said with an apologetic smile.

Mee's heart had melted at the gesture. 'How thoughtful she is, so kind,' she thought vaguely.

A couple of days later, she had woken up in the morning to find herself undressed, her underwear flung indelicately on the floor. Groggily, she managed to dress herself wondering if she had overdone the drinks the night before. Maybe the heat combined with the alcohol had made her strip. After a couple of days the same thing happened. But this time she noticed a man's boxer shorts hanging on the doorknob. It was a deadly red with a bold RUPA written on the waistband. She stared at it, puzzled.

Why would anyone leave their underwear here? Except for

Kuldeepak, there was no male staying in the house. And why would he come up to her bedroom? The questions popped up in her mind only to be diffused by an alcoholic hangover and a splitting headache. Without brushing her teeth, she gobbled some chips that she found on a steel plate on the floor and took a swig of the remnants of last night's vodka, sucking and licking the bottle dry. Fortified, she lurched her way downstairs to wait patiently till Rashmi Pandey was ready to serve her morning tea.

Days were different from nights. Days were ordinary. People came and went. Fatima would drop by, sometimes spending the night. Sunetra had shifted to the upstairs bedroom facing the courtyard and spent most days closeted in her room. Rashmi Pandey would shop, cook, get Kuldeepak to do the occasional dishes by slipping him a twenty-rupee note or a 'paua'... a quart of whisky, slip out to the drug dealer for more ganja, have tea with the cable repair person and generally keep control of Mee's wallet.

The nights, however, were very different. Everyone including Didi, 'dressed up'. Lights were dimmed by covering the naked bulb with coloured cellophane paper, film music, including romantic ghazals by Mehdi Hassan, would be played on the two-in-one recorder that Rashmi Pandey had miraculously procured from somewhere. The two Rajasthani coffee tables would be joined together and with great fanfare, alcohol, snacks, glasses, lighter, cigarettes, ashtrays and on some days even paper napkins would be ceremoniously arranged. Then Mee would forget everything. She was in a land of love.

Rashmi Pandey loved her.

Sunetra loved her.

Fatima loved her.

Didi loved her.

Didi's brother loved her.

This was her family. They lived together and shared the same dreams. So what if Juhibaby, Dada and Cuckoo did not speak to her? So what if her father had died on her without saying goodbye? At least she had a family... It gave her some satisfaction to think that her mother would have an apoplectic fit if she saw her daughter so happy, so joyous with her 'Hindustani' family.

By midnight the party would liven up as more men came in. Sometimes Rashmi would go away upstairs, and then Fatima would heave her weight up the narrow stairs, gallantly supported by some unknown but respectable-looking gentleman. Sometimes Mee had the strange feeling that she was in the midst of several naked bodies, tangled limbs, heavy breathing, sounds of kissing and sucking, in a cacophony of moans. But in the mornings she would wake up alone in her room, with no memories, except a splitting headache which would leave her at least for some time as soon as she had her first swig of alcohol.

And then one day, without warning, Kishore Bohitdar landed up at 22, MHADA. The last time he had seen Mee was at his feet in Pandara Road, where she had fallen after being slapped by her mother. Since Dada had made it very clear to him that he was not in touch with his sister, Kishore Bohitdar had got the address from the ever-cooperative Mrs Shetty who had made several calls, including one to Mr Happy Singh, the estate broker. It was from him that she had got the MHADA address.

Kishore Bohitdar was in a hurry. He had made up his mind to marry his girlfriend, the now ageing Sunanda Sen, and he wanted a divorce. But after he was led up the steep iron staircase into Mee's dark cubicle-like room, and saw her sitting alone on the mattress on the floor, his heart skipped a beat. She had turned incredibly fat, her face resting on three double chins. Her long, once shiny hair was tied in an untidy knot and she was spilling out of a hideous discoloured black and white cotton kaftan. She gazed at him for a long time. He felt awkward under her gaze so without being asked, he just sat down next to her. Moments passed. Downstairs the pressure cooker whistled thrice, a door banged shut, and the TV continued its discordant static. Was this obese woman sitting silently in front of him really the waif-like girl he had once loved to distraction? Something akin to guilt and pity swept over him and he reached out to her. Though she had not forgiven him, something old stirred within her too. They held each other and before long, before either could stop it, they had succumbed to primal instinct.

Something snapped inside Mee that day as her defences slid down. She saw in him the young Kishore Bohitdar, her old friend and well-wisher, the lover who had become a husband.

After a while he spoke in a calm measured tone, 'Thanks for this, but I came here to ask for a divorce. I want to marry Sunanda.'

'So what was "this"?You men are sick bastards...' she spat out, enraged.

'Look, Meehika, don't make this difficult. You know very well that things between us have been over for a long time.'

And then as an afterthought, 'Why don't you find someone for yourself?'

Kishore Bohitdar had fled from her volley of abuses and a shower of shoes, books, bottles.

'I will never forgive you, bastard,' her voice, shrill and

metallic, rang after him as he clumsily bolted down the treacherously swaying staircase.

After he left, she gulped down a quarter bottle of rum, neat, opened a new packet of blades, which she used to shave her legs, found her prominent veins and then proceeded methodically to cut her wrists.

7
Clinger

If in some remote way, Meehika had hoped that her act of self-flagellation would result in an outpouring of sympathy from her housemates, she was in for a surprise. After a week in hospital, when she returned to Cottage 22, MHADA, no one spoke to her. Rashmi Pandey went about her chores with a bruised expression. Didi and her brother were in departure mode as they wandered around the house, picking up remnants of their scattered belongings to toss into their open-jawed suitcases. Fatima breezed in, totally ignored the issue of attempted suicide, ate a shocking amount of piping hot rajma with rice which Rashmi took pains to serve, and prattled about some businessman to whom she had given a hard time. Sunetra spent most of her days closeted with her partner, who had come to take her back to Benaras. Mee had met him briefly on the day she returned from the hospital and had noticed that he was stocky, bearded, intense, had longish matted hair, wore an ochre-coloured choga, and from his neck hung multi-hued necklaces of sphatik, rudraksh and some glittering stone which she could not identify.

'Namaskar,' he had said, his voice soft, a little feminine.

Mee had never set eyes on him before, but felt strangely comfortable with this oddly clad stranger.

Over the days, Mee felt a new sensation of peace enveloping her. Since she had been on heavy antibiotics, she had not had a drink for several days. As the fog of alcohol receded from her brain, she understood with startling clarity that no man was worth the grief of killing oneself. She wanted to forget the terrifying experience of losing consciousness, the helplessness of watching her bright red blood forming rivulets around her feet, her soundless voice, shouting for help. And then the bumpy ambulance ride, the screaming wail of its siren, matching the noises in her head, and the strong smell of corpses and carbolic acid at Cooper hospital. Enjoying her new-found calm, she refused offers of alcohol and most foods, sticking to bread, butter and bananas. Mee observed that though Rashmi Pandey was not speaking to her, yet she did her duty by offering her food at regular intervals. Mee could not help but be touched by her friend's kindness.

On the third night after her return from hospital, she was startled to hear a loud thud very close to her bed. She looked up to see the leering face of Kuldeepak. He was clad in nothing but his underwear, red boxers with RUPA inscribed on the waistband. Mee tensed, wrapping her bed sheet close to herself.

'Kya chahiye?'

Kuldeepak looked her up and down, smiled mysteriously and retreated. 'Sorry, I was looking for my T-shirt,' he said over his shoulder.

'Your T-shirt in my room?' Mee was puzzled.

'Oh, I used to sleep here when you were in hospital, after your suicide attempt.' The last bit carried a hint of mockery.

'Okay, there is nothing here. Please leave.' Mee's tone was sharp.

But before he could move, the sliding door of the room

opposite opened with a sharp whirring sound and in the narrow corridor stood Sunetra. Her loose brownish hair framed her oily face. Under the dim red night-light it looked like a 'fried cutlet straight out of the saucepan' commented Mee's critical mind.

'Get the hell out of here,' Sunetra's soft voice was cold and menacing.

Behind her, from inside the other bedroom, lumbered her partner in a dishevelled choga, the hand which held a half-smoked cigarette trembling a wee bit as he tried to hold her shoulder unsuccessfully.

'Don't touch me, or I will call the police,' Sunetra whispered, her eyes glittering like diamonds in the semi-darkness.

'Please,' begged the man. 'Please.'

She did not say a word, turned back to the room, came out with her suitcase and started to climb down the stairs.

The man briefly glanced at Mee and Kuldeepak in his red underwear and hurried to follow Sunetra. Through her open door, Mee could see Rashmi Pandey standing in front of the main door, blocking it with her spindly arms, holding onto the doorframe on both sides, 'looking like Jesus on the cross', giggled Mee's disoriented mind.

'Let her go. When will you stop clinging to her, you damn chipku?' she demanded contemptuously.

In a wink, Kuldeepak had scurried downstairs and had disappeared into the darkened kitchen. Mee had reached half-way when she stopped short. Rashmi was sounding unusually agitated.

'Why don't you lay off? She is not the one for you.'

'And who are you to interfere in our relationship?' The man's voice was gravelly.

'You come to my house and ask me who I am?' This one from Rashmi.

Instinctively Mee backed up one step. This was not the Rashmi Pandey she knew. Her house? So she thinks it is her house? She, who has stopped paying rent, ever since they moved here. Mee paused, filtering in the news.

'I don't give a fuck whose house this is...Incidentally, don't think I don't know your game plan...feeding and stuffing that poor fat woman with ganja and charas,' the man continued.

Who could he be talking about? Sunetra was as thin as a reed.

'Shut up, you are nothing but a hanger-on, a chipku!' Rashmi's voice was slurring with hate.

'Ha, ha! You saying this, you bitch? At least I don't pretend to be a friend and then drug them. Sunetra has confessed to everything. She is done with your sickness, your orgies. She does not want the bad karma of leeching off that fat woman any more.'

Mee could barely breathe. So she was the fat woman they were talking about. She was petrified that they would turn around and see her. Her heart beat so loudly in her ribcage that on instinct she covered her chest with both hands, willing it to be less noisy.

Then to her horror, in the dim light, she saw a skirmish, a quick shove and push. The man had flung Rashmi aside and gone out, slamming the door. As Rashmi scrambled to her feet, stuttering with rage, to follow him out, Mee turned her heavy body as quickly as she could and hurried up to her room, where she collapsed in a heap. Her heart was beating painfully and she couldn't breathe. Instinctively, she searched for a bottle of vodka but stopped short.

'Oho! So this is what has been happening...my weight gain...alcohol...drugs.' The memory of the boxer-clad

Kuldeepak sent a chill down her spine. Was she being drugged and raped as well? As wave upon wave of realization swept over her, she was drowned by an intense desire to run away. Frantically, she started throwing her things into a suitcase, terrified that Rashmi Pandey would come back and kill her. She was bathed in sweat, her breath came in laboured gasps, she wanted nothing more than to run away to safety, safety from the hand that was drugging her, the friend who had betrayed her so cruelly. Yet she wanted that last drink, that one last ganja or charas or whatever it was that was doled out to her that made her sleep a lot, eat a lot, forget a lot. Where was it? Where had Rashmi Pandey stashed it?

And then she saw him. He was sitting silently on the windowsill, gently paddling his legs, smiling encouragingly at her.

'Bapi, Bapi...' she beamed at him.'When did you come?'

And then a split second later she blinked. There was no one there. This was not her Bapi, her beloved father. Her father was dead. She stood there for a long time, stock-still. As her breathing calmed down she found herself attuned to a different light in the room, something clearer, more luminous.

✦

It was well past midnight when Rashmi Pandey entered the house. She found Mee sitting on the mattress downstairs. Without saying a word she moved towards the kitchen.

'Stop!' Mee felt that her voice did not quite belong to her. It had authority. Even Rashmi was startled for a minute.

'Yes?' she said, sounding more like a boss than a non-paying, paying guest.

'How long will it take for you to pack?' Again Mee could hear her voice from a distance.

'Excuse me...what was that?' Rashmi's tone was incredulous, yet faintly threatening.

'Out! Out! Out of my life!' Mee could not control herself any longer. The memories of the last couple of years came flooding into her mind and she was overcome by rage and self-pity.

'I trusted you and you cheated me...you kept me on drugs and drink...how could you do this to me? What wrong did I do to deserve this?'

Rashmi Pandey did not lose time in assessing the situation. She must save the day. Mee must have overheard her fight with the foolish Clinger and now she must be sucked back into the cycle. She hastened to the kitchen.

Crash! The steel tumbler was pushed out of Rashmi's hand by Clinger who was glowering down at her.

'No, leave her, don't start her off again.' His voice was normal, almost gentle. He picked up the glass, dipped his finger inside, withdrew it and rubbed his thumb against it. He pushed it under Mee's nose: it was lined with a fine white powder.

'Napthapalma, wow, great friendship...drug her back again!'

Without warning, Rashmi Pandey lunged at him, scratching, biting, abusing in ugly Hindi, 'Madarchod...kutta... Why don't you mind your own business? Who has given you permission to come here?'

Total silence.

'Me! I have given him permission because this is my house.' Again Mee observed her voice coming from a distance. One part of her wanted to giggle at her filmy dialogue: 'Yeh mera ghar hai.'

Rashmi Pandey stared at Mee, daring her to continue.

The sheer force of the hostility she projected made Mee shrink with fear.

She is dying. Darkness is enveloping her. She is horribly alone...

Rashmi is saving her...feeding her, loving her.

'You heard what she said.' The spell was broken by Clinger. 'This is her house and she has given me permission to be here. Better leave before she calls the cops.'

For a long time they stood eye-locked, daring the other to move, while Mee stared from one to the other, open-mouthed. With a gambler's instinct, Rashmi Pandey knew when she had met her match. She knew this chipku, this Clinger would follow through on his threat to call the cops. Abruptly, she turned and started throwing her belongings into suitcases which she yanked down from the overhead loft. Next she woke up a puzzled Didi, instructed Kuldeepak to find an autorickshaw, and within forty minutes, the three had left, leaving Cottage 22 resembling an earthquake-hit zone: upturned furniture, empty cartons, rejected footwear, bundles of various sizes and shapes strewn everywhere. Even the kitchen was not spared as Rashmi had thundered through all the shelves and cupboards, pulling out items she considered to be hers. Even in departure, Rashmi Pandey saw to it that she had the power to devastate the fragile Mee.

Clinger put his arms around her. She responded as if she knew this would happen, as if it were the most natural thing in the world. She snuggled into his chest. It smelt faintly of tobacco leaves, beedis and safety: a man's chest. She touched the beads around his neck, the crystal sphatik glowed, inviting attention to its secrets, the rudraksh beads were round, rough and very male. They smelt of the Himalayan jungles. Mee pictured the right hand of Lord Shiva, his wrist looped in rudraksha beads, his clenched palm holding a trident, the holy trishul. Tentatively she touched the hair of his beard. Black, wiry, it twirled feminine-like, near his lips which were partially hidden under a tangled moustache. His nose was retrousse.

'How strange,' Mee thought, feeling a wave of silly giggles looming up. Here is this stranger from Benaras, her friend's partner or lover or whatever their relationship is, holding himself up for her minute inspection, and all she can come up with is Flaubert's description of Minot's nose as 'retrousse'. Try as much as she could, she couldn't remember the name of the novel. Her eyes met his. They were dark pools, almond-shaped and quite beautiful, really. As she gently lowered herself into them, she thought they would have looked lovely on the face of a delicate girl but sat a little awkwardly on this hirsute, dishevelled male.

While she had been looking at him, he too had been inspecting her. He had only seen one of her films in a run-down theatre in Benaras and had not given it much attention. A regular heroine, he had thought, a bit stiff, plastic. Now he gazed at her fat boneless face, her sombre bloodshot eyes and thick unkempt cascade of hair. Her hair suddenly reminded him of his mother and he involuntarily recoiled. An image flashed into his mind of his beautiful Bengali mother with her peaches and cream complexion, they called it 'doodhe altaa rong', having sex with his poker-faced uncle in the storeroom at the back of their house, in a small village on the outskirts of Benaras. That day he had got stomach cramps in school, and had returned home, expecting his mother's reassuring hug as she fussed around spooning him a thick solution of caraway seeds. In later years he considered himself grateful that his mother's naked body had been covered by her hair, but the sight was forever etched in his mind with the message: Women are not to be trusted. His quiet father, closeted in his room, with his spiritual texts, kept his eyes shut to the activities of his hot-blooded exuberant wife, many years his junior.

When he was thirteen, his mother had died in a freak accident. Her death was shrouded in mystery and through hushed whispers, stories of murder, suicide, adultery, blame and counter-blame, floated over an area of a thousand square miles. He had been named Krishna Kant by his father, a Brahmin scholar from Benaras, who was overjoyed that he had fathered a son so late in his life. But Krishna Kant perhaps knew at some subconscious level that his time with his earth mother would be short-lived, so he followed her around annoyingly all the time, thus earning himself the nickname of 'Chipku', Clinger.

After she departed, suddenly and without warning, his life careened off-track. His father, old, pious and aloof, was not exactly equipped to handle an adolescent with raging hormones. Though he earned well as a respectable high school teacher, with property in the village, yet he could not be a mother to his son. By the time Clinger turned eighteen, he had experimented with cigarettes, alcohol, drugs, women and was forever on the lookout for further gratification. And though he managed to gain admission to the famed Benaras Hindu University, opting for a Bachelor's degree in history, he was in reality drawn towards a group of rebel student leaders who had formed a close-door unit, where they read cyclostyled copies of the works of Mao Tse Tung, Fidel Castro and other militant leaders.They were a motley group of novices, joined together by the passion to rebel, and spent a lot of time drinking cups of masala chai, smoking cheap Charminar cigarettes, followed by neat rum at nightfall. During the 1977 Emergency, when the ruling party had come down very strongly on any perceived opposition, Clinger too had been caught and shoved around by the police, even spending a night in jail, only to be bailed out early next morning by his noble father. Thereafter, he had lost interest in rebellion and politics.

Then came a phase when he got attracted to a group of freeloaders like himself, who did amateur theatre, but he soon tired of the frivolity of the members. With the exception of the serene-looking Sunetra. He was attracted to her modesty, her poverty (her father earned a living by burning corpses at Manikarnika ghat), her quiet intensity and, not the least, her suppressed sexuality. But she did not seem overly interested in him and soon they lost touch.

In the meanwhile Clinger met Hariom Baba, who claimed to be a direct disciple of the famous Trailanga Swamy, a kriya yogi, who according to legend, still lived in Benaras though his body was consigned to the flames decades ago. Hariom Baba lived in a spacious four-room house, tucked deep inside the ghats. To reach him, Clinger had to walk through narrow dirty by-lanes full of animal and human droppings, rotting vegetables and fruit peels, and the ever-stubborn hand-cart pullers who careened dangerously through the lanes, maniacally ringing their bells as they manoeuvred themselves away from human beings, lazy stray dogs and an occasional ferocious horned bull, also roaming the lanes in search of food and perhaps salvation. It was said that Hariom Baba liked Clinger's sincerity and perhaps felt sorry for this motherless youth, because he chose to hand over his gaddi, the religious leadership of his sect, to him by giving him his guru mantra, thereby anointing him as his rightful successor.

Clinger loved Hariom Baba with an intense devotion and got back from him the love which he could not get from his taciturn father. And so slowly, almost without being aware of it, he got sucked into the lives of the aghoris: the secret world of the tantric worshippers who were known as 'baampanthis', the left hand of God. Their method of worship was certainly not ordinary, following the path of 'ugra', sharp, 'sheegra', swift, and 'teevra', hard-hitting. In the early days of training in spiritual practice, sadhana, Clinger had to undergo various stages of austerity before he could be purified and declared fit to be inducted as an aghori. It was a lot of fun, actually. He was part of the core group of Baba's followers, six males and only one female, the sister of one of the followers, who was mostly entrusted with the job of cooking. The food, offered as a sacrament to Lord Bhairav and his sister, Bhairavi, always had a feast-like quality about it: goat's meat, curried, after being offered as sacrifice, chicken, eggs, various varieties of fish, and of course, alcohol, tobacco, ganja and charas. These were first offered to the deities before being partaken of as prasad. It was a long haul and they had to undergo an arduous secret training process before they embarked on the final stage of shav sadhana: meditating on the bodies of corpses.

Unlike his guru brothers, Clinger knew no fear. Having grown up virtually alone, without the protective umbrella of parents, he was always the group leader. Satiated with alcohol, drugs and food, meditating on corpses on dark moonless nights next to the gently flowing Ganga, was a practice he enjoyed. It had its benefits. It removed him from fear which happens if one is tied heavily to one's ego. Hariom Baba always taught, 'No ego...no fear.' While meditating he would lose his bodily sensations as he felt himself merging with something dark, something big, something immensely satisfying.

Of course there were other advantages too. Under the able tutelage of his master, it was only a matter of time before Clinger developed his sixth sense. He could clearly read the mind of the person before him and predict the future. At first he had been aghast. Was he hallucinating under the potent mix of meat, alcohol and drugs? But his master had patiently assuaged his fears: an aghori is equipped to enter the subconscious mental field of ordinary people by catching their thought waves pouring from the ether, and thus make accurate predictions. Years later, following the death of his beloved Baba, this vidya, the science that he had mastered, would be the source of his livelihood. Famous politicians, senior bureaucrats and actors would flock to him for advice in matters as diverse as marriage, prosperity or political vendetta. Unlike astrologers, palmists, gemologists, numerologists, tarot card readers, whose job depended a lot on their looking as truthful and divine as possible, the tantric aghori had to look savage while simultaneously instilling deep fear and unquestioning faith in his client. So Clinger roamed the narrow lanes of Benaras in his flowing, ochre-coloured choga, long matted hair and beard, ash smeared on his forehead, multi-hued necklaces jingling on his chest, as he continued to create an ever-growing band of followers.

But when it came to Sunetra, all his spiritual practice, all his power and prowess of understanding the human mind, failed utterly. They had met up again a couple of years after Clinger had left the theatre group. During that time, she had got married to someone who had later deserted her with a small child. Clinger had by then become a name amongst the aghoris of Benaras and so she had been wary at first about resuming contact with him. But this time round, he was more aggressive about his feelings for her, and pursued her undeterred. He told her he loved her and was ready to live with her as her partner, a new concept back then, on the condition that she put her child up for adoption. He was not ready to father some other man's child. Sunetra's conflict between her child and a home and future with him, was what had become an unresolvable issue between them.

After the death of Hariom Baba, the gaddi, or official religious seat came to Clinger, as did the house. He proposed that Sunetra live with him and he would provide her with love and protection, and tutor her to be a tantrik. By now he was earning well. He took cuts from government officials who came to him for favours like stopping their postings or securing a promotion. Clinger would set up meetings with the concerned officials or politicians, and by a combination of self-mastery, mumbo-jumbo, sheer intelligence and street smartness, managed to work out solutions which pleased all parties, especially him, as he happily filled his coffers. This time, however, after a particularly serious misunderstanding, he had followed Sunetra all the way from Benaras to Bombay to coax her to return. But this time things seemed really over. She had made her choice. She did not want him in her life any more.

✦

Clinger glanced at Mee, pressed against his chest, her fingers fondling his necklaces. Their eyes met. They were both wary of relationships and too tired to ask each other any questions, but both were ready to offer their bodies to each other. She closed her eyes.

She was not fat.

She was not used and abused by Kishore Bohitdar.

Nor by Rashmi Pandey and her gang of 'bhayankar auratein'.

She was not a snivelling self-pitying mass under her faded kaftan bought by Rashmi Pandey from the wholesale dealer at Manish market.

This was her body and this was her house. As she gave into Clinger, she faintly heard Juhibaby's voice, 'Whore! Whore!'

'Yes, I am a whore,' her mind whispered back savagely. 'I must get paid for what I am worth. No one will use me or abuse me any more. I give up my need to be weak, a failure, a nervous, dependent wreck. I give up my need to clip my wings, lest I fly higher than them and lose them forever. I agree to lose them if I can find myself.'

She kept her eyes tightly shut. She did not want to see his body or her own. This was not about copulation. This was about her need to be exactly who she was, unfettered by censoring voices all around her. She did not stop to find out what his fight with Sunetra was about.

'I don't need to know anything,' her mind spoke with clarity as her body dissolved dizzily under Clinger's expert lovemaking.

For the first time in a long while she commanded her obese body to go to the kitchen and make a meal, while he cleared up the mess left behind by Rashmi Pandey and her family. Nobody turned up at the cottage, not even Fatima, who had probably received a phone call informing her about the changed scenario. So Clinger and Mee spent entire days eating, sleeping and making love. They occasionally shared a slice of their past: their common interest in theatre, their lack of parental support... small slices, safe slices...but they veered away from the common trauma that had brought them together. Rebound. Both were dealing with rejection from their partners.

His latest fad was painting. Now with only two mouths to feed, Mee bought him several canvases, brushes, paints, turpentine oil, and the whole house began to resemble a children's playschool, a happy space of mismatched form, texture and colour. It was here that they spent peaceful moments shopping for groceries from the small shops lining the lane outside their cottage, ordering food from the thelawala who made amazing ragda pattice, going for an occasional movie at the newly renovated Chandan Theatre, and spending a lot of time in each other's arms.

One evening, she was standing outside the hardware shop in Four Bungalows, waiting for Clinger to pay for some utilities, when she was suddenly seized by such a powerful dizzy spell that she fell onto the bonnet of a car that was parked on the pavement. Clinger suggested that they visit a doctor and that is how she first learnt that she was pregnant. The world around her suddenly started morphing. The hooded lamp on the doctor's table became a one-branch tree. The headgear of the nurse who had conducted the test looked like a long-necked bird about to take flight. Everywhere there were colourful lights which kept flickering on and off. There was a constant buzz, which she thought vaguely came from her chest.

'Oh, the joy! Pregnant? I am pregnant?'

But the smile would not come up to her lips, the buzzing sound in her chest was not allowing the smile to flow to her face. How annoying. She had never been pregnant before. Never.

The enormity of it hit them in the autorickshaw on their way back to the cottage. Clinger was silent, aloof. Natural for somebody's partner to be told that he is fathering her friend's child. Though Mee longed to be hugged and congratulated, she held herself back. She would give him time and space to consider what had happened so naturally between the two of them.

This was the last thing that Clinger wanted. Silently he

cursed himself. He had slipped into a comfort zone with Meehika while they were both nursing their respective wounds but he was in no frame of mind to see her as the mother of his child. In any case, mothers were cheats, they couldn't be trusted. But the dour-faced doctor had told them that the pregnancy was twelve weeks old and abortion was not an option that they should even consider.

Damn her! Why was she so fat and careless? Couldn't she tell by her monthly cycle, or lack of it, that she could be pregnant? A few weeks down the line and a foetus can be scraped out of existence, but twelve weeks, that would amount to homicide.

A few weeks later, Mee gently broached the subject of marriage. He reacted like a mad dog. She retreated into a stony silence. He raged around the cottage, not brave enough to leave. Every month she went alone to the doctor where she was shown the sonography of her unborn child. It was growing in her, day by day, week by week, month by month. Due to her weight and her loose kaftan, her pregnancy by and large remained a well-hidden secret.

Towards her last trimester, when even the single act of walking made her breathless, he turned to her one day. 'Are you willing to shift to Benaras with me?'

Mee was stunned. Such an idea had never crossed her mind. 'We will stay in my father's house in the village, till the baby is born.'

'After that?' Mee's voice was twisted, tentative.

'We'll see.' His response was offhand, irritated.

Next day, when Clinger had gone to buy cigarettes, she phoned A-181, Pandara Road, to give them the news of her 'marriage'. Desperately she lied, saying that she had met a very fine doctor (of course, aghoris cure people) and that they'd had a small marriage in a temple. She did not say a word about her pregnancy.

Beenarani, who had answered the phone, did not sound like her usual self. She seemed detached and indifferent which stung Mee to such an extent that she had to choke back her tears.

'Give the phone to my mother,' she said, implying that Beenarani was not her real mother.

She could hear Juhibaby's voice clearly over the telephone line. After a few minutes, Beenarani came back and whispered, 'Ma is sleeping and the moment she...' Mee disconnected the phone as a huge sob threatened to explode in her chest.

'Okay, we will go the village,' she said on finding Clinger sitting outside on the stoop, smoking a cigarette moodily. Then on an impulse she squeezed herself down beside him, resting her palm on his thigh. She recoiled almost immediately. It reminded her of Juhibaby riding pillion on her father's two-wheeler, her palm resting on his thigh. But Clinger was not her Bapi. Would he be able to love their child in the same way that her father loved her? They both sat silently, each in a private world, staring dully at the little children as they exuberantly rushed around the dirty garbage-ridden courtyard.

✦

6th December 1992. The Babri Masjid in Ayodhya has been attacked. Two communities are at war. There is chaos in Bombay. Satellite TV, which has just made its entry in India, is ablaze in its multi-channel hype, the commentators going berserk with graphic details of the battle between the Hindus and Muslims. It is also the day that Clinger and Meehika are bound on a train taking them up north to Benaras. They only realize the enormity of the mayhem once they reach Bombay Central station. The station is deserted with hardly any passengers. The few red-turbanned coolies loping near the exits are not willing to attend to them and what is ominous is the silent way in which the train is standing, ready and waiting. Mee is due to deliver in a fortnight and because they have given up the rented cottage, they are travelling with a lot of luggage. Mee watches helplessly as Clinger, sweaty, angry, nervous, pushes all the luggage by himself into the quiet train.

Inside the compartment, there is another equally nervous family, clutching on to their children and an enormous amount of luggage. Perhaps they too, like them, are relocating. It is a relief to see several armed police of the Railway Protection Force, sitting at the rear end of the compartment, alert and in control. By the time they cross into the suburbs, the train has been stopped four times. On the advice of the police they pull down the metal shutters of the windows and lock the doors, and in semi-darkness they sit quietly inside, while outside, coming from a distance, they hear the steady sound of banging, shouting, glass splintering, and what seems like hundreds of people running and shouting 'Har har Mahadev', to be immediately echoed by other voices, running and shouting 'Allah ho Akbar'.

✦

Mee had never been to Benaras before. In fact, apart from a sponsored girl guide trip to Kashmir, she had never travelled north of Delhi. Now overwhelmed by the traumatic, sleepless journey, she was nauseated by the noise, colours, crowds and the stinging cold that bit them the moment they stepped off the train. Benaras too had been party to the communal mania of Babri Masjid, and they could see scores of riot police with their helmets and cane shields, manning the station. Before she knew it, they were surrounded by dozens of youth who were swiftly garlanding Clinger, and had also within minutes retrieved all the luggage that they were carrying. Though someone absently garlanded her as well, she was mostly ignored as Clinger strode masterfully forward, an eye-catching figure with his long matted hair, red tilak shining on his forehead, chest hidden under a mountain of marigold garlands, followed by dozens of enthusiastic youth also with long matted hair, some in ochre chogas, others in Levi jeans paired with fluorescent plasticky jackets and pullovers.

By the time Mee had waddled up to the exit gate of the station, panting and heaving, clutching on to her nine-month pregnant belly, the cars were ready, luggage loaded and tied securely to the roof. Clinger, dark glasses in place, was already sitting in the first jeep with several followers. She was allocated the car in the middle, a small Maruti 800, while bringing up the rear were two other cars, stuffed with luggage as well as several more long-haired youth who seemed to be oozing out of the windows 'like toothpaste', giggled Mee's silly mind. The cavalcade moved majestically through the narrow streets of Benaras milling with riot police and general public anxious about news of Ayodhya. A couple of glass-windowed showrooms selling TVs and other electronic items had switched on their largest set, so on every street corner she could see a crowd of tense people gathered together, craning their necks to see the action on the screen. The streets were littered with stones, sticks, bricks, upturned buckets, soda bottles, shards of glass pieces and hordes of people who were mindlessly walking in every direction. Meehika hurriedly rolled up her window as two or three people brought their faces close and leered at her.

'Don't worry, Madamji, they just want to know who is sitting inside the car,' assured the jovial driver of her car. He was not wearing the uniform ochre choga, neither was his hair long, so he was probably not of their sect.

'Aren't you an aghori?' she asked, trying to sound casual.

Honking loudly to distract two cows crossing lazily in front of the car, he jerked his neck towards her, a tinge of pride in his voice. 'No, Madamji. I own this car.' He caressed the steering wheel lovingly. 'These people rent it from me especially when Bade Saab is here.'

So Clinger was Bade Saab.

'So how long have you known him?'

'Oh-ho, Madamji. I know him for so many years. He was a boy then. This small.' He lifted both hands off the steering wheel to show how small. 'Now after Hariom Babaji's demise, he is the leader of the mutth. You know about Hariom Baba?'

Mee nodded vaguely. 'Who else is there in the mutth?' she asked.

'Mataji, his consort...But now...' he lowered his voice, though apart from them there was no one else in the car, 'She is a married woman with a daughter. Bade Saab and she have lots of jhagda-shagda over that.'

Meehika's baby started to kick furiously. An omen or just a reaction to the cramped confines of its mother's position in the small car? She decided not to ask any further questions and quelled the small stab of jealousy that had made an appearance after a long time. At least she had got a sense of the relationship between Clinger and Sunetra. She patted her abdomen soothingly as the car eased its way towards the outskirts of the city, past dazzling emerald green fields on either side of the bumpy road. After about an hour's drive, the cavalcade slowed down as the road got narrower and they entered a dirt track, which wound its way over empty fields, ricketty man made bridges that swayed dangerously as they crossed over slowly, one car at a time. Mee cradled her womb, trying to cushion the impact of the ruthless bumps in the stifling car, far too small for her girth.

After a while, they heard some music coming from a clutch of huts at a distance. People were playing musical instruments and the quiet air amplified the sounds of women singing robustly in chorus.

'Swagat geet...they are welcoming you, Meehika Madamji.'

Mee was startled on two counts: one, the driver knew who she was and two, Clinger had obviously announced her arrival. But the cavalcade drove past the huts in a swirl of dust, as the group of villagers gathered around pleaded with them to stop for refreshments. On a table could be glimpsed several steel tumblers of water and a heap of fresh marigold garlands. After about fifteen minutes, they roared into another cluster of huts, this time a bigger village. They stopped in a kind of central courtyard, where under a large banyan tree, a group of four or five very old men with white beards and frayed turbans sat on charpoys. Close by was a tattered shamiana, flapping in the cold, dusty wind. Under its shade, several dirty, scantily dressed children were running helter-skelter. A film song blared loudly from a horn-shaped speaker tied to a tree. Mee observed flies buzzing around the muddy glass of water she was offered, and though thirsty, refrained. Someone from the group scolded the villager who had offered her the water, and with great alacrity used his teeth to uncork a bottle of a warm fizzy orange drink, which she gratefully accepted. Clinger walked up to the old men to touch their feet in salutation and jabbed his hand near their collective knees. Mee had a sudden flash of memory of Juhibaby's observation of 'Hindustani' pranams of touching knees, so different from the deep, toe-touching pranams of the Bengalis.

Resuming their journey, they zigzagged down a narrow path through a dense jungle. They crossed a stream with a thin trickle of water, and then, turning sharply round a bend, they lurched up a small hill. As they rounded another bend, Mee saw the house. It was an old British colonial house with a slanting brick-tiled roof. The portico, scattered about with old Victorian rosewood chairs and tables, had four majestic pillars with carved lions. A group of men and women holding garlands waited to receive them. A very old man with snow-white hair, wearing a dazzling white kurta pajama, had stepped forward to embrace Clinger who stooped down to touch his feet, while simultaneously accepting the garlands that everyone was drowning him with. He nodded towards the Maruti car.

'Madamji, get down quickly,' there was an urgency in the driver's voice. Mee unstuck herself from the cramped car, pulled her shawl close against the stab of cold air and feeling utterly fat, stupid and ugly, she waddled towards the portico.

'Yeh hai. This is her,' Clinger introduced her. And as an afterthought, 'This is my father.'

She had no idea what to do or say so she bent her neck forward slightly and said, 'Hello.' They all sized her up quickly and averted their eyes. Mee had already started to feel unwelcome, unwanted, a burden.

She was ushered inside. There were several rooms around a large central courtyard, in the middle of which was a shrivelled tulsi tree, drooping morosely from an incongruously freshly painted 'tulsi ghar'. The room allotted to her was large with a high ceiling. An old-fashioned heater glowed in the semi-darkness, filling it with a delicious warmth. There was a large old double bed, a wardrobe and a towel rack. The bathroom was spacious with tiles which must have once seen whiter days, and had an Indian toilet as well as, to Mee's relief, a Western-style commode. A buxom middle-aged lady whom everyone referred to as 'Guddan mausi' was given the charge of looking after Mee. The next time she saw Clinger was late in the night when he looked in to ask if she needed anything. It became clear to her then, that they would not be sharing the same bedroom. Her heart sank.

All of next week she barely saw him. She kept herself occupied with unpacking, sorting her luggage, walking around the large inner courtyard when no one else was around, and eating substantial amounts of the simple but delicious food that was served up from the kitchen, as she waited to give birth. It never occurred to her that the nearest hospital was in Benaras, about seventy miles away, going down the same hazardous route by which they had come. Somehow she felt everything would be all right. The baby would give sufficient notice for them to drive the seventy miles back to Benaras, straight to the hospital, where she would deliver in comfort.

✦

Meehika had torn herself out of her mother's body, under the stairwell of an under-construction portion of Sucheta Kripalani hospital in New Delhi. Her child came out undramatically, almost politely, apologetically, one Friday around midnight when she thought that the sharp pains that she was getting were due to an urgent nature's call. She was in the process of lowering her ungainly body onto the seat of the commode, when she felt something hot, wet and waxy between her legs. And before she could feel the enormity of her pain, her baby slid down in a gush of hot water. When Guddan mausi heard the shriek she rushed in to find Mee sitting on the floor, her back supported by the toilet seat, and between her legs, held together by the placenta, was a wailing red and white newborn baby.

The women talked about it for days.

'Kamaal hai...What, no labour pains? How lucky, I was in labour for sixteen hours.'

'Only sixteen?' said another. 'I was in labour for forty-eight hours.'

'Arre, my daughter-in-law developed such a bad case, that the doctor said to operate immediately otherwise both mother and child would die. You know we had to spend ten thousand rupees, imagine!' said a third.

'I midwifed Krishna Kant and he made such a commotion, how come his daughter is so peaceful?' This came from Guddan mausi, beaming with pride and grandmotherly love.

Mee heard these and sundry other conversations as she lay in bed, too tired to do anything. Though she did feel lighter after the delivery, yet she hated to feel the mounds of flesh that she still could not identify as her own. While Guddan mausi had rushed to bring hot water and scissors to cut the umbilical cord, Mee had held on to her naked baby and then, cold, exhausted and shivering, had assisted in the entire proceedings. After that she did not remember how she had reached her bed.

Next morning, Clinger came to see her with a couple of followers, did not sit down, looked embarrassed at the sight of the infant, smiled wanly at her and departed, entourage in tow. In fact she did not see him much at all during the early months which went in breastfeeding, luxuriant massage sessions for the 'jaccha-baccha', mother and child, nappy washing, nappy drying, daily doses of tonics, tri-monthly doses of injections, rattles, dolls and before long, the baby was lurching around in a walker.

A few days before her daughter turned one, Mee got a surprise call from her childhood friend Pratyusha. They had been in touch on and off, and when Mee was beginning to settle down in the village house , she had given Pratyusha her phone number. The initial congratulations about the baby over, Pratyusha informed her that her family had shifted out of A-181, Pandara Road as Big Uncle had retired from government service, and they were now living in a rented DDA apartment in a new colony on the outskirts of Delhi. She had run into Cuckoo at a social gathering, and she had told her that she and Khokon had moved to Vasant Vihar, where her father had gifted them a house, and that the three old people were really not that old and could surely look after each other.

'I've lived in that stuffy government quarter for far too long, so finally we moved out on our own.'

'What a silly snob she is! Does she think her parents are God's gift to mankind just because they live in a duplex in Panchsheel Park?' Pratyusha was not one to mince words.

No wonder Mee was not able to reach her family to give them the news. They had moved out of her childhood home, they had moved out of A-181, Pandara Road. Not that they had bothered to find out where she was. Unfortunately, Pratyusha did not have the presence of mind to take anyone's phone number, so Mee was virtually cut off from her first family. She wondered how Juhibaby would feel, holding her first grandchild in her arms. About Beenarani, her aunt, she held herself back. She had been hurt by the last telephone conversation and hence angry. Her father, after his magical reassuring appearance in Cottage 22, MHADA, had not shown himself again, though he had left behind his comforting presence.

Here in the village house, her position was not clear. Some referred to her as 'bahurani', daughter-in-law, while others simply called her 'Madamji'. Otherwise life was peaceful, she was looked after, her child was taken good care of, and she had time to read, sleep and detoxify her body from the abuse of her recent past. In summer she had delicious cool 'bael sherbat', crushed from the large fruits that grew in abundance around the house. Also growing in clusters were blackberries, gooseberries, guavas and litchies, which she ate in generous amounts, adding to the glow in her cheeks as well as her patience. 'Fruits calm one down,' she heard Juhibaby's faded whisper. In the chilly winter afternoons, Mee joined the women of the household as they sat around a wood fire in the open courtyard, eating warm freshly roasted peanuts and roasted sweet potatoes dipped in rock salt.

Since she did not have family elders around her, Clinger's mother, a beautiful Bengali woman, being a photograph hanging in his father's sitting area, and her own mother and aunt, out of range, the onus of the name-keeping ceremony, the 'naam karan sanskaar', fell on Guddan mausi, who found out that according to the planetary position of the baby's astrological chart, a name beginning with 'K', would be propitious.

So it came to be that Krishna Kant's daughter was named Krishna. However, unlettered village folk often miss the 'h' sound, and so Krishna became 'Krisna'. The name-keeping ceremony was attended only by the servants and their families, as Clinger's father was away at their other farm in another district, and Clinger himself came with his entourage much after the puja and havan ceremonies were over, and then proceeded to noisily eat dozens of hot poories and spicy potato curry followed by the mandatory sweetmeat, the dazzling, fluorescent boondi laddu.

Guddan mausi was not happy with the name 'Krisna'. 'You

people don't understand,' she had declared to all and sundry. 'Krisna is her father's name. It will bring her bad luck. But since you people are adamant, so I shall be too. A good name with 'K' is Kasoori, so I shall call her by that name.'

Kasoori... Krisna-Kasoori. Little Krisna would chant her name in cute giggly bursts the whole day. It had a lilting sound and every time Guddan mausi called out to her, little Krisna would clap her milky white chubby hands and chant back 'Krisna-Kasoori... Krisna-Kasoori.'

The days passed in a haze as Krisna became the centre of the household. Mee's day would start with her and end only after she had fed her, sung to her and put her to bed.

After putting Krisna to bed, Mee would feel pangs of restlessness. Where was Clinger? His room was in the front portion of the house, next to the portico, so often she would not know whether he was in the house or not. It was only when the servants suddenly got very active, scurrying across the large courtyard from the kitchen end to the outside portion with trays laden with food and drinks, that she guessed Clinger and his entourage were back.

Of late she had started to monitor his activities. He would leave around noon after breakfast, only to return by around nine-thirty at night with large amounts of fresh raw meat. While the servants got busy with cooking the meat, Clinger and his entourage would open bottles of imported whisky and vodka, and party till the early hours of the morning. He never came to meet her, let alone invite her to join him. Mid morning, she read the Hindi newspaper hungrily. It always arrived a day or two late, and she would get it only after Clinger, having read it first, would fold it clumsily and hand it over to a passing servant to give it to her. It was from the servants that she frequently heard the terms 'janana' and 'mardana'. She was a woman, so her portion of life, her room, her area of dominance was inside the portals of the house: janana. He was a male, a mard, so his world was the portion outside, the guard to the fort: mardana. Even to step out of the janana, Mee would have to ask a servant to check if the coast was clear and no unknown male was present.Only then could she wander into the mardana. It was also at times like these that Guddan mausi would run behind Mee with a shawl or dupatta, once even with a tablecloth, to cover her head in case she encountered Clinger's father on the way. Though she had grown up seeing Juhibaby cover her head as a mark of respect in front of Big Uncle, as a young woman she had sworn never to follow these ancient rules of patriarchy. But now as someone or the other covered her head for her, she quietly accepted it as long as she could get closer to Clinger and check what he had been up to. Slowly, she was falling in love with him.

She needed to talk to him, to feel his arms around her, to inhale his heady breath under his tangled beard like she used to in 22, MHADA. Then there was no entourage, no servants, no Krisna-Kasoori, only the two of them. He had opened her eyes and saved her from Rashmi Pandey and the gang of 'bhayankar auratein'. Seconds later she would be overwhelmed with dread. Was he still in love with Sunetra? Where was she? Was he seeing her? Insecurity and jealousy were eating into her. She needed to know. She must find a way to talk to him. This was not her plan. She had agreed to come to Benaras with him but not to be shut up in a janana, closed to the outside world, her only companions being servants and caregivers. Surely there was more to the arrangement than this.

One lonely evening an old memory came back to her as though from the depths of a bottomless well:

'They're gonna put me in the movies
They're gonna make a big star out of me...'

She clenched her teeth in agony. She had started to hate herself: her face, her misshapen body, her oily skin, the gnarled hands, the dry hair. The more she hated herself, the more Clinger edged away from her. If she tried to hug him, he would hold her at arm's length, as one would one's sister. The more detached he became, the more desperate she grew to get his love. Her life was on hold, she had no goals of her own, her one-point mission was Clinger. He was her god, her saviour, the father of her child, how could she let go?

She thought he would love her if she were slim and beautiful...her stomach churned...like Sunetra...Where was Sunetra? Her last image of her was on the landing in 22 MHADA, suitcase in hand. Could it be that she was back in Benaras and back in Clinger's life? It was an excruciating thought.

Then one day, a stray article about post-partum depression, alerted her about her state. No, she must not fall into depression like her mother. She would not give in to weird sleep patterns and weirder behaviour. She had to be alive and well for Krisna-Kasoori, she had to be the perfect mother to her perfect daughter. And so she went on a reckless diet, to look stunning for Clinger. She barely ate, sometimes surviving only on oranges and bananas for days on end. Though by the end of it she did manage to shed a reasonable amount of weight, she also managed to lose a lot of hair, her face became gaunt with sunken cheeks, she developed ghost-like dark circles around her eyes and what was worse, her breath stank, which made Clinger stay away even further.

Before she knew it, Krisna was nearly of school-going age. She would turn three that winter and there were no schools close by. Mee began to get desperate. Her plan to diet and get back to being the glamorous 'heroine' she once was, was going awry and Clinger was not getting any friendlier.

Finally, one day he gave into her pleading that she needed to talk to him about an important matter, and came to her room. He sat stiffly on a chair, his body language—head and shoulders craned towards the door—betraying his need to slink out at the earliest opportunity. Maybe if he could manipulate a fight, then storming out would be easy.

But Mee was determined not to let that happen. She must be patient, hang in there, not let him go. Summoning up her courage, she said, 'Krisna is going to be three soon. She needs to go to school.'

A very pregnant pause gave birth to a rush of anxiety. What did she have in mind, he wondered.

'Would you consider relocating back to Bombay? I still have my apartment there.'

A shorter pause. 'My life is here.'

'What life...life with Sunetra?' Mee could not stop the tremor in her voice.

'My work is here,' he continued, more in control. 'However, we could move to the Benaras house where I can get her admission in Besant Theosophical School. There you could also do the things you like...'

Without a thought, she beamed, 'Yes, sounds perfect.'

He gave her a small tight smile and hurried out of the room.

✦

Benares, 1995. It was a joy to be amidst the noise, colour and vibrancy of the city after three years of a quiet rural life. Mee was charmed by the narrow lanes with shops selling exquisite handwoven Benarasi sarees, musical instruments, sweetmeats of such colour and variety that she wanted to taste each and every one. Every now and then, through low doorways hung with metal bells, the entry to ancient temples, men and women emerged, heads bowed, foreheads smeared with kumkum paste, holding copper plates of fruit, flowers and incense. The air vibrated with the sound of conch shells, temple bells and aartis sung in the praise of the divine. She loved to negotiate her way through the crowded lanes, her senses soaking in the new experience, holding on tight to little Krisna's hand.

The house itself was located deep inside one of the lanes leading to Assi ghat, and though one had to enter it from the crowded lane side, the courtyard opened miraculously in front of the river Ganga. Mee's jaw had dropped the first time she had seen the watery expanse just a few metres away. A broken boundary wall divided them from the river and on the rocky steps leading to it were scores of people, sitting, chatting, eating peanuts and soaking in the balmy air.

Clinger was true to his word, and Krisna was admitted to the Besant Theosophical School without any problem. Mee's heart ached with joy when she saw her little daughter in her neat school uniform, waving cheerfully as she climbed into the cycle rickshaw with Guddan mausi, now her official nanny, who would wait outside the school to escort her back. This left Mee a couple of hours to do, what Clinger had obliquely referred to as, 'the things you like'. Again, she noticed with consternation that once he had settled them in this magnificent house facing the Ganga, he himself seemed to spend a lot of his time back at the village house. He was civil with her, yet distant, as if regretting his decision to father her child. With Krisna he was loving, but in a strange way, tentative, not sure whether it was safe to let himself love her as he should, or keep her at a distance. Mee longed for him to trust her but he locked her out emotionally, his unfailing motto being 'women can't be trusted', and she seemed doomed to a life of isolation. No amount of lengthy massages by the garrulous Guddan mausi could remove the perpetual knot of dread she felt in her stomach.

It was Pratyusha who woke Mee up to herself in one of their lengthy telephone conversations one day by prattling on about her job at the bank and how much fun she was having in her life. At that very instant, the knot inside her unravelled and she decided to take charge of her life. What was it that she liked? After years of living aimlessly with no clear plan in mind, she decided to put pen to paper.

LIKE:
Singing
Dancing
Acting
Writing
DISLIKE:
Cooking
Cleaning
Exercising
Buying provisions
Deciding the daily menu
Serving meals and clearing up
Supervising Krisna's homework
Checking school uniform every day
Doing the laundry account

There were more, she thought, and all of a sudden she started writing. As words poured out, soaking the pages like the long-awaited rains on parched soil, she inwardly started to pray to the Goddess Saraswati and to Lord Ganesha, the remover of obstacles. She remembered how Saraswati had deserted her on the day of her last MA exams on Lytton Road. Hiding inside her books, she had tumbled out of Mee's indifferent hands, out of the rickshaw. Offended, ignored, Saraswati had kept away for so many years; now cajoled, remembered, she quietly slipped back and settled on her fingertips, as Mee surrendered to the words and emotions that flowed out of her pen.

One day, seeing her hunched over a sheet of paper, scribbling away, Clinger suggested that if she liked writing, why didn't she try writing for a magazine. Probably to get her off his back and assuage his own feelings of guilt for neglecting her, he spoke to the editor of *Meri Saheli*, a popular local magazine for women. His introduction was enough to get her an interview and the next day, she arrived at *Meri Saheli's* office, nervously clutching her resume which she had taken pains to put together. She was ushered into the office of a scowling lady, who softened up when she glanced through Mee's CV.

'Hindi? Do you write in Hindi?'

At once Juhibaby showed up, gurgling derisively. 'Now after a posh English education, you want to write in a *Hindustani* magazine?'

Mee gathered together the remnants of her frazzled ego and murmured an affirmative. She had to do something with her life, otherwise she would surely go to pot. Besides, those wretched months with Rashmi Pandey, and three years of having to read a Hindi newspaper in Clinger's village house, had borne some fruit—her Hindi had vastly improved. Still, she hesitated.

It took her a few days to pluck up courage to call the

lady and tell her that, after thinking it over, she was ready to try her hand at it. She bought herself an English to Hindi dictionary from Krishna's school bookstore, and thus armed, started her column 'Dain-Nandini', the diary of a mofussil housewife, a title which the editor loved.

With Saraswati on her side, Mee was unstoppable. Every week she despatched delicious little stories on the life of a mofussil, small-town housewife. She spoke through a character called 'Noton', a pseudonym for herself, as she did not want Clinger to be embarrased by her writing in his hometown. This gave her unlimited freedom to write what she wanted to, portraying in words all the experiences, all the stories of the dozens of women she was meeting in this new juncture of her life.

Noton goes to school to get her daughter admitted. They ask for a hefty donation. Her husband tells her that since she has given birth to a girl child who would be of no use during their old age, she should be kept at home to do housework.

Noton stands in the ration line, waiting for kerosene, as gas agencies are on strike. Here she meets many Notons like her.

Noton has to cook, clean, help her child with homework, wash clothes at four in the morning when the municipality opens its water supply, stitch blouses to earn an extra hundred rupees, while her husband who does an occasional job, prefers to sit in front of the TV.

Noton has to cook for numerous in-laws who arrive without warning and stay till they are edged out by a fresh batch. Noton continues to cook and serve wonderful dishes on a near non-existent budget.

Noton wants a little extra cash because she wants to perform 'uddyapan', the culmination ritual for the Goddess Santoshi Ma. Her husband refuses, feigning excuses, while his mother pointedly shows off a new saree, gifted to her by her son, her insensitive husband.

After a long hiatus, Mee was thrilled to earn a thousand rupees a month, two hundred and fifty rupees per article, per week, paid in cash. This she stored in a bright green biscuit box on which she hadwritten in her neat hand 'Noton's Good Luck Money' with a smiley under it. She had been told by the editor that people loved her articles and the magazine's sales had gone up. Her life was smiling a bit.

Clinger pretended that he knew nothing about her writing and she played along, pretending too. Desperate to please him, she struggled to be the perfect housewife she had never been. If this was the way she could keep her man, so be it. So she woke up at dawn, bathed, donned a saree, did Ganga aarti, and cooked Clinger a hearty breakfast, while Guddan mausi got Krisna ready for school. When Krisna returned from school in the afternoon, Mee was in the thick of her writing schedule. She barely had time to give the eager little girl a quick hug but not before telling her that she was grubby and stinky as well. Once Krisna had come back from school, her knees bruised and bleeding. Guddan mausi had told her that the child had hurt herself while playing kho-kho. Mee had panicked and barked an order, 'No sports for you. You are too much of a delicate darling.' Whereas years ago she had reacted tempestously to her mother calling her voice a broken cymbal, a bhaanga kashore, Krisna merely giggled and jumped into Guddan mausi's lap, flailing her chubby arms upwards, waiting for her uniform to be removed.

For someone who had been paranoid about cooking, Mee had turned dictatorial about food. She insisted that Krisna got all her vegetables, milk and fruit at the right time, in the right order and right amount. Without realizing it, she began spending more and more time in the kitchen, learning and perfecting the dishes that Clinger liked, and less and less time with Krisna. She was taken aback when one day the generally quiet little girl remarked, 'Why are you always in the kitchen?'

Another time Krisna had come home with a card inviting her for a classmate's birthday party. Without looking up from her Noton article, she had murmured, 'Wonderful. Go and show it to Guddan mausi.' She had not noticed Krisna's crestfallen look.

'Will you read to me, Ma? You read English so nicely and I understand so much better,' Krisna had asked her one evening.

'Mmmmm...okay, take out your books,' Mee had answered absently.

'What is this, a new book?' She turned the book around.

'This is my Class Four book.'

'Oh my God, you have gone to Class Four?' Mee blinked stupidly. And then to cover up, rhetorically, 'How time flies, my darling.'

'You don't remember because you had a deadline that day so you had sent Guddan mausi to attend the parent–teacher meeting and afterwards she bought all the books.'

This sent a chill up Mee's spine. Had she been so self-absorbed in the last couple of years that she had sent Krisna's nanny to the PTA meeting?

Her heart melting with guilt and love, she turned to clasp her little girl, but before she could do so, she heard the familiar commotion of loud voices and the blaring of car horns, announcing the arrival of Clinger and his entourage. She pushed Krisna aside and rushed to the kitchen to serve up the various delicacies that she had prepared. She must remember the order in which he liked his food served. The fries, followed by the lentils then the kebabs, then the mutton... Guddan mausi must hurry up with the poories, otherwise the food would turn cold. And the raita must be whipped up fresh, just as he liked it.

Unknown to herself, Mee had become the person she had resolved never to become.

Mee had become Ma.

8
Descent

'Ma, all my teachers were saying that your mother writes so well.' Krisna sailed into the room, a panting Guddan mausi in her wake, clutching on to the heavy schoolbag and a large parasol.

'How fast Kasoori now runs, baba, I am getting too old to keep up with her,' grumbled Guddan mausi, mock angrily.

'Okay, now go and change your uniform while I quickly finish this last paragraph. After all we have to continue to prove to your teachers that your mother writes well.'

Mee winked at her daughter, trying to look attentive while her entire mind was focused on her article. If Krisna observed her mother's abstracted look behind her polite solicitiousness, she made no protest, skipping off obediently while Guddan mausi bustled to the kitchen.

As on most afternoons, Mee ignored the comforting clatter of plates and spoons that announced that Guddan mausi was serving lunch. She did not join them as they settled themselves in front of the TV, eating their paratha-subzi and watching Krisna's favourite cartoon show, Shinchan. Mee did not approve of the silly Chinese cartoon character, who spoke in an annoying sing-song manner but since she had one of her eternal deadlines to meet, she held back her sermon for another day.

Noton's story this week was about her mother-in-law who constantly abused her, accusing her of being in an illicit relationship and therefore, a whore. Noton's friends encouraged her to fight back, like the women in the saas-bahu shows on TV, but this bahu decided that the only way to spite her mother-in-law was to turn into a model housewife. If she became 'bahu number one', her mother-in-law's script of 'You are a whore', would surely have to end.

Mee had recently taken a three-month crash course in computers from a one-room institute down the road, and was now sufficiently proficient to hammer out her articles with one finger, on a large computer with a web of wires that Clinger had got installed for her. But today, Noton was not her usual generous self, serving up words and phrases so that the story almost wrote itself. Today, as Mee sat at her table, doodling, she was stumped.

Was her character really a whore?

Did she have extramarital sex?

Did that make her a whore?

What if her husband was a sly, cheating non-provider?

Was she not entitled to her own happiness?

Was the mother-in-law trying to create a rift?

The Ganga too failed to provide her with any answers that afternoon as she sat staring out of her window. The grating sound of Shinchan's dubbed dialogues all but drowned out the river's quiet murmuring. The early evening sunlight was rippling on the waves as a cool breeze drew out more young people towards the riverfront, eating peanuts, surreptitiously locking hands behind cones of bhelpuri as stray dogs, cows, buffaloes, food vendors, holy men all meandered along in a strange sort of orchestrated dance. With a soft click, that part of her mind which was kept locked and labelled, 'Ma, Dangerous', opened and there stood Juhibaby, larger than life, in a green saree mismatched with an orange blouse, glowering down at her, 'You are nothing but a whore!'

Instinctively Mee rubbed her cheek, the memory of that stinging slap still fresh, as she quickly pushed Juhibaby back into her mental closet.

'I'll show you,' said Mee of the Quiet Voice. 'I'm not a whore. I am a wife, a mother, a housewife par excellence, I don many hats. And do you know, I even cook better than you? So there!'

'I invite you to my home in Benaras,' the Voice continued, and suddenly Mee found the conclusion to the article which had been eluding her all afternoon.

Daughter-in-law would throw an open challenge to her mother-in-law.

Mee would challenge Ma.

In a flash arrived Macbeth's three witches, her spinster aunts, her mother's sisters.She would invite the three sisters to her house and set herself up in a subtle competition with her mother. In order to put Juhibaby down, the envious sisters would sing her praises, then everybody would get to see who was a whore. Excited by her plan, she spoke to Clinger about it.

'Do you mind if I invite my mother and her sisters here for a week or so? Krisna is going to be ten, and she has never met the family...' Her voice trailed away at the bit about 'the family.'

'Sure,' replied Clinger. And again, 'Sure.' And with that he had sped away from the room as though his life depended on it.

'Suniye...suniye,' she had silently pleaded. 'Listen for God's sake! I need you to hold me, I need some love, dammit!'

Inadvertently she was following her mother's script, except from the Bengali 'Shono' it had become the Hindustani 'Suniye'. Ever since she had come to Benaras, she had not called Clinger by his name. Guddan mausi, on whom had fallen the mantle of 'mooh-boIi-saas', surrogate mother-in-law, had made it amply clear, very early on, that calling one's pati-dev by name was not acceptible. Of course 'Suniye', was in no mood to listen and so Mee was left licking her wounds and organizing in her mind the next course of action.

The three sisters were hugely surprised to receive Mee's invitation to visit her in Benaras but accepted with alacrity. They were dying to know how Juhibaby's daughter was faring. How come she had remembered them after so many years? If things were awry which in all likelihood they would be, with some one as wayward as Meehika, it would give them enough gossip to enliven the rest of their barren lives. So they stood in queue at the station to book their tickets, and packed their meticulously starched 'taant' and 'dhakai' sarees in brand new airbags, specially purchased for the trip.

In the meanwhile, Pratyusha had managed to get the phone number of the rented flat where Mee's family had moved, so one afternoon Mee plucked up courage and called. No one answered. After two days, she called again, and this time, Juhibaby picked up the phone. Mee panicked and hung up. Next day, more fortified, she called again, and this time, when she heard her mother's voice, she forgot that day, many years ago, when she had vowed never to call her 'Ma'.

'Ma?'

A pause.

'Hahn...yes.'

Another pause.

A multitude of emotions passed back and forth in that thousand-kilometre, decade-long pause.

'My daughter will be celebrating her tenth birthday on the sixth of next month, and since you have never seen her, I want you to be there.' Mee's words came out in a rush.

A pause.

'Hello, Ma, are you there?'

Another silence, then, 'Hahn...yes.'

'So you all will come, right?'

She heard her mother's shudder and then a small voice, 'Dekhi...let's see...'

'Book your tickets for Benaras immediately. I will come to the railway station to pick you all up...hello...hello, Ma?'

'Hmm...' Ma murmured and the line went dead.

Mee grinned to herself. The first hurdle had been crossed. Now she had to plan meticulously so that she could give her aunts a fabulous time. In return, they would give her golden points which would wipe out her shame and her mother would be humbled forever.

The aunts had not been keen to share the limelight with Juhibaby, so they booked tickets to come early and leave the day after the birthday. Juhibaby, Beenarani and Rajeshwar would come one day before the birthday, and stay on for a week after that. All plans were in place. The cake had been ordered, the invitations to Krisna's friends sent, the birthday dress bought, the day-by-day menu chalked out, two gypsy vans were hired for the whole week and Mee was in a happy mood.

Mee gave her aunts a royal welcome, befitting the guests of honour who would redeem her life. She took Krisna with her to the crowded station to receive them. Mee tutored

Krisna to touch the feet of her grandmothers, Bengali style, away from the eyes of Guddan mausi according to whom, in their culture, virgin girls, kanyas, did not touch the feet of elders before their marriage. Bengali versus Hindustani. Mee would have it her way this time. Happily, Krisna herself wove three garlands for her grandmothers, something she was not tutored to do.

Mee spared no effort to give her aunts the time of their lives. They kickstarted the holiday by visiting the famous Vishwanath and Sankat Mochan temples, window-shopped at Gadholia, crossed the Ganga by boat to reach Ramnagar and witnessed the preparations for the famed Ram Leela festival. She showed them the old quarters of Benaras: Revditala, Bhelupura. Madanpura, areas where the old Muslim weavers sat hunched on their wooden machines, weaving priceless Benarasi sarees. She bought her aunts a saree each with the money from her 'Noton' account. One day she planned a perfect picnic to Sarnath, twenty-five kilometeres away, where the young Prince Siddharth had become Gautam Buddha after attaining self-knowledge. Guddan mausi did not let her down as she cheerfully guided a band of hired women to cook lavish multi-course meals every day.

Mee had booked tickets for a concert where the famous exponent of the rudra-veena, Padamshree awardee Raghvendraji, was to play to an exclusive gathering on the banks of the Ganga. The soul-stirring performance had ended late and Krisna had fallen asleep in Guddan mausi's lap, a fact noticed by her middle aunt. Mee caught her staring pointedly and worried that this may cost her a few minus points, she hurriedly took Krisna in her own lap which, being less cushiony, caused her to yelp in surprise. Mee patted and cooed her back to sleep, the perfect loving mother.

Since they had reached home late, Guddan mausi and Krisna mutually decided to bunk school the next day. But early morning found Krisna alert and happy, playing with a small white-coated owl that had flown into the house.

'Ooh...Lokkhi...lokkhi,' squealed the eldest aunt.

The owl, according to the Hindu pantheon, was the official vehicle of the Goddess Lakshmi, pronounced 'lokkhi' by Bengalis, and as such regarded as an auspicious sign.

'Baajey kautha...Rubbish,' rebuffed the middle aunt. 'To see an owl in the daytime is a bad omen,' she declared emphatically.

The owl, a beautiful bird with sharp, round, yellow-black eyes, was in and out of the house all morning. Towards midday, the phone rang. Mee, being closest to it, picked it up. It was Dada at the other end and it was Dada again who was the harbinger of bad news. Beenarani had died. Again he spoke to his sister and gave her the news as one would to a mere neighbour. He also told her firmly that her presence was not necessary.

It was with a sense of déjà vu that Mee booked a ticket for the evening flight to Delhi, just as she had done when her father had passed away. Her aunts too decided to fly back to Calcutta the same evening. The fun was over. Marks were shared between the three. Juhi's daughter had a decent life and she had, wonder of wonders, turned out to be a good housewife and mother.

Alone on the flight, Mee wept copiously. Beenarani had been like a second mother, someone who always provided succour when Juhibaby rejected her. Yet she never criticized her sister-in-law, but would merely say, 'Your mother needs rest. Let her sleep.' How divine was her nature, and Mee's last words to this childless mother had been, 'Give the phone to "my" mother.'

Guilt and shame swept over her. Now it was too late to say sorry, to tell her how much she loved her. She was gone. And then other concerns filled her mind. With both his younger siblings gone, what would Big Uncle be feeling? And Juhibaby, how would she cope alone, without her best friend, her closest companion, her husband's sister?

Years of struggle had taken a toll on Beenarani, the days of poverty in Shimla when there was uncertainty about the next meal, the stress of waking up at 4 a.m. each morning to cook lunch for the entire family before going off to teach scores of naughty, demanding kindergarten children, returning home late afternoon, laden with groceries, vegetables and fruit. Yet no one heard her complain. Even when she could no longer lift the bags as effortlessly as she had done in the earlier days. She specially hid it from Juhibaby, her brother's beautiful wife, her best friend. By the time she had become noticeably breathless, and had roused an alarmed Juhibaby to call in their family physician, it was too late. There were severe blockages in her arteries, and at her age, surgery was not an option.

She had been feeling ill since the previous night, but looking at Juhi's gaunt face, she had refrained from sharing her pain. In the morning she had casually mentioned that she should see the doctor. While Juhi leapt out of bed in a panic, Beenarani took time to get dressed, located her reading glasses, organized her medical papers neatly in her purse, and only then did she call the taxi. Big Uncle was not at home so the two old ladies left his lunch in a covered plate on the dining table, took the spare set of keys and set off to the doctor.

Beenarani never made it. Five minutes before she reached the hospital, she gazed mutely at Juhibaby, put her head on her shoulder, and died. The frightened Sikh taxi driver offered his plastic bottle of water with which Juhibaby tried desperately to revive her, but the water trickled out through her parched lips. Her heart had stopped beating and it was useless to try and revive it.

Mee didn't see the face of her beloved aunt. Dada had cremated her before she landed in Delhi. Now instead of A-181, Pandara Road, the taxi driver took her through crowded roads in bumper-to-bumper traffic, till they finally reached a middle-income group housing society, very obviously called MIG, in a remote part of east Delhi. Mee's heart sank. They were new to the locality and there was hardly anyone to grieve for her aunt who had always been a popular and well-loved figure on Pandara Road. She found Juhibaby dry-eyed, sitting quietly in a sparsely furnished house. She was in her trademark mismatched ensemble, an off-white saree worn over a deep blue petticoat and a lemon yellow blouse. She had lost a lot of weight and her once beautiful face was gaunt and shrunken. As Mee entered, two neighbours stared at her, trying to recollect where they could have seen her, but out of courtesy they made a quick exit.

Dada and Cuckoo came in an hour later and did not hide their annoyance on seeing Mee sitting with Juhibaby. There was a family crisis, they declared. Having lost both his precious siblings, and perhaps thinking that it would be inappropriate to live alone with his brother's widow, Big Uncle had joined a band of sanyasis as they toured the country with their guru. This was something completely unexpected and it affected Dada the most. If Big Uncle went away, who would stay with Juhibaby? He and Cuckoo had shifted out of the house. Big Uncle could not be persuaded to stay back, he had already withdrawn his savings and himself from the family he had nurtured for over six decades. Mee did not meet him: there was a deadline for some forms that he was filling up at the guruji's ashram.

Juhi did not speak much to Mee and they slept fitfully that night in separate rooms. Mee woke up with a start to realize that it was close to noon. Hurriedly, she brushed her teeth, changed and was heading towards the kitchen to make tea, when she stopped short. Dada and Cuckoo stood on either side of Juhibaby who was seated at the dining table, with heaps of paper in front of her. Mee saw her signing the official-looking documents as Cuckoo kept turning page after page and Dada pointed to the place where she was to sign: a perfect synchronized dance. And Juhibaby, her mother, without even bothering to peer in her shortsighted way at the papers, was signing blindly, page after page.

Mee stood stock-still. What papers were Dada and Cuckoo making her mother sign? Cuckoo saw her first and was not quick enough to hide the expression of guilt on her face. Juhibaby looked up blankly, the hand holding the pen suspended in mid-air. Dada stopped short and expressed his irritation with a cluck.

'Thaamley kano? Why have you stopped? Keep signing,' he commanded.

Juhibaby continued to sign as Cuckoo kept turning the pages.

'What are you signing? '

'Ma has given me the power of attorney to sell Baba's plot of land.' Dada's voice was sharp, not encouraging more questions.

An 'Oh!' escapedMee.

Cuckoo was the first to break the silence that followed. 'Well, your father nominated Ma as his successor. She can do whatever she likes with it. She can give it to whoever she likes.' Under Dada's stare, she trailed off.

'In any case, has it occured to you, dear sister, how our mother will live ? Who will provide for her?' And then, 'You?'

The last word was so contemptous, that Mee stood paralyzed. He had stabbed her in her solar plexus, and she swayed a little as a thousand thoughts tangled in her mind. Why was he always so angry with her? Why was he forever trying to put her down?

'But she has our father's pension money.' A sliver of common sense slipped its way out of her mouth.

'A mere eight thousand rupees a month, do you think it will take care of her rent, food and diabetes medicines?'

Before she could filter the news, Cuckoo spoke up, 'She refuses to stay with us in Vasant Vihar. We can spare a room for her if she likes.'

Mee looked at her mother who had not lifted her eyes from the documents.

'Tai ki...is that so, Ma?'

'Yeah, yeah, go ahead and cross-check. Do you think your Dada and I are lying? Do you think we are the kind of people who want to snatch an old woman's measly property? My father can give us ten times the amount.' This time Cuckoo ignored Dada's stare.

'No, no...let me speak. Enough is enough! What does she mean by landing up here and questioning our intentions?'

' My aunt's body is presumably still warm under the funeral pyre. I came to say goodbye to her.' There was a tremor in Mee's voice.

'Well, say your goodbyes to all of us as well. Don't worry about Ma. I will look after her as I have always done.' Dada's voice rang out, loud and pompous.

'Why...haven't I done anything for her?' Mee's voice was a squeak.

'Sure you have. You ruined my wedding by exposing your affair. You hurt her in front of her family and friends...You took off to whichever city you felt like going... You say you are married and now you have a daughter...'

Before Mee could say anything, Juhibaby spoke up for the first time. Her tone was deathly cold. 'Meehika , I suggest you carry on with your own life as you always have. Don't worry about us, we will manage our own affairs.'

Then turning to Cuckoo, 'Bouma, could you help me with my eye drops please?'

Cuckoo made no attempt to hide her smile, a big victorious smile which spread across her face and stayed that way till she had helped the frail, slightly bent Juhibaby out of the room.

For a long time, brother and sister stood there, waiting for the other to make a move. Then Cuckoo called out to him from the bedroom and throwing her a cold look of disgust, he walked out stiffly. Chilled to the bone, her heart breaking with anguish, Mee went to pack her things. This time there was no ritual of petals from the feet of the deity, 'thakoorer phool', no gifts for the married daughter come home. Her mother had categorically told her to stay away. Another version of the slap. Her heart was wrenched once more and she hated her mother with every pore of her being.

She left without a word of farewell. She spent the journey in a daze, till she felt the plane touch down at Benaras airport. She thought vaguely of picking up something for Krisna, an apologetic birthday cake for her truncated birthday party, but finding a rickshaw driver who would wait as she shopped would be difficult in the rush hour, so she decided to go home.

The main door was closed, latched in the secret way privy only to the family. So Guddan mausi and Krisna were not home. Wearily she came into the main room, mechanically switched on the computer and sat staring into the Ganga. In the inky darkness, the sight of boats moving serenely in the distance like glowing ducks, soothed her nerves. She had cried so much that now she felt dead inside. Her mother had pointedly rejected her over her brother. She was hopelessly helpless in front of her non-love.

She went to her bedroom and as she switched on the light, she saw Sunetra coming out of Clinger's embrace, both scrabbling to cover their nudity. Her shock was so instant and her relief so great, that she almost laughed. At least now she knew...after all the years of guessing and fretting...at last now she knew what perhaps she had always known.

'Okay,' said her mean mind, mimicking Shinchan's sing-song voice, 'All the doors are closing on you. First your mother and now Clinger.'

Mumbling with embarrassment and humiliation, she hastily shut the door behind her and ran to the solid comfort of the neutral computer.

Shortly afterwards, she sensed them slipping out of the house. In a while, Guddan mausi returned with Krisna and another young girl, who looked a little older than Krisna. While Krisna came running to hug her, Guddan mausi stood by the door, uncharacteristically quiet, shuffling her feet. Finally, she edged towards Mee and whispered, 'I have to tell you a secret.'

'I already know.'

Guddan mausi's eyes grew round. 'How?'

'They just left from my bedroom.'

Guddan mausi glanced sideways at the little girl. 'They left without her?'

Now it was Mee's turn to be surprised, 'Who is she?'

'Sunetra's daughter. Bhaiya brought her here to play with Kasoori.'

Through a haze Mee glanced at the little girl as she stared back sombrely, hands clasped in front of her. So finally the jigsaw had fitted in their puzzled lives. Clinger had accepted Sunetra's daughter. They were a unit. Krisna and she were out of the pack.

'What's your name?' Mee managed a fake composure.

'Actually, my real name is Sulakshana but Rashmi mausi changed my school name to Reshma to match with her name, Rashmi, so now I have two two names.'

She spoke in chaste Hindi.

The walls of the room were narrowing down on her, brick by brick, inch by inch.

'Rashmi, who Rashmi?'

'Rashmi Pandey, my mother's best friend.'

Mee could hear her heart banging inside her ribcage. So finally after so many years Rashmi Pandey had caught up with her. She had a clear recollection of Rashmi Pandey's face contorted with hatred and humiliation as she had left 22, MHADA, over a decade ago. But now she had surfaced, to stalk her, to take revenge. She had used the age-old ploy of controlling a naive parent: pretend to love their offspring madly. She had got Clinger to accept her best friend Sunetra on her terms: with her daughter. While simultaneously taking her revenge on Mee for evicting her a decade ago, the motherless woman also got the pleasure of reuniting Clinger with Sunetra and the adoration of Reshma for free. A sob started to build deep inside Mee's chest. What about poor Krisna? What was to become of her? Did she not deserve her father's love?

In panic, she ran towards the kitchen and started to open the windows. 'You need air...You need air,' her frantic mind insisted.

In the dark she tried to find the ghada, the earthen pot

whose natural cool water she always preferred over refrigerated water. She found the pot but could not find the long-handled ladle, so she dipped her bare hands in and splashed her face. By now she was shivering in shock, the image of Clinger and Sunetra's naked bodies on her bed mocked her, teasing her, reviling her. She took a step forward and slipped on the water that she had spilt. She fell to the floor with a loud thud. Normally Guddan mausi would have rushed to her in panic. But now there was an eerie silence. Not even Krisna ran to her rescue. Where could they be?

✦

Sprawled on the floor face down, she meets her ghosts again. They are several dark fractured shadows but she is transfixed by two of them: one has the fat square body of the refrigerator, the other is tall and thin and bears the appearance of the crockery cabinet. The refrigerator speaks like Shinchan, grating and sing-song. The cabinet is nasal, very familiar but she can't place the voice. Now they hover over her, left and right, dark and shade, looming shadows.

'Pack your bags,' says the referigerator.

'Stay and fight for your rights, you coward,' whispers the cabinet.

'It's all over. Face it,' quavers the refrigerator, a steel grey shadow.

'A woman must never quit her marital home,' the cabinet's nasal voice is prim.

The refrigerator roars a deep metal-rumbling laugh, 'She is not married. She is not married to him.'

'Run...run...run!' whispers the refrigerator. 'They are coming for you.'

'Who is coming for me?' Mee hears her own soundless whisper.

'She...they...she is coming!'

This is followed by sounds of rustling and scuttling. Somebody is running towards her.

'No,' she pleads. 'Don't leave me. You saved me from my husband...from the "bhayankar auratein". You can't leave me now... And your daughter, don't you care about your daughter? See, how pretty she is...Please! I beg of you... I touch your feet...'

Mee grovels at his feet, desperately trying to hold on to them as he walks away, dragging her behind him. She is thrashing on the floor, flailing her arms in the air.

✦

Click! The light was switched on. There was nobody else in the room. Guddan mausi and Krisna were standing there, gaping down at her. The other girl was not with them.

Guddan mausi's face was expressionless. 'Get up and start packing. Quickly.' There was an urgency in her voice.

Krisna ran to her mother and held her tight. 'It's okay, Ma. Guddan mausi has told me everything. From now on she has to take care of Reshma, not me, so we must go.' Her voice was sweet and calm.

'Go? Go where?' Mee is bewildered.

'Go back to where you came from. You will be safe there.' Guddan mausi lowered her voice. It had a tinge of sadness.

'Safe? From whom?' Fear is ripping Mee's gut.

'Don't waste time. Let me help you pack. Tomorrow morning we will send you by the aeroplane. Bhaiya has given me money for you.'

So that is where Guddan mausi and Krisna had gone...to drop off the child. Clinger had even paid off Guddan mausi to switch her affections overnight from Krisna to Reshma.

9
Mumbai

In the years that Mee was away in Benaras, Bombay had become Mumbai. The millennium ushered in good news: 'India shining' was the hysterical proclamation and as its commercial capital, Mumbai too began to shine with new bridges and mushrooming metro stations, criss-crossing every highway, squeezing the narrow island city even further. With newer and bigger malls, huge hoardings from which the faces of popular film stars smiled down, Toyotas, Fords, Renaults, moving majestically on wide cemented roads, India had arrived. Everything was suddenly upbeat and sparkling: the poor had colour TVs and banks were generously handing out credit cards to fulfil the consumers' demand for better and newer cars, TVs, houses, fridges, designer clothes and sunglasses.

Mee had left Bombay with Clinger on the historic day that Babri Masjid had fallen, 6 December 1992. She had been nine months pregnant then. She returned to Mumbai with her ten-year-old daughter on an ordinary Thursday morning on 20 December 2002, with two suitcases and a heartful of anguish. Of course, Clinger had provided her enough money as though to compensate for the unusual circumstances in which she had made her exit.

This was Krisna's first experience in an airplane, and she was enjoying every minute of it. Seeing her daughter's rapt, innocent face, Mee momentarily forgot her own anguish and the trauma of the previous night. She had to continue to keep a grip on herself so she behaved like she did when under stress, talking too much and too loudly, much to the silent discomfort of her daughter.

From the airport they took a taxi to Ghatkopar East. It was the only safe haven Mee could think of: the home of Mrs Shetty. It took them a long time to reach, the roads though familiar had been broadened and intersected with half-built bridges and skywalks. Krisna gazed round-eyed at the huge malls dotting the highway. Finally they reached their destination but almost missed it, because three other buildings had come up around it—thin, tall, brand-new buildings with identical tiny windows and box balconies.

When they had left Benaras it was a cold winter morning. Here in Mumbai, the weather was pleasantly warm. So, peeling off their woollens, she ushered Krisna into the familiar cantankerous lift up to the fifth floor. She couldn't wait to meet Mrs Shetty and see her reaction. And then the surprise... introducing her to Krisna.

The front door was open but the flat was empty. Mee's heart sank as they stepped out of the way of workers lugging a large cupboard out of the room. 'Aunty kidhar hai?' she asked one of the workers.

'Buddhi ma beemar hai...soyi hai...,' he gestured towards the bedroom.

Holding Krisna's hand firmly, Mee ran to the bedroom. On a mat on the floor lay a shrunken figure, facing the wall. Next to her on the floor was a plastic bottle of water and a polythene carrybag stuffed with gold- and silver-coloured strips of tablets.

Mee squatted on the floor and hesitantly touched the sleeping figure. 'Aunty?' she whispered.

Moments passed, then the figure slowly turned and squinted at her. 'Kaun, who is this?' She was barely audible.

Mee was stunned to see the transformation. Gone was the plump, active, curious, loving Mrs Shetty. In her place was an old white-haired trembling skeleton.

'It's me, Meehika. Don't you remember me?'

The eyes stared at her for a long time. Faded grey pools within pools. Then there was a slight flicker. 'You came back?'

Mee had to strain to see the lips form the words. 'Yes, Aunty, I came to meet you. Look who I have brought,' she pulled Krisna forward. 'This is my daughter Krisna.'

Mrs Shetty's mouth formed some words which Mee could not decipher. Halfway through, she fell asleep, snoring gently. Mother and daughter waited uneasily as the workers continued to noisily shift out the furniture.

In a while, Chinky, Mrs Shetty's younger daughter, came in, fat and breathless. It took her a few minutes to recognize Mee. The two women hugged each other, moist-eyed.

'Cancer. Doctor has given her three months. She lost the will to live after Appa passed on last year.'

'So where are you moving now?'

'We have sold this flat, now that she cannot live on her own. Now, sometimes she will be with me and sometimes with my sister till...'

'I see.' Mee tried to keep calm. She could not tell Chinky that she had been banking on Mrs Shetty to provide her a roof over her head, till she found her feet.

'Were you planning to stay here?' Chinky must have seen Mee's dazed look, along with the suitcases.

'Yes, actually...I've had a problem with my marriage...my other relationship...' she stopped, embarrassed.

'No problem, Didi. The person who has bought this place is currently abroad. We don't have to hand over possession immediately—we had got an extension due to Amma's health situation. Don't worry, I will inform him. But we don't have anything left here now...'

'That's okay, we will manage.' Mee felt a wave of relief, grateful that they would not have to spend precious money on a hotel.

They spent the night on a dhurrie that Chinky retrieved from Mrs Shetty's possessions. Next morning Mee cautiously peeped into the flat next door, her first marital home, and was welcomed by a large Bihari family with several children of different ages. Mrs Kalawati Jha, from Chhapra district, was a warm-hearted lady who asked her no questions primarily because she was too busy answering her chattering brood.

'Mummy, where have you kept my pencil?'

'Mummy, shall I have a red toffee or a green one?'

'Mummy, where is my charger?'

When Mrs Jha got to know that this very flat had once been Mee's, she very graciously loaned Mee a mattress, a sheet, one set of plates, spoons and glasses, and told her she could use her gas stove for an hour in the morning for the day's cooking, for free.

Aware that she was on the streets, quite literally, Mee had to think quickly. Mr Happy Singh of Happy Rentals popped into her mind. She set off for Versova in search of him. He had moved to a larger, swankier office where she found him looking very successful, very dapper in a Reebok T-shirt and shiny Nike sports shoes. Unfortunately, he did not have happy news for her. Her once luxurious flat on the beach had been lying vacant for a long time because it needed major repairs which Mee, of course, had not been around to attend to.

Now bigger and fancier buildings had come up and people were looking for better deals. She had the option to either sell, renovate or settle for a lower rent. Mee could see Happy Singh's business mind ticking away to gauge which was the best deal for him. Without divulging too many details, she told him that since she was currently short of cash, he should go for a cheap rental and, with the deposit money, find her a small apartment, preferably near a school.

Looking at the ravaged woman sitting across the desk from him, Mr Happy Singh's business-minded heart softened for a moment. He had known her when she was successful and in her prime. Now it was obvious that she was in trouble. He quickly found her a flat in Bangur Nagar in Goregaon West which belonged to a friend of his. When she obliquely mentioned the tragic circumstances in which she had left Benares, without being able to get a school transfer certificate for her daughter, he made a call to another old acquaintance, a trustee in Janki Devi School. So Mee and Krisna moved into a new phase in their lives.

The first floor 1-BHK in Goregaon was mercifully fully furnished. The rooms were large and airy and the kitchen cabinets were a cheerful yellow and green. After she had paid the rent and brokerage, Mee found there was very little left of the money Clinger had sent her through Guddan mausi. Then there was the expense of Krisna's school books, bag and bus. So Mee dispensed with any household help and decided to do all the cooking, washing and cleaning herself. This turned out to be a blessing in disguise because it kept her ghosts at bay. She was desperately lonely and longed for Clinger's presence, however indifferent.

One muggy, pre-monsoon morning, when Mee was moping around, feeling too lazy to bathe or clean the flate, she was surprised by a visit from Mr Happy Singh, accompanied by a pale insignificant person with a bald head and long nose, whom he introduced as the director of a TV show. They had come to ask if she was interested in playing the role of a grandmother. Mee was aghast. She was only in her forties. But the meeting had a good outcome because in the course of conversation she mentioned her 'Noton' articles, which by God's grace she had remembered to pack in that catastrophic exit from Benaras, and thus landed herself a part-time job as the writer's assistant for the TV show. She was introduced to the concept of ghost-writing, where one got paid but did not get a title or credit. It worked well for her. Still struggling with low self-esteem, her out-of-shape body, Juhibaby's rejection, the shock of losing both the men in her life, Kishore Bohitdar and Clinger, and the inability to love her daughter deeply, Mee was happy to reconnect with her last role: the content, busy writer–housewife, the role which had crashed on seeing the naked dance on her bed. On lonely nights she would fantasize that she was in Sunetra's place and then for a brief moment she would feel better. She was happy to write the long, meaningless dialogues which the actors on the show mouthed. Writing paid some bills, and it kept the ghosts from emerging from the shadows and overpowering her.

✦

Six years went by. Six years during which they neither saw nor heard from Clinger. In the beginning, Mee would count each day, each month, that Clinger did not make any attempt to reach her or Krisna. But as the months turned into years, she slowly settled into the routine of writing her scripts, cleaning and cooking, taking care of Krisna. Not so slowly, Krisna grew from a ten-year-old into a teenager. It came as a shock to Mee when Krisna came reeling home one day with stomach cramps and blood-stained underwear. She had turned thirteen that year and they had celebrated by having pani poori from the corner stall. Mee had not told her about the monthly cycle, presuming she would find out the way she had, when she had been her age. Because Juhibaby had not been explicit about the grand moment of a girl's life, Mee fumbled when her part came and was as unprepared as Krisna when it happened. Of course, sharing this milestone with Clinger was out of the question. As though he cared about his daughter, she wept inwardly. It was three years, two months and twenty-one days and he had not once contacted them.

Another three years went by, and Krisna turned sixteen. This time, mother and daughter celebrated with a meal at a not-too-expensive Chinese restaurant nearby. Looking at her across the table, Mee felt a glow of pride. Though Juhibaby had never seen her grand-daughter, Krisna had inherited her genes. She was a beauty.

✦

Kishore Bohitdar too had his ghosts, albeit very different from Mee's. His 'I-am-such-a-terrific-guy' self-image had taken a beating when Mee had thrown him out of 22, MHADA, with the harshest, shrillest exit line that anyone had given him: 'I shall never forgive you, you bastard!'

She had never given him a divorce. She didn't have to. He wouldn't need it.

That day he had run for his life, bounding down the treacherous, heaving staircase, panting, sweating as he jumped into an auto and headed straight to Sunanda Sen's house. By now they had got very brave about their relationship and would meet often at her place. Her good husband, Prakash

Chand, had retired as the Dean of the School of Art, and they now lived in a nice old bungalow on a quiet street, adjacent to Bandra's flower market. She had taken him in her arms, soothed his furrowed forehead and made him a cup of her special coffee. He was aroused by the experience of meeting Mee, their ferocious animal-like copulation, and without the least bit of guilt, he reached out to Sunanda. She acquiesced in her unhurried maternal way. Then she caressed his creased shirt into place and patted him off. The ex-Dean would be coming home soon.

Pampered, happy, satiated, Kishore Bohitdar had no clue what was coming. Sunanda provided him everything: food, drinks, sex, guidance, glamour, friendship, the thrill of secrecy and most importantly, security. They belonged to each other, forever. Nobody could take that away. Or so he believed.

But the silly young art student from France, who had come to tutor under Prakash Chand and was their house guest for a few weeks, succeeded in doing just that. In less than a fortnight, he had seduced Sunanda and convinced her to return to Paris with him. It was scandalous. He was even younger than Kishore and far more good-looking. Perhaps a better performer in bed as well. Kishore Bohitdar refused to believe it even as it was staring him in the face. Soon he found himself in the intensely awkward and humiliating position of being pitted alongside the Dean as Sunanda and Patrick, for that was the white devil's name, frolicked right under their noses. Of course, Sunanda denied it. But then she had denied her relationship with him as well. So he joined the Dean and entered the rank of Cuckold Number Two.

After Sunanda disappeared to Paris with the Frenchman, Kishore Bohitdar drifted aimlessly for a long time, stunned and lost. His mother had died a few years ago, perhaps from heartache, ever imagining the pride of her eyes fornicating with someone her own age. His father, old and stubborn, was too parochial to leave his homeland, Orissa. By now, Kishore himself, by some quirk of fate, had become the Dean of the very institute where he had studied. But unlike the prim and proper husband of his erstwhile lover, he wore his hair long, matching his salt and pepper goatee, and was always seen with his students smoking cigarettes, drinking vodka and rolling joints. Most evenings would find the more favoured students sitting on the carpet in a circle in the Dean's large drawing room, discussing art, eating and drinking.

One day, quite by chance, as he was entering the house of one of his ex-students who was now teaching animation painting at the school, a woman with a young girl brushed past him and he could swear she looked like Meehika though older and slimmer. The art teacher verified that it was Krisna and her mother. The name meant nothing to him. Yet some instinct drove him to find out her address, and a few afternoons later, he rang the doorbell of the Bangur Nagar flat.

Meehika, just out of her bath, head wrapped in a towel, was expecting the computer repair engineer, so unlocking the door, she rushed to the kitchen where the pressure cooker was letting out one hysterical whistle after another. When she found that the engineer had not gone to Krisna's room as he normally did, she impatiently ducked her head into the hall and froze. Standing calmly in the centre of the hall was Kishore Bohitdar. A hundred thoughts jostled simultaneously in her mind. She was disturbed by his greying hair and beard, irritated by his tiny paunch that stood out under his purple silk kurta worn over well-fitting jeans but what completely unnerved her was the authoritative manner in which he was standing in the middle of her daily life, without so much as a 'May I?'

He was the first to speak. 'Sorry, I was not sure if this was your flat, so I am not carrying anything.'

'Oh! No need...please have a seat,' she stammered.

'Nice place,' he remarked.

'Thanks.'

Just then Krisna burst into the room, a dishevelled, radiant teenager, struggling to remove her heavy backpack bursting with books.

'Ma, has the computer uncle come?' She stopped short on seeing Kishore Bohitdar.

Mee was at a loss. How should she introduce him? 'Krisna, meet my deserting, cheating ex-husband?' She had not spoken much about her past to Krisna and the girl knew nothing about Kishore. So she merely said, 'Er...this is Kishore Uncle.'

A shy 'hello' from Krisna.

'What's your name?'

'Krishna Kishori.'

Krisna's English-speaking teachers and classmates had laughed out loud at the rustic 'Krisna Kasoori'—so she had quickly learned to pronounce the 'h' in her name.

'Lovely name. Who has given you this name?'

Krisna looked questioningly at Mee but her mother remained silent. Finally she said, 'My Guddan mausi.'

Krisna was still standing awkwardly, clutching her bag, glancing down at Kishore Bohitdar while he gazed up at her when suddenly Mee saw it. It hit her so hard that for a second she thought she would hit the floor. She flopped down on the chair closest to her.

Why hadn't it crossed her mind? Why hadn't she seen it? Was she blind?

Krisna had her father's eyes. Kishore Bohitdar's eyes. Identical. All the while she had thought that her daughter's eyes were like Clinger's mother, the photograph on the wall. But now there was no denying it. Her gaze rushed to Kishore's feet in his open sandals, and there she clearly saw an older, male version of Krisna's feet, the second toe tilting towards the big toe, exactly like hers. Mee's world was whirring, she could barely breathe.

'Can I go, Ma?' Krisna asked shyly. Mee managed a nod.

He watched her go. 'So you called her Kishori...as a memory of our relationship, may I dare to hope?'

Again Mee's head started to reel, harder than before. Had she lost her mind?'

In the desperate years of trying to please Clinger the thought never crossed her mind that the child could be anybody's but his. But the Fates knew who the father was, and manifested it through Guddan mausi's name-keeping ceremony. 'Kasoori' was the rustic version of 'Kishori', the feminine counterpart of Kishore.

'I don't envy you anything, Meehika, I envy you your Kishori...And I envy her father...whoever he is...' And with that he had pulled out his visiting card, placed it on the table and walked out, shutting the door behind him.

Mee could hear the muted voices of Krisna and the computer engineer, then the sound of tap water and the flushing of the toilet. Soon, Krishna would have changed out of her school uniform, ready for lunch, expecting Mee to fuss around her while she chattered about her day in school. But Mee couldn't move. She held onto the arms of the chair with a vice-like grip. Was this a page out of a novel or a movie, or was this her life?

She had a vague recollection of the day when Kishore Bohitdar had come to 22, MHADA, to ask for a divorce. They had mated and all at once she remembered the savagery, the anger and the hatred that had overpowered her. But out of that, a rose had been born. How incredibly powerful a woman is, thought Mee. She was the only one who knew the truth. But her power to discern, to intuit, had been robbed by Rashmi Pandey's 'drug her and keep her in control' game. Suddenly the latent seeds of suppressed rage against Kishore Bohitdar started to throb. And all at once she felt vindicated by this knowledge, her secret. She would never share it with a soul. She would die with this secret locked in her bosom. She would not delete it from her mind but place it alongside Juhibaby in the compartment marked 'dangerous'. So she clicked the button in her mind: Off... Kishore Bohitdar and Krisna-Kasoori would have to go on their separate journeys.

Krisna was at her computer, fiddling with the wires. She claimed that it always broke down whenever she had a project. It was a third-hand piece, donated to them by Shuklaji, the director of the TV show for which Mee wrote. When Krisna was at school, Mee would sit down to do her one-finger typing. Now, seeing her daughter frowning at the aged machine, she felt a pang of guilt. She would work overtime to raise money to buy her a brand new computer, she vowed. She looked closer. The shape of Krisna's head was like her own but the long sensitive fingers tapping the keyboard, were Kishore Bohitdar's. As she stared at her daughter through a chink in the curtain, she was overcome by the sequence of events. She had been on drugs then. What if her child had come from an unknown source? The red underwear marked RUPA, flashed before her eyes. It could have been Kuldeepak. She shuddered involuntarily. The room began to grow hazy, and she fell forward, grabbing the curtain for support. It came crashing down with her, the metal rod missing her head by inches. In a trice, Krisna was at her side, her face frozen in horror.

'Ma...Ma...are you okay?'

Mee could see her daughter's face but she was numb and dizzy. She tried to speak but only succeeded in releasing a mouthful of saliva. Krisna was saying something to her, and much as she tried to hear, there was a loud banging sound coming from the ceiling which was threatening to break her head into pieces. Again she tried to speak. This time she could feel her head tilting off to a very faraway place. Krisna's eyes were round with terror, her lips moving up and down. She must remind Krisna to brush her teeth after dinner.

After a while there was no one in the room. She tried to get up but everything was blurred. She tried to blink and the moment she did that, her vision split into two. There were two sofas on which two Kishore Bohitdars had sat that afternoon, there were two of everything. She peered long and hard, her neck stiff and outstretched, far away from her head which was staring up at the ceiling from where the hammering was coming.

Bapi was strolling around peacefully. He was wearing his favourite old brown overcoat. Was it winter already? Mee was confused.

'Get up, Meethurani,' Bapi said.

'I can't Bapi, parchhi na...they have stuck glue on the floor.'

He smiled, his warm smile lighting up his eyes. 'Come, come with me.'

She was pulled up gracefully and carried down the stairs as she felt a wondrous peace and lightness enveloping her. Suddenly the radiance was too much to bear. There was a bright orb on her face. Like the sun, up close. It was blinding her. Behind the light stood a couple of shadows, looking mutely at her. They opened her eyes wide, tapped her hands, knocked her head, pressed her chest, pumped her stomach, tugged at her legs, pulled out her tongue, tweaked her ears. Then they jabbed something sharp and cold in her arm and she went floating back to a place of peace.

✦

'Ma...Ma,' Krisna's voice was anxious.

Mee opened her eyes and was startled by the unfamiliar surroundings. Hospital? Was this a hospital? She tried to speak but a young South Indian nurse with flowers in her hair, put her finger on her lips and hushed her down. 'Lay-ter, lay-ter, rest now,' she spoke with a soft Telugu accent.

Krisna was standing near her, holding her hand from which protruded a needle and a long tube which went all the way up to an inverted bottle that hung over her head. From it at regular intervals dripped something the colour of pale urine.

'What happened?' Krisna could see the question in her mother's dilated panic-stricken eyes. She bent close and whispered, 'You have had a little problem...with your heart. Don't worry now and rest. I am here. Don't worry.'

Mee closed her eyes as everything faded away. She must find her heart and wish it a speedy recovery. But it is so white and so cold. Maybe it is snowing. That is why Bapi was wearing his greatcoat. But where is her heart and why is it bruised? Who hurt her heart? If she tries hard enough she will find it for sure. But for now, she should sleep. It was going to be a long haul. She would not be able to find her heart easily.

Listening to her mother's incoherent mumblings, Krisna felt more alone and afraid than ever. Apart from Mee, there was no one she could call her own. Even Guddan mausi had gone away to Reshma. When Mee had collapsed, the first thing she had done was to run to the next door neighbour's house to call up Happy Singh uncle. When he had not answered the phone, she had run back home in a panic. Entering the hall, her eye fell on Kishore Bohitdar's card which he had left on the table. She ran back next door and tried his number, but he too had not answered. Overwhelmed by his meeting with Meehika and her daughter, Kishore Bohitdar had returned home and consumed a heady mix of dope and alcohol and was noisily snoring on the couch.

Krisna knew Clinger's phone number by heart. She hesitated briefly before calling. It was answered after the first ring.

'Hello, kaun? Who is this?'

'Reshma Didi, it is me Krisna.'

'Kaisi ho? All well?'

'No, Ma is in hospital. Can you give the phone to Papa?'

'Papa has gone shopping with Mama. He has left his mobile at home by mistake. I will ask him to call you as soon as he gets back.'

'Thank you, Didi. Please save this number. Okay, bye, I have to run back to the hospital.'

By this time, the neighbouring aunty had called the nearest hospital and her sons carried Mee down the stairs and into the ambulance.

Lying on the hospital bed, Mee looked serene, there was no sign of pain on her face. But Krisna was worried. How would she be able to manage school and taking care of her mother? And how would they pay the bills? She thought of calling her three grandmothers in Calcutta but realized she didn't have their number. Just then the chief doctor and his assistants came in, followed by Happy Singh, Shukla Uncle and two other people she had not met before. The doctor examined Mee and wrote down a long list of medicines on his notepad. Krisna was vastly relieved when Happy Singh Uncle, without even glancing at her, pulled out a huge wad of notes and told one of his companions to run down to the hospital chemist shop for them.

'Silent ischemia,' the doctor was saying, 'it comes suddenly and without warning, mainly due to accumulated stress. Let her stay here for a few days and then we will take a call.'

Fortunately the hospital was walking distance from the flat and when Krisna reached home the next morning, the next door aunty told her that there had been several calls for her from one Kishore Bohitdar and a Krishna Kant from Benaras.

'My father,' said Krisna softly.

When Krisna had called, Clinger was out shopping with Sunetra in Benares. He was by and large happy, except when he had to buy things for Reshma. That was when he would have stirrings of guilt about the way he had treated Mee and his daughter. It was puzzling and uncomfortable: both girls had the same skin tone and hair and could easily be mistaken for blood sisters. Sunetra always pretended to look away while Clinger surreptitiously bought a few small things for Krisna as well, with the hope that he would meet her one day. But whenever any paternal feelings towards her arose, he would quell them. He had found Sunetra after a long time and he was not willing to let her go away again, and so he tried to please her in every way, especially by pampering her daughter. With Sunetra, he suffered from supreme insecurity and fear that like his own mother, he would see her having sex with somebody or in a tragic repeat of karma, she too would die on him, thus reinforcing his internal litany, 'women can't be trusted'. Whereas with Mee he had been relaxed. He had never really been in love with her so apart from the child they shared, they had nothing in common. Sunetra was his love, his life, yet he found himself always running away, from whom and why? The damning question was, why did Mee keep swimming up on the surface of his consciousness? He was forever grappling with the dilemma that whenever he was with Sunetra, he thought of Mee and vice versa. He felt doomed.

He had thus been in a pensive mood when they returned to the village house, laden with the bags of shopping that they had done in Benaras, when Reshma told him about Krisna's call. Sunetra could not help but notice the panic-stricken way he kept calling up the number she had left, but he couldn't get through.

'Damn, I should have bought her a mobile at least!'

'Perhaps you should go to Mumbai and see how she is doing.' This came from Sunetra.

Clinger gave her a long probing look. She gazed back steadily.

'I mean it. After all, she is the mother of your child.'

After several calls, he had finally connected with Krisna.

'I will be coming soon...beta...' He was stunned by the choked emotions that he felt, which he covered up by loud throat-clearing.

'Thank you, Papa,' she had replied softly.

When Clinger arrived at the hospital, Mee could not recognize him. She was heavily sedated as the doctors feared that she may go into another seizure. Clinger stood awkwardly at the foot of the bed, and made a quiet exit as soon as Happy Singh, Shuklaji and others came bustling in. But he took Krisna to a nearby store to get her a mobile, a brand new one with all the accessories a young girl could ask for. He wanted to stay in touch with his daughter, he was sure of that now.

On his next visit, he was accompanied by Reshma, and the two girls were happy to see each other again. While

Clinger stayed in a hotel in Andheri, Krisna insisted on Reshma staying with her, so after a few days he returned to Benaras alone, leaving the two girls to take care of Mee who had been discharged from hospital. After the hectic hospital stint it was peaceful to be at home, as they cooked her oil-free meals together and monitored her medication meticulously.

Whether they were watching or not, the TV would be on the whole day. One or the other girl would finish her chores, stop by, flick the channel, stare at it for a moment and then move onto a video game that Reshma had brought from Benaras or toy with some application on her mobile. They also took turns on the ancient computer. Soon, Clinger would be coming to take Reshma back to Benaras, something neither girl was looking forward to.

One evening they were both lying on their stomachs in the hall, earphones on, heads propped up on their elbows, with a large bowl of McDonald's French fries sitting companionably between them. They were watching Pogo TV, munching their fries, checking messages on their mobiles, all effortlessly at the same time, and Reshma was also intermittently helping Krisna with her delayed school project.

'I'll be going soon,' said Reshma, her mouth full of fries.

'Don't go, na, Didi, we'll tell Papa to come after ten days.'

'I feel weird to call him Papa. He's not really my Papa, you know.'

'Why do you say that, after so many years?'

'Because my mother is not married to him. She really gets upset about it and then they fight.'

'So what, even my mother is not married to him, but he is still my Papa.'

'So much fun if they got married, na? They really love one another.'

'Yeah,' Krisna's voice was reflective.

It was only when they saw Mee tottering close to them that they yelped in unison and helped her to a chair. She was stunned by the uncomplicated, non-judgemental love between the two girls. Whose marriage were they talking about? Sunetra's or hers? At once she was filled with a wild yearning for Clinger. No... No... She would not let go. Clinger was her god, her rescuer.

The stress of getting up from her bed and walking to the hall had been too much. She felt dizzy and the same familiar numbness started pressing against her, rendering her immobile. Again everything started doubling, then bifurcating. The seat of the chair on which she was sitting started to spiral downwards and as she struggled to get up, her knees folded over her chest. She couldn't breathe. The girls were not in the room. They had deserted her. In terror she called out for help but the sound that emerged started bifurcating, dividing into first two, then four, then sixteen, till all she could see were wisps of sound hanging cobweb-like in the shimmering air.

✦

With superhuman effort Mee pushes herself out of the chair and to her horror she sees herself divided into two. One part of her, what she thought was her, the whole of her, leaps out of herself and stands facing the Her stuck helplessly on the chair.

'Who are you?' asks the terrified Mee of the chair.

The figure in front moves close to the wall and in a moment begins to rapidly change its shape and form: electron, proton, neutron, shiny dazzling stars, snowflakes, dewdrops, dizzily moving cylinders, spheres, orbs, all whirling at tremendous speed till it coalesces into a dark black form. It is Mee herself looking at herself.

'I will tell you who I am,' says She of the sixteen voices and in a fraction of a second wraps itself around the chair. 'I am you...I live in you...I feed off you...You and I are one... I am Noton...Don't throw me out.'

With supreme effort, Mee of the chair pushes her off, and She revolves and rotates with the speed of light and turns into a blazing ball of fire.

'My daughters... My daughters,' screams Mee of the chair.

But She of the fireball, dazzling, seductive, scorching, circles around Mee of the chair, enters her and slowly burns her bit by bit, inch by inch.

Then somewhere from inside Mee of the trapped chair, something snaps. Some clear thought like a vibration or frequency emerges like a tremendous white torrent and stares back at the blazing inferno, which suddenly and without warning crashes on the floor with the sound of glass being shattered. Mee watches in horrified fascination as Noton dissolves into a greyish smoke. Suddenly she feels light, free and slightly hungry. Something long, painful, snake-like and life-sucking had wrapped itself around her for years and now that invisible entity, her men-in-black who freely roamed her gut, had uncoiled and burnt itself out.

✦

Mee could feel each sense, each cell in her body come alive. She could hear voices, someone whistling and the room was filled with a wonderful aroma. Two soft hands were holding her upright. She was sitting on a mat on the floor in front of the softly droning TV and Reshma was precariously holding a bowl of piping hot Maggi noodles in front of her. Krisna was in the kitchen pouring tea into three cups. Noton was nowhere in sight but the stench of burning was strong.

'Burning...burning...she was trying to burn me.' Mee's voice was barely audible.

'Who was trying to burn you?' Krisna came in with the tea tray which she set down on the floor beside her mother.

'Noton.'

'Who is Noton?' The girls exchanged a quizzical glance.

'Don't you smell something burning?' whispered Mee.

Krisna sniffed. 'No, Ma, there is no smell of burning.'

'Aunty, they are showing *Terminator* on HBO. You must be dreaming about the fire and smoke.' Reshma flicked the remote and switched off the TV. At once a calm replaced the noisy static. Mee tried to get up. There was something in her mind, something of vital importance which she needed to discuss with the girls. Later. Perhaps after half an hour, after a small nap.

She dozed fitfully and when she awoke, the girls were not in the room. She could hear their voices in Krisna's room, they were busy chatting. Good time to make her two phone calls. She eased herself up from the mat and with slow steps reached the table where Reshma's phone lay. She dialled a number.

'Haan, beta?' Sunetra's voice was bright.

'This is not your beta. This is Meehika. You have taken my daughter away from her father. I will take your daughter away from you. If you want her back you have to come and fetch her. Immediately. Both of you.' She disconnected and switched off the phone so that Sunetra wound not be able to call. Next she needed to call Kishore Bohitdar. But not now. Perhaps after half an hour. After another nap.

✦

It is late evening. Mee is feeling so much better after a warm bath. Krisna has helped her drape a saree. It has been so long since she had worn one. This one had been an all-time favourite which she had picked up years ago from Vama, a high-end store in South

Bombay, when she was a successful actress with a loaded wallet. The saree is a delicate silk weave with an unusual muted grey-black border set against a mango-coloured background. From somewhere Reshma had got a wreath of exquisitely perfumed mogra flowers and had pinned it to her bun.

In the next room she can hear the steady hum of activities as the girls go about softly attending to their chores. The front doorbell rings a couple of times. She can hear the door being opened and shut. From a distance, the sound of the conch shell can be heard from the Bangur Nagar Kali temple, heralding the aarti, the evening prayers. The evening is soft, balmy, full of secrets.

'They are coming...they are coming!' Krisna comes charging into Mee's room, her eyes shining with excitement. She helps Mee up and as they reach the hall, Reshma, as if on cue, throws open the front door with a flourish and there, standing with grim, anxious expressions, are Clinger and Sunetra. Without a word, Reshma takes them both by the hand and leads them inside the room where on the floor sits a panditji, putting the final touches to a beautiful improvised mandap, made of banana leaves and garlands of bright yellow marigold flowers. Around him are assorted copper vessels, a tray full of flowers, two boxes of sweetmeats, milk, honey, curd and on another tray, two beautiful handwoven garlands of fresh red roses.

The girls seat the stunned Clinger and Sunetra on the mats in front of the mandap where a shining copper vessel holds a pile of sandalwood waiting to be lit. Before they can say anything, the girls urge the priest to start the rituals and with the lilting shloka, 'Mangalam bhagwan...Mangalam Vishnu...' he begins.

He places their hands on each other's and lights the symbolic fire. On cue, as if stage managed, Kishore Bohitdar makes his entry. He emerges from the havan smoke that has engulfed the room, a dazed and comical figure, squinting as he tries to find his bearings and the reason for this unexpected invitation. Mee waves him towards herself and in a very familiar manner places her hand on his thigh. If he stiffens, he doesn't show it, but Clinger's eyes meet Mee's and he stares at them, not knowing how to react. Mee smiles back graciously while still fondling Kishore Bohitdar's kurta.

'Relax,' she breathes over the sounds of the mantra.

'This is Kishore,' she adds, artfully stressing on 'this', to suggest someone special. 'Kishore, this is Krishna Kant, Krisna's father. The girls wanted this marriage to happen.'

Reshma stays close to her mother, her face radiant with happiness. Krisna moves around busily, attending to the requirements of the pandit. She is looking very pretty, dressed in her only bit of finery: a powder pink lehnga choli which Mee had saved up to buy her for some school function. She pauses to smile shyly at Kishore Bohitdar as she hands him a glass of water. Their fingers touch briefly. Mee averts her eyes. She will never let them know, the secret is hers to keep. Clinger's eyes are also on Krisna standing near Kishore. His eyes are darting, guilty, a little jealous. Mee pulls Krisna between herself and Kishore and gathers both of them close. Across from them are Clinger, Sunetra and Reshma. Two families, sitting on opposite sides of a sacrificial fire, the havan.

The pandit asks who will do the kanyadaan, the giving away of the bride. Mee gently asks Kishore he is willing to do it. Before he can protest, Mee takes his hand in hers and leads him to the mandap, stumbling a little. And as the mantra increases its speed and intensity, Meehika, sitting with her husband Kishore Bohitdar, releases Clinger from his guilt of abandoning his daughter. The guilt that she bears of knowing that Krisna is not his daughter will be recompensed by this simple give and take; she will assuage her own guilt by assuaging his, and this she will do by assuring him that she is going back to Kishore Bohitdar thus ensuring a stable life for his daughter.

Sunetra, the parting of her hair a brilliant sindoori red, exchanges garlands with her blushing bridegroom, and the nuptials are complete. Sunetra stands there, a new, vibrant bride, Clinger is patently ill at ease.

Rituals over, Krisna plays the perfect hostess, serving the wedding feast of moong dal khichdi and potato curry. Midway through, they are joined by Happy Singh, Shuklaji and some of the TV crew who enter merrily with a big cake on which is inscribed in pink cream, 'Happy Birthday'. When they discover that it is a wedding and not a birthday to which they have been invited, Shuklaji gamely orders whisky and more food from Sreeji restaraunt. By the end of the evening, everyone is drunk and merry.

✦

Kishore Bohitdar met Clinger with a strange mix of envy and relief and concluded that he was a stupid man to leave his own daughter to father someone else's child. Relief, that the road ahead of him was clear. Meehika was giving strange come-hither signals. What could that mean? He really liked Krisna, felt some sort of connection with her. Maybe she would look up to him as a father figure. Quickly he pushed the thought out and flushed the commode. He had already gone over his quota of drinks and now after a small bite, he should head home. He hadn't switched on the bathroom light because he was groggy and unable to locate the switch and now as he groped in the dark to open the door, he saw the two girls standing in front of the washbasin outside, scrubbing something, their backs to him. Feeling like a voyeur, he craned his neck to hear what they were saying.

'You are not feeling bad, na, that your Papa married my Mama, tell me honestly?'

'No, Didi, seriously, I am not feeling bad. Papa loves Aunty more than he could ever love my Mama.'

'How do you know?' Reshma's voice was laced with a wisp of sadness.

'Arre Didi, that day na, Ma sat me down and told me, "See Krisna, it is important to be a transition person. Don't follow traditions blindly, follow your heart. Don't follow old tired scripts, write new scripts so that in the future generation, many lives will be changed for the better. If your Papa loves Sunetra Aunty more than me, it is his rightful choice and we must honour individual choices. This is my dream for you".'

'Wow, Aunty is super educated!'

'She is a writer...maybe she read it somewhere.'

Kishore stood stock-still, spellbound, as both girls giggled, gave each other a high-five and melted away in different directions.

From the corner of her eyes, Mee watched Kishore coming out of the toilet, wiping his hands. Gleefully, she hugged her secret to herself. He was so close to knowing his daughter, but she would never let it happen. He had spurned her when she had needed him most. Idly she wondered where Sunanda Sen could be. He had the slightly unkempt needy look of the middle-aged single man. Their eyes met briefly. She quickly averted hers and started giving directions to no one in particular. In a while Kishore said his goodbyes and left. The others too noisily took their leave, drunk and merry. Happy Singh insisted that the newlyweds spend their 'first night', in a swanky flat whose key he was privy to and dragged them away. The girls, still highly charged up after their successful event management, proceeded to clean up, rinsing and wiping the plates and glasses and dragging the furniture back in place. Krisna was relieved to see her mother like her old self, relaxed, laughing as she did a postmortem of the momentous evening.

Just when Mee was turning in, Pratyusha called on Krisna's cell phone. Mee had added her in her contact list. 'So how did it go?' Pratyusha was slightly tipsy, merry and bursting with news.

'Fantastic! You should have seen their expressions change from belligerence to open-mouthed shock.'

'Well, I have news for you too. Sorry to burst the bubble, but I just heard that your brother and his wife have put your mother in an old age home for the blind.'

'I don't fucking care...' A pathetic wail pierces the air, rooting the girls, napkins in hand, to the spot.

10
Games Toys Play

Instantly Krisna was at her side. Taking the phone from her she spoke to Pratyusha and asked for the address of the old age home. Mee was sobbing angrily, trying to speak between big gulps of breath, 'I don't care... Let her rot there for all I care. She told me to mind my own business.'

'Ma, don't get agitated. You have barely recovered.'

'I knew it...I knew they would do something like this,' and then piteously, 'They made her sign away my father's property and then they abandoned her after she turned blind...She is blind!'

'Ma, calm down, I beg of you. You will fall sick again.'

'She always chose Dada over me...The good son... the chamcha son...and now see what the good son has done.'

'Ma, your mother needs you. You should go and help her.'

'And have her slap me again?'

'Who slapped you, Ma?'

'You don't know anything. She hates me!'

'Ma, if you turned blind and were in trouble, wouldn't you want me to leave everything and rush to you?'

Her daughter caressed her, gave her water and wiped

away her tears. For a long time they sat together, hugging each other close.

✦

Once she had recovered from her initial shock, Mee was determined to fight this out on her own. It was decided that while Clinger would go back to Benaras, Sunetra would stay back with the girls, till Mee's return. Single-handedly, she would take on Dada and Cuckoo and Juhibaby too, if need be, but if her mother were to take Dada's side once again, then it would be over with them forever. Krisna helped her pack her suitcase and her medicines, neatly writing down the names, dosage and timings on a sheet of paper which she put into Mee's handbag. The plan was that Mee would spend a few days in Delhi with Pratyusha who was in the same kitty group as Cuckoo and would therefore be able to help her find Juhibaby.

Mee met Pratyusha after forty years, with a sense of surprise, even awe. The little Pratyusha who used to skip along with her, hiding in corners for a quick smoke, had evolved into a trim, smartly turned out mother of two handsome teenage boys, who shyly loped beside her, hands in their pockets, shuffling their feet. Pratyusha had worked with Citibank all her life and had recently retired because, she said, she now wanted to live off her husband's earnings.

'I have looked after the family plus my career. Now is my time to chill!' she informed Mee gaily. While the boys got into the front of their gleaming Mercedes, which the older boy drove with panache, Mee and Pratyusha sat in the back, unable to take their eyes off each other.

Pratyusha lived on the first floor of a large bungalow on the Ring Road, close to Vasant Vihar. The house was beautifully furnished with teakwood furniture, elegant sofas, paintings, mirrors and blinds made of embroidered raw silk. Mee was given the guest room, again artistically done up in different shades of blue. Mee thought of her tiny rented one-bedroom flat in Mumbai and winced mentally.

She only met Pratyusha's husband and boys at mealtimes, which were rather formal affairs, when they sat around a stately dining table and were served hot, perfectly round rotis by two uniformed servants, followed by different desserts at the end of each meal. Mee noticed that Pratyusha did not play the role of the busy homemaker, fussing around the table, and conducted herself more or less like a familiar guest. The rest of the time Pratyusha and Meehika were ensconced on the guest room bed. Though they had been in touch sporadically over the years through the telephone, they had to share all the juicy details of what had happened in their lives for almost forty years. There was so much to catch up on.

After the trauma of her recent past, being with the carefree, high-spirited Pratyusha was turning out to be highly therapeutic for Mee.

Two days later they set out for Dada's house. Pratyusha, the ever-resourceful ex-banker, had successfully managed to procure the address. The medicines kept Mee's heartbeat under control and this time round she was determined not to get rattled by Dada or Cuckoo.

The house was in a quiet, leafy lane in Vasant Vihar, a squat two-storeyed bungalow sandwiched between two taller buildings on either side. A board which read 'Arjun Kumar Chowdhury, BA, LLB' hung crookedly on the wall. Oho! So for all the big talk, Dada's father-in-law had not given him ownership of the house. The lawn in front looked unkempt and neglected. They walked up to the front door and rang the bell. No one answered. After several rings, they went around to the back of the house and from one of the open windows they could hear the whirring sound of a ceiling fan. So someone was at home, after all. Again they went back to the door, pounding it with their fists and calling out loudly but they were met with an eerie silence. Just as they were about to leave, a car screeched to a halt outside the gate and Cuckoo strode out. She stopped short on seeing Meehika and Pratyusha.

'What?'

'Where is my mother?' Mee tried to make her voice as cold and dignified as possible.

'Why are you asking me? Ask your...b...brother.' Cuckoo tried to match Mee's cool confidence but faltered on 'brother'.

'Where is my brother?' Mee was in superb control.

'Just in case you don't know, your brother has been suffering from clinical depression for the last so many years. Now I am sick of it all...sick of his behaviour...sick of his moods...sick of his temper and of his sleeping for days on end.'

Her voice rose as she spoke. Two men lazily pedalling their cycles, slowed down momentarily on hearing the commotion.

'Let's go inside, we can talk peacefully.' This from Pratyusha.

Cuckoo turned back towards the car. 'Ma, Ma! You better come in. This is going to be longer than I thought.'

The window rolled down and an elderly lady with eyebrows dyed jet black and a fashionable haircut which would have done wonders on a teenager, but on her only accentuated her flabby jowls, stared at them. The uniformed chauffeur leapt out of the driver's seat to open the door and after a brief struggle the woman managed to squeeze her obese body out of the car and lumbered towards the group in a dark green Murshidabadi silk saree, reeking of Chanel No 5.

Cuckoo unlocked the door and they faced a dark, cavernous drawing room, which would have been large had it not been stuffed with furniture of the 1980s: a dark heavy sofa set with frayed tasselled cushions and scalloped crochet back covers, heavy mismatched side tables, a broken plastic TV trolley. The room was airless, musty and suffocating and Mee could feel a familiar panic rising.

'Where is my brother?' she asked again.

'Follow me,' commanded Cuckoo authoritatively, having got some of the wind back in her sails, and Mee meekly followed her down a corridor and stood obediently as she opened the door to a room at the far end.

The curtains were drawn, and it was dark inside. In the centre of the room, under a noisily whirring ceiling fan, a crumpled form lay on a bed, curled up foetus-like. Fear gripped Mee. That huddle on the bed could not be her self-possessed, arrogant, older brother, her Dada.

'Get up! Get up!' Cuckoo's voice was shrill. And then enticingly, 'Look who is here to see you...'

But the figure did not budge. Cuckoo went up to the bed and poked him sharply. He rolled over without waking. Mee saw her brother's face, aged, lined, frozen in sleep. He was so motionless that he could well have been dead.

'So now you know. This is what has been happening. He sleeps for days on end. How long will my father cover up for his non-performance at work?'

While this was going on, Mrs Mimi Chowdhury, Cuckoo's mother, panting with the effort, had squeezed herself into the small space by the bed.

'We had warned her not to marry him. Now look what she has to deal with,' she spat out. Mee stood agonizing over her brother's condition. What could she say or do? She had come in angry, prepared for a fight. She had not in her wildest dreams bargained for this.

'Come on, finish what we had come here to do. Collect your things and let's go.' Mrs Mimi Chowdhury's voice was paper-thin, slicing the air which was thick with tension. Mee's heart went out to her brother.

She could feel a deep sadness choking her chest. Obviously, under the circumstances, how could Dada and Cuckoo look after Ma? They could barely look after themselves.

'Tadatadi kauro...Let's hurry up, shall we? Your father is waiting for us. We have a dinner party to attend.'

Cuckoo opened a wardrobe near the window and mechanically started throwing things into a suitcase which she had pulled out from under the bed. Except for Mrs Chowdhury's staccato breathing, a waking version of a snore, there was silence all around.

'Wait a minute...If you leave him in this state, who will take care of him?' Mee was distraught.

'My daughter has been doing it for a long time, poor girl! We could have got her married to the classiest, wealthiest family, but look at her now.' Mrs Mimi Chowdhury's tone was a bitter whine.

'Ma, maybe I should wait for a few days.'

'Choop kaur! Quiet! What rubbish. Your father and I are exhausted with your dilly-dallying. In any case when he wakes up, he will come straight home and eat his whole week's quota of food, like always. Let's go.'

'Where have you put Aunty?'

This was Pratyusha's second sentence in all that time. Her voice was quiet, grave.

Mother and daughter stopped for a second. Cuckoo blinked. Mrs Mimi Chowdhury blew out her cheeks, 'Savitri

Vriddha Ashram, home for the aged. It's on Ajmal Khan Road, on top of Bata Showroom. You can ask anybody...'

And with that she jerked her daughter away from this most unnecessary family meeting, and moved off like a monster ship in full sail, her scanty hair blowing like a grotesque flag at its helm.

✦

The two friends sat in contemplative silence over lunch at a newly opened restro bar in Khan Market, now a posh shopping place. Pratyusha had insisted on their revisiting their old happy hunting ground and so they had driven past Pandara Road, Shahjahan Road and Modern School. The single long lane which connected Pandara Road with Khan Market, via Shahjahan Road, on which, as children and then as teenagers, they had spent so much time, had now over the decades become broader, cleaner, quieter. The colony now housed government officials of middling and high ranks. Other people had moved into A-181, Pandara Road. If only she had been able to love Dada more as a child, then perhaps things may have been different. If only she had not been so self-obsessed then... If only...

'Come on, cheer up! We'll go and meet Aunty now.' Pratyusha could detect the deep sadness in her friend's face as she tried to cover her own through mock cheer.

She put on her reading glasses with their stylish frames to help Mee with her medicines and now the two middle-aged friends gently locked hands as they walked towards a very difficult purpose.

They found Savitri Vriddha Ashram with a little difficulty, having missed a turn. They had never seen so many old people herded together under one roof. Cotton mattresses lined the floor on both sides of a narrow room crowded with geriatrics of both sexes. Some were sitting quietly, staring sightlessly ahead. Others were slowly moving around, chatting in low hoarse cough-laden voices. Some fiddled around with their steel trunks and dilapidated suitcases, fondling their belongings of an entire lifetime: a few sets of well-worn clothes and photographs of children and family who had discarded them.

One woman suddenly reached out and clasped Mee firmly, starting to weep. 'You look like the carbon copy of my daughter. Oh my child! Just hold me, only for one minute, just hold me.' She smelt of dandruff and decay. A matron-like person in a dirty white saree separated them.

'Kisko dhoond rahe hain? Who are you looking for?'

'Her name is Juhibaby. She is about seventy-two years old.' Pratyusha glanced at Mee for confirmation. Mee only nodded, too shaken to reply.

'Oh, that one? Poor thing, her son has gone mad and her daughter-in-law is such a harami, a real bitch, none of us like to deal with her. Come this way... By the way who are you?'

Talking non-stop, without waiting for an answer, the matron lead them through several small rooms chock-a-block with old people, sprawled, curved, hunched, supine, heaped erratically on filthy mattresses like leftover food on a platter. One really old woman was sitting, clutching a cracked mirror, meticulously plaiting her wispy grey hair with a fluorescent pink ribbon, another one was hunched over a battered trunk, scrabbling to find something, her glass bangles ringing hollow. Near the outer doorway, two slightly younger women were sitting on their haunches, facing each other, jabbering away in rapid Punjabi. It was obvious to the matron that Pratyusha and Mee belonged to the upper strata, with their sunglasses, smart clothes and lingering perfume, so she voluntarily supplied information with the hope of getting a generous tip.

'This is the ladies' wing,' she pointed to the left, 'and that is the gents' wing. We are full the whole year round. Once these oldies come here, nobody wants to take them back. Very sad. Now take my case, for example. I have three children but my husband left me for another woman. I raised them single-handedly but who knows, they may leave me tomorrow to rot in one of these homes.' She shot them a piteous look.

'Don't worry, meet me on the way out.' Pratyusha knew how to deal with such situations.

'Okay, madamji, you are very kind. Now I will take you to the special ward. Only six people sharing one room and bathroom. This is for people who are bekaar, worthless... dumb, blind, lame, you know...'

Before Mee could even digest the shock of her mother being labelled 'bekaar', Pratyusha pulled the matron away, fumbling in her purse for the promised tip, thus saving themselves the shame of having to own up to their relationship with the worthless old woman who had been dumped in the home for the aged. The matron stared greedily at the hundred-rupee note, turned it around in the sunlight to verify its genuineness, folded it six times, tucked it into her bra and only then parted her lips into a big tobacco-stained smile.

'Here,' she said, opening a door at the rear end of the corridor. 'Visiting hours are there...but for you people all okay.' Giving them a broad wink, she sashayed off.

An unbelievable stench met them as they entered the room. Facing them were six hospital-like steel cots, each separated from the other by tattered, faded curtains. Through the grimy, broken windowpanes, emerged the steady roar of traffic from the perennially busy Ajmal Khan market below. And there, right opposite the door, lay Juhibaby. She had become so shrunken that it took Mee a long minute to recognize her mother. She resembled a thin rag doll with her mother's clothes hanging ridiculously loosely around it. Glassy-eyed, the form was staring sightlessly at a fixed point on the ceiling. It was as though someone had nailed Mee to the ground, she stood there rooted and stumbled slightly when Pratyusha gave her a gentle push.

'Is that her?' Pratyusha whispered in shock.

'Arrrrrgh.' A strange sound escaped Mee by way of an answer, surprising both Pratyusha and Juhibaby, whose eyes now came down from the ceiling and hovered somewhere between Mee's lips and chin. Pratyusha stepped forward.

'Aunty... It's me, Pratyusha, from Pandara Road, Meehika's friend, do you remember me?'

Juhibaby's gaze slowly shifted from Mee's lower chin to Pratyusha's lower chin. Her eyes were opaque, like two grey pebbles. Slowly she broke into a smile, suddenly reminding Mee of a little pink and white leather purse that she had been very attached to as a child. Her mother's once roses and peach complexion had turned leathery.

'Protuussha?'Ma had always stressed the middle syllable, like a true Bengali.

'Yes, Aunty... I found out you were here, so I came to meet you.'

'Bhalo...bhalo...nice of you, I wish I could see you though...my vision has more or less gone.'

'How are you, Aunty?'

Pratyusha was standing next to the cot, holding Juhibaby's pencil-thin hand in her own.

'Khokon, my son, you remember Khokon? Well, he said, my leg was close to becoming gangrenous...I have diabetes you know...so he had me admitted to this hospital...'

'Ma...Ma...Maaaaa!'

Mee fell on her mother's frail form, sobbing uncontrollably.

'Who? Meehika? When did you come?'

She struggled slightly. It seemed to Mee that her mother was involuntarily recoiling at her touch. Pratyusha gestured to Mee to control herself. Wiping her tears, she managed a nod and rose from her mother's body.

'Ma, this is not such a great...er... hospital. I will take you to a wonderful one and you will get well soon.'

'No, no. Khokon will get very angry and then he and Bouma will fight.' She was barely audible.

Pratyusha pinched her nose, implying 'bad smell' and gestured to Mee to pull back the soiled bed sheet that partially covered Juhibaby's body. It was just what they had feared. For a moment both of them reeled with the impact of the stench emanating from Juhibaby's legs and feet which were covered by pink and purple welt-like wounds, which someone had clumsily swabbed with cotton wool, leaving clumps of it sticking on the raw bleeding flesh. Seeing Mee in a state of frozen horror, Pratyusha again indicated with her hands 'let's get her out of here.'

'Ma, I have come to take you with me.'

'Okay,' she said simply, like a child. 'Can you take me to Mamoni? She is waiting for me...she says she will not die without seeing me for the last time.'

'But Kolkata is very far. How will we...?'

Pratyusha again indicated quickly, 'Say yes...say yes.'

'Theek acche, Ma, I will take you to Kolkata.'

There was a long waiting list at Savitri Vriddha Ashram so they were not unduly perturbed to see Juhibaby go. A freshly deserted senior citizen who was capable of engaging in stitching, sewing dolls and weaving cane items like the 'healthier' inmates, was of more value than Juhibaby who was in the 'bekaar' category. Nobody paid attention when Juhibaby was wheelchaired out into a waiting ambulance, straight into hospital. In all the tension and haste, Mee missed the superb irony. The hospital to which Juhibaby was admitted was the Sucheta Kripalani hospital, where Pratyusha's sister was the resident medical officer. Where half a century ago, Mee had burst out of the body of a half-dead Juhibaby under the stairs of its under-construction wing.

Pratyusha was her angel. Not only did she clear the hospital bills, claiming that due to her sister, they were discounted, she made special arrangements to fly Juhibaby to Kolkata. She came to the airport to drop Mee and Juhibaby and the two women once again hugged each other for a long time. Pratyusha knew the days ahead would not be easy for her friend.

✦

Her eyes and legs ravaged by the deadly diabetes, Juhibaby could not see the aircraft in which she would be making her first journey by air. She was pining for a glimpse of her beloved Khokon. Mee wondered vaguely if she knew the depth of Dada's manic depression. Juhibaby herself swung from bitter anger to sweet compassion, two opposite ends of an arc that she was too dazed to comprehend.

Chhayamoni's son, Debu, came to receive them at the airport in a taxi. Mee had last seen him at Dada's wedding and tried to erase the memory of the humiliating slap that she had received from her mother in his presence. He looked older, paunchier, and had grey-green stubble, matching his limp, greying hair. Nobody spoke much as they travelled the long distance from a sparkling Dumdum airport, past Rajarhati, on the brand new expressway towards the city centre. Their destination: 156 Rashbehari Avenue.

The Calcutta of yore had changed dramatically into a modern metropolis, renamed Kolkata. Though it still retained its old-world charm: the 'tung-tung' sounds of the trams as they criss-crossed each other sedately, running neck to neck with aged buses, navigating through hand-pulled rickshaws as they fearlessly plunged through the traffic, Mee was fascinated by the expensive-looking shopping centres that had taken the place of the old New Market she remembered, the movie halls which had turned into multiplexes, and the huge posters with stunningly beautiful Bengali women modelling even more stunning jewellery and sarees.

To her, Calcutta still signified crowds, high-decible conversations in Bengali, where everyone from the pedestrian to the high-end shop owner, spoke loudly, dramatically, gesturing wildly with their hands to illustrate their meaning. To her the throb of the city included the smell of pungent fish, fowl, ripened fresh fruit, local vegetables, flowers, sweetmeats, fried condiments, the delectable 'kochooris, loochie-aloor dom', but most powerfully of all the scent of the sweet pink yoghurt, the 'pinky doi', and of the fruit-bearing trees of 156, Rashbehari Road.

The large forbidding mansion of her childhood had strangely shrunk. In place of the familiar low wall facing the quiet street, her cousin made the cab stop in front of a small gate carved out of a high wall, plastered with posters of a smiling chief minister of West Bengal with her signature hand wave and limp cotton sarees. There was no tree-lined courtyard any more. In its place were rows of warehouses, regimental and grim. Mee's cousin pointed to the Small House, the house in which Juhibaby had been raised.

'That is our office.' His tone was grave as though he had just introduced himself as the prime minister of India.

'Kothai...kothai...where is your office?' Juhibaby, eager, wanted to see.

'Chhoto badi. The Small House.'

Juhibaby fell silent.

The mansion had been boxed in by the dozens of warehouses that Debu had got constructed around it. He had decided to live off the rent coming in from these properties, rather than pursue a career, and was more interested in dabbling in politics than maintaining his family home. The Small House was where he conducted his political affairs. So now the mansion stood shabby and eroded with peeling plaster and a coat of green moss on its lower walls. Debu carried the frail Juhibaby in his arms as Mee supervised the luggage. The house did not look like the large, airy, sparkling Big House of her childhood, but smelt cold and damp as though ignored by its inmates.

Before entering the mansion, she went to look at the Small House. As children, visitors from Delhi, they had not been encouraged to go there. To Mee, it had just been a regular outhouse, the kind of servant quarter she had grown up seeing in the government houses on Pandara Road and Shahjahan Road. She could never understand why it was off limits for them. Now as Mee stood in front of the Small House, she recalled that Juhibaby's skirting around any discussion about it was what gave it a certain air of secrecy, most unbefitting for a structure so mundane. She could clearly visualize Juhibaby calling out, 'Khokon, Meehika, come back here.'

'Ma, but we want to play here.' Dada's squeaky baby voice is plaintive.

'Choop kaur! Quiet now...That is not a place to play. Come into the house.'

'Noooooo...'

'Are you coming quietly or shall I come to fetch you?' The children did not want to take a chance with Ma's menacing tone.

'Okay, baba, we are coming.' They scurry inside.

✦

She found Juhibaby seated next to Chhayamoni on her king-sized bed in the west wing of the house and was instantly struck by the fact that her aunt looked younger and more beautiful than her mother, though she was a good fourteen years older. Nobody could have guessed that Chhayamoni had been afflicted by a terminal illness with the doctor giving her only a few months to live. She had rejected medicines, surgery and alternative therapy and relied only on prayers and the leaves of the holy basil. It was heartbreaking to see Juhibaby old, emaciated, a wrinkled bag of flesh, being held and caressed by the person who she perhaps bonded with the most, her sister-cum-surrogate mother, Chhayamoni. Mee had last seen her aunt at Dada's wedding, and the same image imprinted itself in her mind of the two sisters ensconced on her parents' queen-sized bed in A-181, Pandara Road. Now once again, years later, both old and diseased, the two sisters sat holding, caressing, crooning to each other in perfect comfort, oblivious to anyone outside their sacred circle. Watching them Mee, idly wondered what it would be like to have a sibling of the same sex. Would she have preferred an older sister or a younger one? Her train of thought was broken by Chhayamoni's sweet voice. She wondered how anyone at the age of eighty-six could have such a melodious young-girl voice.

'Meehika ma, bhalo to... Doing well, my dear?'

Mee bent down to touch her aunt's feet, seeking her

blessings and, according to custom, touched Juhibaby's feet as well. She noticed with relief that her wounds were drying. Since Juhibaby could not see where Mee was standing, her arm raised to give blessings awkwardly groped the air. Instantly, Chhayamoni took Juhibaby's groping hand and placed it on Mee's head. Mee glanced at her beautiful aunt. Her eyes in a rose pink face were clear and sparkling, revealing no sign of distress on seeing her sister blind and lame. She held Juhibaby to her and gently stroked her back. Mee thought it best to leave them alone for a while. She had barely turned when she heard her mother's voice, childlike, clear, talking about Khokon. Damn! It always had to be about her dear brother.

She ate a quiet lunch by her self, served by her aunt's part-time cook, a newly married young girl with a radiant face and bright sindoor in the parting of her frizzy hair. She introduced herself as Chompakoli and Mee was happy to tuck into a pure Bengali meal after a long time. After a while she wandered into her aunt's bedroom to check on her mother. She saw Juhibaby fast asleep, her mouth slighted parted, snoring gently. Her aunt noticed her and graciously patted the bed on which lay several old black and white photographs and an ancient velvet-bound album.

'Bosho, ma... Sit down, my dear. Your mother and I were revisiting our childhood.'

Mee picked up an old sepia-toned photograph closest to her. It was a photograph of what seemed like a theatrical performance. Several men and women, dressed in magnificent costumes, their faces chalkily made-up, were frozen in various poses in front of an ornamental painted backdrop. Absently, she turned the photograph and at the back, written by an unlettered hand, were the numbers 1925.

'Who are they?' Mee was curious.

'Well, this one here is my mother, your grandmother. And that one there, in the embroidered kurta pajama, playing the harmonium, is my father, your grandfather.'

'Why are they all dressed up so weirdly?'

'They are dressed up for their parts...they are professional actors. Have you heard of jatra?'

'Yes,' Mee nodded. 'It's a theatrical folk form of Bengal, right?'

'Well dear, we were part of a jatra troupe. Those days there were no cars so we performed our mythological plays travelling from village to village in wagons. Truth be told, your mother was born in a wagon.'

She laughed merrily, softly so as not to disturb Juhibaby who was sleeping peacefully by her side. Mee was taken by surprise. Her mother had never mentioned this.

A trifle irritated, she picked up another picture. It was of a matronly woman with arresting features and masses of dark curling hair rolled up on both sides of her forehead like horns. She tilted the photo towards her aunt.

'Ah! Look at this... This is a picture of our mother Ruma. How pretty she used to be! She died when you were very small.'

'Where are they...your sisters? My three aunts?'

'Oh, they live in Sealdah, in the suburbs. Debu has informed them about your visit. They will be coming to meet you both in a day or two.'

'Why don't they stay here? It is such a large house!'

Chhayamoni paused for a longish moment, looked down at her sister sleeping peacefully and spoke in a low whisper. 'Your mother exhorted us never to tell anyone the truth and especially to you. Somehow she was always fearful that you would not be able to handle it.'

Mee looked questioningly at her aunt.

'Truth be told, beta, I came into this grand Big House as a housemaid. Back then we were horribly poor, the jatra had to pack up giving way to the bioscope... Nowadays you call it cinema. But by the grace of the Almighty, the mistress of this house chose me as her daughter-in-law. You see, your cousin Debu's father was a paraplegic... But a very good man, bless his soul. So they allowed my parents and my four sisters to live in the Small House, the outhouse on the east side of the garden. They lived there as servants.'

Mee took her time filtering this shocking bit of information. Oh! So this was her mother's shameful secret which she had hugged tight to her bosom, never letting her children know. Mee wondered if her father knew. She picked up another photograph. It showed a pretty little girl of five or six curled up on a verandah, asleep, hugging a pair of shiny sandals.

'Why is this kid hugging her shoes?'

Her aunt plucked the photo out of Mee's hand and exclaimed, 'Why, this is your mother! See how beautiful she was! This was on the day of my wedding. She did not want me to get married so she kept tugging my saree and would not let go. So my mother, jittery as she was that day, really walloped her. Poor thing kept crying and crying till she fell asleep, holding her first pair of shoes. My poor mother! In her last days as she lay dying she regretted treating your mother so badly. But it was too late to bridge the past. I was sharing all this with your mother a little while ago.' She sighed deeply.

For some unknown reason Mee's hackles rose. Simultaneously she wanted to weep.

'Why did my grandmother, treat my...my... mo...mother so badly?' She fumbled.

'Beta, things were different those days. There was never enough to go around. And your mother was the fifth daughter...maybe she was pining for a son, who knows.'

She sighed again. She started to put all the loose photographs into an ornate brass box with a curved handle. With her free hand she gently patted Juhibaby's head.

'Kee re, kheeday teeday pacchey na? Aren't you hungry?'

Juhibaby stirred sleepily, her grey pebble-like eyes moving sightlessly in their sockets as she opened her mouth wide in a deep satisfying yawn.

'Mamoni, I was dreaming of Benushaib.'

'Was he neighing?'

Both the sisters laughed merrily as they rocked one another. Mee could not help feeling a little left out and jealous. Why does my mother always lock me out?

✦

The three spinster aunts came the next day with special sweetmeats and 'pinky doi'. As she savoured each spoon of the delectable yoghurt, Mee thought of Krisna. Had she been able to give her daughter any such memory to give to her own children one day? What if Krisna had had a sibling, like Ma had her sisters, and she had Dada? Seeing her aunts again after so long Mee was reminded about her own thwarted plan to humble her mother in front of her sisters, by inviting them to her home in Benaras. It was not necessary any more.

Mee took a picture of the five aged sisters with their snow-white hair matching their crisp white sarees, on the porch of the Big House. Far in the distance, could be seen the Small House. She would not hide its truth from her daughter. The past was nothing but a road to the future.

✦

A couple of days later Chhayamoni had to go to her naturopath for her monthly check-up. Debu accompanied her. They would visit the Kalighat temple and be back by evening. Chompakoli had prepared all the meals and had taken the rest of the day off after giving Juhibaby her breakfast. Mee had dozed off after a hearty breakfast of doi-cheede, flattened rice and yoghurt, when she heard her mother calling Chompakoli from the bedroom. She splashed some water on her face and went to see what she wanted.

'What is it, Ma? Why are you calling Chompakoli? Have you forgotten today is her day off?'

'Day off? Why wasn't I told that it is her day off?' Juhibaby's tone was querulous.

'Ma, of course you knew. You were there when she asked for leave... Anyway tell me what you want...I will do it.'

'Paikhaana...toilet...' Juhibaby yelped, desperately trying to scramble off the bed.

Mee pushed her back on the bed. Her tone was firm. 'What are you doing, Ma? You know very well that you can't walk to the bathroom. Please do your business in your bedpan. I will clean it.'

' Nooo...don't touch me!' Mee was startled by her mother's reaction.

'Why not?'

'Go away... I don't want you. Send me back to Khokon. I want Khokon.'

Mee was astonished, hurt beyond belief. Here she was, the saviour, the child who had rescued her parent from an old age home where she had been abandoned by a sibling, and this is what she was getting in return?

'Theek acche...very well,' she said, her tone dripping with bitterness. 'I will send you right back to the old age home where your darling son left you and from where I picked you up.'

Juhibaby's face slowly turned in the direction of Mee's voice.

'Old age home?' It was an uncomprehending whisper.

'Yes, dear Ma. Savitri Vriddha Ashram, home for the aged. It is on Ajmal Khan Road. You had become gangrenous. That was not a hospital.'

'Not a hospital? But Bouma said...' Her face started to crumble.

'Your darling son and his darling wife abandoned you. Just because you had turned blind and could not see where you were. Do you want it in writing? No problem, I will send you back! I am sick of not being loved by you... sick of being pushed away... sick of being unwanted. And guess what, unlike you, I love my daughter and I have no desire to leave her alone in Mumbai while I sit here and tolerate your bullshit!'

Mee was riding on a giant crest of emotions, the long closed dam of her heart had burst and she was helpless against it as her pent-up rage, jealousy, frustration poured out in uncontrolled torrents.

'You never loved me. All I heard from the time that I was born was that I almost killed you. Was I responsible for what happened at my birth? Answer me! You slapped me in front of everyone. You called me a whore. You never once called me in all the years that I was struggling and suffering on my own. Did you hear my end of the story? Did you ever pause to wonder what kind of life your daughter was leading? Did you care if I was alive or dead? Okay, so I may have made a few mistakes, married the wrong guy... Maybe I was too young and immature but does that mean you crucify me? And then when I came to Delhi after Beenarani's death, and innocently asked what was it that Dada was making you sign, you remember what you said? You said, "We will manage our own affairs". Is this how they managed your affairs for you? Left you on the footpath, blind and gangrenous?'

Even as she was releasing five decades of hurt and anger against her mother, something was urging her to use her words kindly. But she wanted to hurt her mother, to shake her out of her apathy, to demand her place in her heart, her rightful place.She stood there panting, spent, utterly, exhausted.

'Meethuma, can you clean me up please?'

Mee froze. For the first time in her life, Juhibaby had borrowed her husband's nickname for his daughter... Meethuma.

Then she saw the shame, sorrow and helplessness flitting over her mother's face as she futilely paddled her forearms to get off the bedpan. Mee helped her up. She did not mind the smell that met her nostrils, she did not mind picking up her frail mother and cleaning her bottom like a newborn baby's. She powdered her mother carefully, noticing the tiny red veins on her buttocks, and then fitted her with an adult diaper. Juhibaby lay there, naked, immobile, calm. This act of intimacy had broken down her wall, the wall of shame, guilt and inadequacy that she had built around herself as long as she could remember.

'Tell me about your life.'

Her voice was clear, almost. Overwhelmed, Mee tentatively put her palm on her mother's skeleton-like, vein-ridden hand, expecting her to shrug it off any minute. But Juhibaby did not move her hand away.

'How is your marriage? I don't see Kishore around.'

'Mine is a very long, pretty sad story.' Mee sighed. 'You must be tired now. I am sorry if I hurt you. I am really sorry. I didn't mean to.' She could feel hot tears scalding her cheeks.

'Kedona ma, don't cry... I know you are crying... You have always been my feisty daughter. You have been what I could not be. I am proud of you.'

Mee was stunned.

'But Ma, my relationships did not work out. Kishore and I have not been together for years now.'

'That's okay. Things like that happen. At least you had the opportunity to be a wife and mother. As for me, I was too young when I got married and things more or less happened to me...almost without my say... But you must be at the helm of your life. You can create anything and everything that you want. That is your birthright.'

Mee could not believe her ears. Was her cranky, indifferent mother, loving her, honouring her, accepting her? She felt a rush of something flowing through her, something clear and sweet and electric. It felt strange, as if something was moving through her very fast, as if the emotional deluge had cleared away any clot, any knot that had come between her and her heart. What had her pain tried to tell her heart? Maybe she hadn't listened to her heart. Maybe she had not listened to anybody or anything. Maybe she was too busy meeting her own agendas. But now the wall around her heart, that stood between her and Juhibaby, had been broken, she was not going to ever let it come up again.

After Juhibaby had been sponged and fed, Mee went to her room and started sorting out her things. It was time to go home... And time for Juhibaby to meet her 'Hindustani' grandchild. When Debu returned in the evening, she would ask him to book their return tickets. It had been a long day but strangely she was not tired at all.

'They're gonna put me in the movies
They're gonna make a big star out of me
The biggest thing that ever hit the big time
And all I have to do is act naturally.'

The song was on Mee's lips as she thought about what she would do when she returned to Mumbai, this time with her mother. Life was short. Life was beautiful. She would enrol in a gym. She would get her hair styled differently and get a new wardrobe. She would go on a holiday with Pratyusha. She would look after Juhibaby and love her insanely.

From her room Juhibaby smiled to herself. It had been a long time since she had heard her 'bhaanga kishore' sing.

✦

They left two mornings later. Juhibaby clung to Chhayamoni's hand as the taxi slowly moved out of 156, Rashbehari Avenue, taking her to a city where her only grandchild was waiting for them, Mumbai.

As the Airbus 320, lurched upwards with tremendous gravity-defying force to meet the sky, Mee instinctively reached out for Juhibaby's hand, but she was fast asleep, her head thrown back, snoring gently. Mee tilted her head a little to gaze at her sleeping mother. With Chhayamoni's tender care, the colour had returned to her cheeks, and her pink complexion and silvery-white, freshly shampooed hair glowed warmly under the dimmed cabin lights. She was proudly wearing the brand new cream and maroon dhakai silk saree that Chhayamoni had given her as a parting gift. Mee had teamed it with an orange blouse which had become so loose that it had to be held together with safety pins, and a pink petticoat. She was sure the deviant colours would have met with her mother's approval.

The simple way in which her aunt had unlocked the secret of over five decades, that she was the daughter of a humble servant family, opened something in her chest and she could swear that despite the cabin pressure which always made her claustrophobic, her breath was flowing like a calm river. Chhayamoni's revelation made her look at Juhibaby with new eyes. For the first time she had a glimpse of her mother's inner darkness, her neglected childhood, her yearning for the love of an indifferent mother, and Mee felt utterly humbled by the pain that her mother had never once shared with her children.

Back home Sunetra was packed and ready to leave as Reshma had been missing school. As the taxi entered the building compound, Krisna ran forward holding a garland of flowers for her grandmother. But Juhibaby was in a querulous mood. The long flight, the queue for the taxi, the disturbed eating pattern had her trembling with exhaustion. Quickly, they helped her up to the flat.

'Ma, this is my friend Sunetra and this is her daughter Reshma. They were here with Krisna while I was away.'

Juhibaby, calmed by a cup of hot tea and biscuits, smiled and waved her hand in blessing.

'And where is Krisna?'

Mee gestured to Krisna who shyly came forward, touched her grandmother's feet and straightened up. Juhibaby, unable to figure out where exactly Krisna was standing, awkwardly groped near her feet. Mee took her mother's hand gently and raised it up all the way to Krisna's head.

'What? She is that big?' Juhibaby exclaimed.

'Ma, Krisna is going to be sixteen soon.'

'Aaaaah! I missed seeing her growing up,' said Juhibaby simply.

Sunetra had kept the house neat and tidy. A well-stocked

fridge and hot rotis, dal and vegetables awaited them in the kitchen. Suddenly Mee found herself tongue-tied. She could not find the words to thank her. They had become family. She knew deep down that though they were not connected by blood, yet they were bound by an unspoken loyalty, loyalty not bound by roles or rituals but something more fundamental. The girls parted reluctantly, with promises to meet each other soon. Mee watched mistily from the window as the taxi bearing Sunetra, returning back to a life with Clinger as his lawfully wedded wife, with her daughter Reshma, disappeared into the thick Mumbai traffic.

Grandmother and grand-daughter slept on the double bed in the small bedroom, while Mee slept on the sofa-cum-bed in the hall. Mee could hear them chatting late into the night.

'Hum jab chhota tha na, hum mathematics se bahut darta tha.' Krisna would laugh softly at her granny's memories, spoken in lilting accented Hindi.

'Silver Nani.' That was Krisna's special name for her granny who had silver-white hair.

Silver Nano was the brand name of the new Samsung refrigerator that Clinger had got installed in the flat as a 'thank you' gift, no doubt. Krisna had creatively joined together the two sparkling new additions in her life: a fridge and a grandmother and created her own name for a grandmother who she was seeing for the first time in her life.

'Silver Nani, tell me about my mother when she was a child. Was she naughty?'

And Juhibaby would speak in Hindi, using tense and grammer in such unique ways that Krisna would soon be rolling on the floor with mirth, shortly joined by the hysterically giggling Juhibaby herself, scrabbling to sit up on her elbows.

'Bas, bas, mai more jayega, I will die laughing... Okay enough of Hindustani bhasha, now I will teach you Bengali, your mother tongue... now repeat after me "Au...aa"...'

Before long Mee would have tuned off to the comforting sound of her mother and daughter teaching each other Hindi and Bengali. Juhibaby had come full circle; she had no choice. Her grand-daughter was a pure 'Hindustani', and she had fallen in love with the soft-spoken, artistically inclined Krisna.

The Kali temple, which was a stone's throw from the flat, was a spiritual and cultural hub for the hundreds of Bengali expatriates who had settled in the suburbs of Mumbai. They collected, 'chanda', donations from every Bengali in their book and celebrated each festival, particularly the Bengali ones, with gusto. Juhibaby had been excited to hear the hauntingly beautiful conch shells being sounded at dawn and dusk and wanted to visit the temple. Krisna took her there one evening after school. After that there was no looking back. The Bengalis who lived outside of West Bengal, the 'probaashis', gravitated towards one another with a gusto matched only by the Punjabis and Tamilians. In a very short time, Juhibaby had made many friends who referred to her as 'mashima', maternal aunt. Dolly, Rekha, Putul, all middle-aged women, around Mee's age, would drop by to have a cup of tea or chat with Juhibaby. Sometimes Mee would return from an errand or script meeting to find several Bengali women in their lovely taant sarees, sitting around her mother as one of them prepared tea for them all in the kitchen. Mee was happy to note that her mother was not a sad blind woman, but a rather chirpy and entertaining magnet who drew so many people to her. Since she herself rarely made an effort at friendship, they would be awkward around her. Very often, on hearing sounds of visitors, Mee would sneek back downstairs and go and sit on the children's swings in the garden, waiting for them to leave. She sensed that her mother was not as comfortable with her as she was with these strangers and it angered her a bit. Juhibaby was happy to wear Krisna's salwar-kameez and keds and go for a leisurely walk with her. In all her life Mee had never seen her mother in anything but a saree. She even wore one to bed. Now seeing her at this age, in this new avatar, sunglasses perched on her pert nose, cane in hand, walking confidently with her grand-daughter, Mee felt a stab of envy. 'Why does she always lock me out?'

And then one day the inevitable happened. Krisna stopped for a second to save a little puppy from being crushed under the wheel of a flying car and left Juhibaby's hand for a split second too long, and, sightless, she walked straight into the car and crushed her hip bone. Mee was at one of her interminable script sessions and so her phone was on silent. Only when she saw sixteen missed calls did she realize there was an emergency and rushed home in a panic. Juhibaby had been taken to the hospital on SV Road by some bystanders who had seen the accident, and there she lay, her one thin leg up in a cast, suspended from the ceiling. She had been heavily sedated.

In the weeks that followed, Krisna and Mee had a difficult time juggling school, home and deadlines at work. They were saved miraculously by the Bengali circle who took turns to be with their 'mashima', often bringing steel tiffin boxes filled with payesh and other Bengali dishes. Even Happy Singh, ever solicitous, visited the hospital, enquiring after Juhibaby's health. With her diabetes level shooting up, an operation was not advisable, so Juhibaby was discharged from the hospital in a cast and a suitcase full of medication.

During the hottest and wettest months of May, June

and July, Juhibaby had to be in plaster, bound to her bed for twelve weeks as ordained by the orthopaedic doctor. All day long she lay in bed, writhing in pain, except for the few hours when the painkillers made it bearable. Krisna had thoughtfully downloaded some Bengali songs on her computer and this she would switch on for her grandmother, stuffing her own ears with cotton wool before sitting down to study.

Sitting by Juhibaby's bedside while Krisna was busy in the kitchen making dinner, Mee felt a rush of gratitude for her daughter. 'Ma would have been happier to have a daughter like Krisna, rather than me,' she mused.

Suddenly in the middle of her reverie, her mother's voice floated into her consciousness. She was holding two invisible balls in her hands and was saying, 'Fluffy, fluffy hot kachories, large malpuas with cream, samosas with green chillie chutney and one dry sweetmeat.' Then she abruptly wound up, 'Yes, that's it, I guess.'

And then as Mee pieced together the fragments of the menu, she realized that her mother had been referring to the snacks that she wanted served to mourners when they would congregate to pay their final respects to her departed soul. Ma started giggling. Like a little girl. Something like how Krisna used to giggle as a child, warm and fruity. It was so infectious that Mee couldn't stop herself smiling, but said in mock anger, 'Are you actually giving me the menu you want served on the chautha puja, after you leave us?'

'Yes.' Ma too had a surprised look on her face. 'I suddenly remembered that my mother-in-law, your granny, used to say that after one's death, the family should put the favourite food of the departed soul under the peepal tree. It helps the soul to ascend.'

Suddenly Mee felt very alone, a bit scared, so she changed the topic.

'Ma, sing me a song...any song... I always yearned to sing like you.'

'Song? At my age?' Juhibaby demurred, waiting for the proverbial prodding.

'One minute.'

Mee ran to open the door and called out to Krisna to join them. 'Silver Nani is going to sing for us,' she whispered.

'Is that you, Krisna? See I am going to sing for you a Hindustani song. It is from a film of my favourite hero, Rajesh Khanna.'

And she sang,

'Ye shaam mastani
Madhosh kiye jaa
Mujhe dore koi kheenche
Teri ore liye jaaye.'

Though her voice was feeble and her notes shook ever so slightly, the pure yearning of her heart reached out and touched both her daughter and grand-daughter. The three of them sang well into the night, the magic of music bringing them closer, wrapping the three generations in its ageless fold.

✦

Juhibaby died exactly five days after her plaster was removed. She had been excited as a child to experiment with the second-hand walker that Happy Singh had thoughtfully brought for her. After being bedridden for almost twelve weeks, she was at last able to take wee steps at a time, with support from Mee and Krisna. All of a sudden she had started blooming. Her skin had cleared remarkably and all her new friends from the Bengali circle who took turns to visit, swore that their Mashima was glowing.

Two days before she died, she had stepped into the kitchen

and taught Krisna how to make her special version of the rice payesh which she loved.

'The trick lies in the garnish. Add a couple of bay leaves and some crushed cardamom into a tablespoon of hot ghee, toss it into the pudding, immediately cover it and let it stand.'

Afterwards, she had sliced a small fistful of almonds, cashew nuts, and pistachios and sprinkled these over the dish so masterfully that Krisna had whispered in Mee's ears, 'So much dry fruit...have you got a new assignment?'

'No, this is called "Lokkhir guna", means my mother is abundance incarnate. She can make a fistful appear to be much more than it is...'

A day earlier, Ma had suddenly become very agitated about Khokon. 'What does he mean by leaving me here? Can he not phone at least? I understand they lead busy lives but a phone call, is that too much to expect? And what about my pension, where is that may I ask?'

Mee had tried to calm her down. There was no use telling her about Dada's condition. She had not heard from them all this while. She wondered if he was better and back at work. She decided to ask Pratyusha to do a little snooping around, now that they knew the Vasant Vihar address. She noticed with relief that Ma never mentioned her darling Bouma even once.

On the day she died, she had asked for some water and then tea. In between the time it took Krisna to give her Silver Nani a glass of water and then to make her a cup of tea, exactly the way she liked it, she slipped away. For some time, Krisna thought that she had dozed off, like she often did, her mouth slightly open, snoring gently. But when Krisna returned after twenty minutes to find her grandmother in exactly the same position, lying supine, hands across her chest, her head tilted on one side, an alarm rang in her mind. She was looking different, too still. Krisna shook her gently by the shoulders, trying to wake her, and then slowly the truth had dawned. Her Silver Nani had gone. Mee had gone to town that morning to meet a producer for a film script, and by the time she could take a taxi and rush home, Krisna, with the help of the Bengali circle, had done the needful. The Gangajal, along with the leaves of the holy basil, had been put in Juhibaby's mouth. Her ears and nose had been blocked with cotton wool, to ward off negative energies seeking to enter through these orifices and tamper with her 'ling deh', the soul element, as it prepared for its onward journey. All this Krisna gleaned from the solemn wisps of conversation that was floating between the ladies.

When Mee finally rushed into the house, the first thing she felt were dozens of eyes focussed on her face, trying to gauge her reaction, ready to merge with her sorrow or perhaps a voyeuristic curiosity to view another's grief, from the safety of detachment. Self-consciously she sat down on her knees on the floor next to her mother. Juhibaby was lying there, a half-smile on her face, glowing. For a moment Mee was hopeful. Was there a mistake? Was her mother alive after all? She touched her face and put her ear to her heart, with the dull hope that she may catch a faint throb. She looked up to see Dolly, one of her mother's favourites, who choked on a sob as if to say, 'She has gone, really she has gone.' But seconds later she was calmed by the whispers, the swish of cool cotton sarees worn by the Bengali circle as they moved around the house, attending to all the rituals required for a funeral. While someone was calling up the priest who would officiate in the funeral rites, another was ordering provisions. Everyone was huddled together, crying softly, comforting the other. Mee was astonished to see how popular her mother had been. These people whom she had met so recently were genuinely sorry to see their 'mashima' go.

In a while, Krisna came and sat next to Mee. Both were tearless. Once again Mee trailed her palm over her mother's face, her chest, her arms, her soft inverted belly, her legs and by the time she reached her feet, something snapped. She grasped her feet with both hands and sobbed inconsolably.

'Ma, I am sorry... I am very, very sorry, I have not been a good daughter. Forgive me, Ma!'

For once, Mee was oblivious to the people around her, oblivious to her own naked grief. Krisna did not stop her, merely caressed her gently till her sobs subsided. Mee continued to sit at Juhibaby's feet for a long, long time, till the purohit accompanied by several men, husbands perhaps of Ma's Bengali circle, came with a stretcher, white cloth, rope, flower garlands, ready to take the body to the crematorium.

'Wait! I have to inform my Dada. He must see her one last time.'

Mee had no telephone numbers so she called up Pratyusha, giving her the news and asking her to rush to Vasant Vihar to inform Dada. Pratyusha called back in half an hour saying that the house was locked up and no one knew where Cuckoo's parents lived. Time was running out. Mee was informed that unless they cremated her mother before sundown, they would have to keep her body on ice slabs the whole night. Her mind was in turmoil. What if she kept Ma on ice the whole night only to be told the next morning that Dada was still untraceable. She looked at Juhibaby who seemed to clearly indicate, 'Take me now...take me now... I hate ice...I'll catch a chill.'

'Let her go,' Krisna whispered to Mee. 'She told me she hated the cold.'

So amidst chants of 'Bol Hari... Hari bol, Bol Hari, Hari bol', Juhibaby, born in a remote village of Mednipur in West Bengal, was carried away by friends and well-wishers to be cremated at the electric crematorium in faraway Goregaon West, Mumbai, Maharashtra.

✦

The flat suddenly felt so empty. Sunetra, Reshma, Clinger and now Ma, all had gone their own ways. The Bengali circle had graciously done their duty and had gone home to rest. Mee called Chhayamoni to break the news.

'Ma has gone.'

'Good. I shall follow her soon.' Her voice was gentle, calm.

'Don't say that. I need you.' Mee's voice quivered.

'Thank you once again for bringing her here to meet me. I wanted her to go before me. Meyta bhishon bheetu...this girl has always been very fragile.'

'This girl', Mee took a second to ponder on the fact that since her mother was more like Chhayamoni's daughter, it would then make her more of a grandmother than an aunt. In a flash, she thought of her biological grandmother, Ruma, the beauty, who had been careless with her mother. Somehow she did not feel so bad this time.

'I shall bring Krisna to meet you soon,' Mee promised.

'Bhalo thakeesh, God be with you.' Her voice rang strong and clear. Mee hurredly disconnected. She did not want her aunt to hear the sadness in her voice.

The next day, she went to Four Bunglows market to place the order for the snacks that Juhibaby had wanted for her chautha. Kachories, malpuas, samosas and one dry sweet, her mother had been clear and specific. She guessed that about fifty to seventy-five people would attend the prayer service that was